THE ELEMENT OF NEGOTIATION IN THE PACIFIC SETTLEMENT OF DISPUTES BETWEEN STATES

THE ELEMENT OF NEGOTIATION IN THE PACIFIC SETTLEMENT OF DISPUTES BETWEEN STATES

AN ANALYSIS OF PROVISIONS MADE AND/OR APPLIED SINCE 1918 IN THE FIELD OF THE PACIFIC SETTLEMENT OF INTERNATIONAL DISPUTES

by

Dr. P.J.I.M. DE WAART

MARTINUS NIJHOFF - THE HAGUE - 1973

Translated from the Dutch with a grant from the Netherlands Organization for the Advancement of Pure Research by C.R. Sibson M.A.

ISBN 978-94-015-0371-6 ISBN 978-94-015-0947-3 (eBook)
DOI 10.1007/978-94-015-0947-3

CONTENTS

CHAPTER III

PACIFIC SETTLEMENT OF DISPUTES BETWEEN STATES — IMPLEMENTATION OF LAW

ABBREVIATIONS

AFDB	African Development Bank
a h	ad hoc provision
A.J.I.L.	*American Journal of International Law*
Annuaire	*Annuaire de l'Institut de Droit International*
Arb. A.	Reports of International Arbitral Awards
ASDB	Asian Development Bank
ASIL	American Society of International Law
Benelux	Belgium, Netherlands and Luxembourg (economic union between)
BIS	Bank for International Settlements
B.Y.I.L.	*British Year Book of International Law*
diss.	dissertation
Doc./Docs.	Document/Documents
ECOSOC	Economic and Social Council
ECSC	European Coal and Steel Community
EEC	European Economic Community
EFTA	European Free Trade Association
EURATOM	European Atomic Energy Community
European Convention	European Convention for the Pacific Settlement of Disputes
FAO	Food and Agriculture Organization
GA	General Assembly
GATT	General Agreement on Tariffs and Trade
GT	General treaty
IADB	Inter-American Development Bank
IAEA	International Atomic Energy Agency
IBRD	International Bank for Reconstruction and Development
ICAO	International Civil Aviation Organization
ICJ	International Court of Justice
I.C.J. Reports	International Court of Justice, Reports of Judgments, Advisory Opinions and Orders
IDA	International Development Association
IFC	International Finance Corporation
IGO	International (Governmental) Organisation

ILC	International Law Commission
ILO	International Labour Organisation
IMCO	Inter-Governmental Maritime Consultative Organization
IMF	International Monetary Fund
ITC	International Telecommunication Convention
ITU	International Telecommunication Union
Liber Amicorum Martin Domke	*International Arbitration, Liber Amicorum for Martin Domke*, The Hague 1967
L.N.T.S.	League of Nations Treaty Series
LoN	League of Nations
Mélanges Rolin	*Mélanges offerts à Henri Rolin, Problèmes de droit de gens*, Paris 1964
NATO	North Atlantic Treaty Organization
N.T.I.R.	*Nederlands Tijdschrift voor Internationaal Recht*
OAS	Organization of American States
PCIJ	Permanent Court of International Justice
PCIJ Series	Permanent Court of International Justice, Series of Judgments, Advisory Opinions and Orders
PEASLEE	*International Governmental Organizations*, by A.J. PEASLEE, 2 vols., The Hague 1961
Post-War Treaties (PT)	*Post-War Treaties for the Pacific Settlement of International Disputes*, by M. HABICHT, Cambridge 1931
Proc. ASIL	Proceedings of the American Society of International Law
R.d.C.	*Recueil des Cours de L'Académie de Droit International de la Haye*
Res.	Resolution
R.G.D.I.P.	*Revue Générale de Droit International Public*
SC	Security Council
SG	Secretary-General
SP	Special provision
Suppl.	Supplement
Survey I (SI)	*Systematic Survey of Treaties for the Pacific Settlement of International Disputes 1928-1948*, United Nations 1948
Survey II (SII)	*A Survey of Treaty Provisions for the Pacific Settlement of International Disputes 1949-1962*, United Nations 1966
Symbolae Verzijl	*Symbolae Verzijl, présentées au professeur J.H.W. Verzijl*, The Hague 1958.
UAR	United Arab Republic
UK	United Kingdom of Great Britain and Northern Ireland
UN	United Nations
UNCTAD	United Nations Conference on Trade and Development

UNESCO	United Nations Educational, Scientific and Cultural Organization
UN series	Organization and Procedure of United Nations Commissions, 12 vols., United Nations 1949-1950
U.N.T.S.	United Nations Treaty Series
UPC	Universal Postal Convention
UPU	Universal Postal Union
USA	United States of America
USSR	Union of Socialist Soviet Republics
Varia Juris Gentium	*Varia Juris Gentium, vraagstukken van Internationaal Recht, Liber Amicorum aangeboden aan J.P.A. François,* Leyden 1959
vol(s)	volume(s)
WFUNA	World Federation of United Nations Associations
WHO	World Health Organization
Yearbook	*Yearbook of the European Convention on Human Rights*
Z.f.a.ö.R.V.	*Zeitschrift für ausländisches öffentliches Recht und Völkerrecht*

KEY TO CODE

A	Arbitration
C	Conciliation
J	Judicial Settlement
P	Mention of obligation to settle disputes peacefully, although this is not elaborated
I	All disputes
II	Legal disputes
III	Political disputes
—	Application of arbitration and/or judicial settlement depends on cooperation of all parties
+	Application of arbitration and/or judicial settlement does not depend on cooperation of all parties
⁙	Special measures have been taken to obtain cooperation of parties in the application of arbitration and/or judicial settlement
GT	General treaty, *i.e.* treaty of which pacific settlement of disputes is the sole or main subject
SP	Special provision, *i.e.* provision in a treaty in a specific sector — e.g. transport or trade — which aims at the pacific settlement of disputes arising from the interpretation and application of that treaty
ah	ad hoc provision, *i.e.* provision on the application of a method of pacific settlement whenever a dispute arises

FOREWORD

The system of the pacific settlement of disputes contained in the United Nations Charter — confirmed in 1970 in the Declaration on Principles of International Law concerning Friendly Relations and Co-operation among States — is based on agreement between the parties on both the method to be applied and the acceptance of its results. From the juridical point of view states are free in this system to establish in advance their choice of the application of one or more methods to a dispute and their willingness to accept the result in respect of all or certain groups of disputes or only to determine their choice when a dispute arises. The functioning of the International Court must be regarded in this light.

The practice of pacific settlement shows that there is not too great a distance between the standpoints of the Soviet countries, who emphasise direct negotiation as the starting point in settling disputes, and that of the Western countries, who lay particular stress on judicial settlement as such, because the Western countries usually make the application of arbitration and judicial settlement to a specific dispute dependent on the cooperation of all parties, in obtaining which negotiations are essential.

This conclusion is based on an analysis of the use that states have made of their freedom of choice. In the analysis, a great number of bilateral and multilateral agreements on pacific settlement and their application since 1918 — about 600 — were investigated to see to what extent the application of the method agreed upon and the acceptance of the result were made juridically dependent on the cooperation of parties. The measurement of the element of negotiation shows that the present organisation of the interstate settlement of disputes still fully reflects the principle of the sovereign equality of states.

The quantitative way in which the study is constituted means that the result is intended to be valid irrespective of the theoretical position the reader may choose. Depending on his point of view, he will see the result as a confirmation of or an exception to the view he holds. Nevertheless, I felt the need to place my investigation against the background of a theoretical legal consideration of the significance of mutual consent for creation of law and implementation of law in general which has guided me in my work. This consideration is based on the conviction that the phenomenon of law is a form of communication between men, just like language, art and play. In this, legal security comes to the fore as an example of the comprehensibility and trust that are the basis of communication between men. In the hope that this comprehensibility, and thereby communication, which must also be considered indispensable for the functioning of the international legal system, will be promoted, this attempt has been made to survey the agreements between states on the pacific settlement of disputes, the guiding principle being their freedom of choice.

The book is a version of a thesis in Dutch with which I graduated as a Doctor of Law under Professor A.J.P. Tammes at the University of Amsterdam in September 1971. I am most grateful to him for the stimulating advice and critical guidance he gave me as my supervisor. The English translation of an abridged version of the thesis was made possible by a subsidy from the Netherlands Organization for the Advancement of Pure Research. Mr C. Sibson, M.A., has produced a highly satisfactory translation. Finally, I wish to thank my wife, not only for her support during the many years of preparation of the thesis, but also for her help in adapting it for this publication and for drawing up the bibliography.

Leidschendam, May 1973 P.J.I.M. DE WAART

CHAPTER I

THE SIGNIFICANCE OF THE ELEMENT OF NEGOTIATION IN THE PACIFIC SETTLEMENT OF DISPUTES BETWEEN STATES

Part. 1.

The significance of mutual agreement between parties in applying methods of pacific settlement of disputes between states

Article 33, para. 1 of the United Nations Charter lays down that the parties to a dispute

> "shall, first of all, seek a solution by negotiation, enquiry, mediation, conciliation, arbitration, judicial settlement, resort to regional agencies or arrangements, or other peaceful means of their own choice".

The Charter does not indicate any order in which the methods should be used. Art. 36, para. 3 merely urges that

> "in making recommendations under this Article the Security Council should also take into consideration that legal disputes should as a general rule be referred by the parties to the International Court of Justice in accordance with the provisions of the Statute of the Court".

During the preparatory discussions in San Francisco in 1945 on the contents and form of the Charter and the Statute of the International Court of Justice (ICJ) as part of the Charter, it was stated by the delegations of the Great Powers, particularly the Soviet Union and the United States, that they had strong objections to the inclusion in the ICJ Statute of a provision obliging parties to submit to the jurisdiction of the Court legal disputes which could not be settled in any other way. They let it be known that it would be difficult, if not impossible, for them to accept the Charter if the principle of compulsory jurisdiction, with or without the possibility of reservations, were included in the Statute, which after all would be part of the Charter.

Since the UN was founded the Soviet Union and the countries within her sphere of influence have kept to this position. In 1946 the United States made the declaration accepting the compulsory jurisdiction of the ICJ which was optional under Art. 36, para. 2 of the Statute of the Court, albeit with the important qualification that the declaration did not apply to

"disputes with regard to matters which are essentially within the domestic jurisdiction of the United States of Ameiica *as determined by the United States*" [1].

In 1945 the UN had 51 members. Since then this number has more than doubled, particularly since the early 1960s, when many Afro-Asian countries became independent. These countries of course had no direct influence on the content and form of the UN Charter. In view of this, it is also understandable that since 1961 the Afro-Asian countries, supported mainly by Czechoslovakia and Yugoslavia, should have urged at the UN General Assembly that the study of the "principles of friendly relations among states" be undertaken. On 16 December 1963 the UN General Assembly unanimously adopted a resolution — No. 1966 (XVIII) — setting up a Special Committee on Principles of International Law concerning Friendly Relations and Co-operation among States. This was done under Art. 13, para. 2 of the Charter, which instructs the General Assembly to undertake studies and make recommendations with a view to :

"... a. promoting international co-operation in the political field and encouraging the progressive development of international law and its codification".

Bearing in mind the principle of geographical distribution and the need for representation of the main legal systems of the world, the Committee was made up of representatives of 4 countries from the 'Eastern bloc', 9 from the 'Western bloc' and 14 from countries which do not belong to either bloc, and therefore represent the 'Third World'.[3]

[1] *Survey I*, p. 1150 (author's italics). The declaration is still in force as originally worded.

[2] Cf. Doc. A/5746, para. 3. The resolution recommended the "Governments of the States designated members of the Special Committee, in view of the general importance and the technical aspect of the item, to appoint jurists as their representatives on the Special Committee". The International Law Commission for its part applauded the constitution of a special committee because "such topics as peaceful co-existence and friendly relations are predominantly political in nature and ought to be left to a body more amenable and susceptible to political influences than the "International Law Commission". (See L.T. LEE, "The International Law Commission re-examined", in *A.J.I.L.*, 1965, p. 560). There was thus the noteworthy spectacle of jurists emphasising the political aspects and politicians emphasising the juridical aspects.

[3] Report of the Special Committee on Principles of International Law concerning Friendly Relations and Co-operation among States, 1964 (Doc. A/5746 of 16 November

The Committee considered 7 principles, including the one that is the basis of Art. 2, para. 3 of the Charter :

"All States shall settle their international disputes by peaceful means in such a manner that international peace and security and justice are not endangered".

Important points discussed by the Committee while this principle was being considered were whether it was necessary and appropriate to lay special emphasis on direct negotiation as one of the methods of pacific settlement of inter-state disputes — a viewpoint defended in particular by the Eastern bloc countries — and whether it was desirable to appeal to states to accept the compulsory jurisdiction of the ICJ, a point emphasised in particular by the Western countries and a few smaller Third World countries.[3]

The discussions of these points at the Special Committee's conferences in 1964, 1966 and 1967 are very similar to those during the Hague Peace Conferences of 1899 and 1907. The pronouncement of the Serbian delegate at the 1899 Hague Peace Conference

"La médiation en tant que préliminaire d'une intervention a toujours suscité des méfiances marquées et justifiées de la part des petits États"

would not have sounded out of place at the 1966 New York conference.[4] The heartfelt cry of the Dahomey delegate during the 1966 New York conference

"The world, and especially the weaker and poorer countries, needed a high judicial authority which would ensure that justice prevailed — a goal which was one of the purposes of the United Nations"

would definitely have been topical in 1899 — apart from the reference to the purposes of the UN.[5]

The smaller states still need protection against the larger states.[6] This need is also expressed in the small states' efforts to have the word

1964, in particular paras. 155-163 and 166-178, and Annex B), 1966 (Doc. A/6230 of 27 June 1966, paras. 195-206 and 210-220), 1967 (Doc. A/6799 of 26 September 1967, paras. 369-382), 1970 (Doc. A/AC. 125/L. 86 of 1 May 1970, p. 7 and A/L. 600 of 24 October 1970, pp. 12, 13).

[4] O. Hoijer, *La solution pacifique des litiges internationaux avant et depuis la Société des Nations*, 1925, p. 68.

[5] Doc. A/6230, para. 269.

[6] H. Blix, "The Principle of the Peaceful Settlement of Disputes", in the WFUNA publication *The Legal Principles governing Friendly Relations and Co-operation among States in the spirit of the United Nations Charter*, 1966, p. 60 : "Nowhere is the juridical principle of equality of states better respected than in an international tribunal". This is very much the question now that the refusal of one state to accept a norm can hinder its adoption as valid law.

'justice' included in provisions relating to the pacific settlement of disputes. When Art. 2, para. 3 of the Charter was being drafted during the 1945 San Francisco conference, for example, the word 'justice' was added at the instigation of Bolivia, which wanted to prevent the actual maintenance of peace taking precedence over all else in the settlement of disputes, at the expense of the small states. During discussion of pacific settlement at the Special Committee's meeting in New York a number of states asserted once again that

"medium and small states attached considerable importance to the concept of justice in connexion with the settlement of disputes and that the word 'justice' should therefore be included in the statement of the principle".[7]

Despite the small states' preference for judicial settlement it was not denied at both meetings of the Special UN Committee on Principles of International Law concerning Friendly Relations and Co-operation among States that both valid international law in general and the system of Chapter VI of the Charter in particular leave states completely free to choose the pacific method by which they intend to settle a dispute.[8] In the final text of the 'Declaration on Principles of International Law concerning Friendly Relations and Co-operation among States in accordance with the Charter of the United Nations' established by the Special Committee on 1 May 1970 and adopted by the General Assembly on 24 October 1970, the freedom of states to choose the method of pacific settlement of a dispute is emphasised :

"International disputes shall be settled on the basis of sovereign equality of States and in accordance with the principle of free choice of means".[9]

It is still true, in other words, that in modern inter-state relations states are free to choose the method of peacefully settling disputes. The declaration also states :

"The parties to a dispute have the duty, in the event of failure to reach a solution by any one of the above peaceful means (i.e. those mentioned in Article 33 of the

[7] Doc. A/6230, para. 180. BLIX, in the article referred to, points out rightly that "politically understandable as this provision is, it is not easy to define what kinds of settlements would be unjust and therefore ruled out. Presumably any settlement approved by the General Assembly or the Security Council would not be open to challenge on this ground", (*op. cit.*, p. 50). Also H. KELSEN, *The Law of the United Nations*, 1951, p. 366.

[8] Doc. A/6230, para. 186. See also L.M. GOODRICH, *The United Nations*, 1960, pp. 199-200, A.J.P. TAMMES, *Internationaal Publiekrecht* (Public International Law), 1966, p. 182, and OPPENHEIM-LAUTERPACHT, *International Law*, part 2, 1952, p. 6.

[9] Doc. A/AC. 125/L. 86, in which the consensus of delegations on the text of the declaration is given on the basis of informal consultations, p. 7, A/L. 600, p. 13, and Res. 2625 (XXV).

charter — author), to continue to seek a settlement of the dispute by other peaceful means agreed upon by them".

This implies that if a dispute arises there must be agreement not only on the method to be used, but also on acceptance of the result achieved. This agreement can be reached on an ad hoc basis when a dispute arises, or can be laid down in advance by parties in bilateral or multilateral treaties of which pacific settlement of disputes is the sole or main subject — referred to hereinafter as *general treaties* — or in provisions which are part of bilateral or multilateral treaties in specific sectors — e.g. transport, trade, the economy — and which aim at the pacific settlement of disputes arising from the interpretation and application of these treaties, hereinafter referred to as *special provisions*.

In order to be able to go into the import of the result of the recent definition of position — 'codification' — with regard to the pacific settlement of disputes, which is contained in the above declaration, an attempt has been made in this study to quantify the use made by states of their freedom of choice of a method of pacific settlement of disputes and of their freedom to accept the results of these methods. To this end, an examination has been made, without attempting to be exhaustive, of a number of general treaties (301 in all) and special provisions (258 in all) and a number of cases of conciliation, arbitration and judicial settlement in practice (173 in all), taken for the most part from the period between 1918 and 1965. This period was chosen to enable the development of conciliation and arbitration since the founding of the first international organisation, the League of Nations, and the first international court, the Permanent Court of International Justice in the Hague, to be investigated.

Taking as a starting point the freedom of choice of parties, the guiding principle observed in the analysis of the general treaties and special provisions was to group the methods of pacific settlement of disputes under 2 headings :

I. methods under which parties reserve to themselves the decision which can end the dispute;

II. methods under which parties entrust this decision to third parties.

In this the degree of institutionalisation has been investigated, i.e. the measures taken by the parties in advance to facilitate or ensure the application of the methods concerned.

The fact that in contemporary inter-state relations mutual agreement between the legal subjects is central to creation and application of law in respect of pacific settlement of inter-state disputes, as appears from the above declaration and will be confirmed by this analysis, implies that the organisation of the community of nations can be described as anti-authoritarian. In other words : the organisation of present-day inter-state relations is based on the sovereign equality of states, which means that an arrangement of relations between states is based on negotiation and joint action between states. In this process, however, the individual is receiving more and more attention and, as a citizen of his state and within non-governmental international organisations, he is trying to create or increase influence on the development of international law as part of public international law, which regulates relations between states.[10]

In national legal systems with an established reputation too the tendency can be detected to give a central position to the individual as legal subject in attempts to explain the basis of the legal system. This can be illustrated with the aid of a number of recent studies on the normative character of law, representing the analytic, functional and existential-phenomenological theories. Before analysing mutual agreement between states in the formation and implementation of law in respect of the pacific settlement of inter-state disputes, we shall also consider the significance of mutual agreement between legal partners in the creation of law (part 3) and implementation of law (part 4) in general.

Part 2.

THE NORMATIVE CHARACTER OF LAW

In inter-state relations the individual faces the fact that, as a citizen of a certain state, he can confront a citizen of another state without their personal relationship giving rise to this situation and without either feeling that they can exercise any influence on, let alone be personally responsible for, the course of events, even though they may live in a democracy. Relations between groups of people living in different countries can be felt by the individual persons and the groups to which they belong to be beyond their control, even at a time when technology offers more and more ways of intensifying contacts between people in different countries. An example of this is the fatalism reflected in remarks such as those heard in the Netherlands to the effect that anti-Vietnam War campaigns, for example, are futile because the individual and the countries which do not belong to the Big Two, Three, Four or Five cannot exercise any influence on events. In such an uneasy atmosphere international law seems to be an illusion in which

[10] J.J. LADOR-LEDERER, *International Non-Governmental Organizations and Economic Entities*, 1963, in particular Chapter X, "The Legislative NGO", pp. 82-89.

small countries in particular want to believe, and in any case the question as to the basis of this law (and therefore of law in general) becomes pressing.

Ideas of international law vary. Some deny the existence of international *law*, some recognise it as weak, incomplete law, as law based on the will of states, or as a natural law.[11] In other words, the existence of international *law* is by no means undisputed. Among those who are prepared to admit its existence there are some who warn that a crisis in international law may arise or who feel that one is imminent.[12] It seems still common knowledge that, in the most favourable circumstances, international law is at best weak and incomplete law. This is not unconnected with the way in which the close link with politics shows itself in this branch of law. This relationship, however, is nothing special for law as such, although the jurist living and working within a national legal system will not always realise it (or want to), for in such a system the conflict of interests is fought and kept in check in the legislature, which normally provides an anchor for the jurist in his work. In a national legal system, furthermore, the distribution of functions between the legislature, the judiciary and the executive is not usually so unsatisfactory that jurists and citizens in general do not yield to the temptation to ignore the relationship between law and politics and regard law too much as an independent entity, as something outside the individual which can protect him against himself and against other individuals, acting both individually and in organised groups. The need for law as an independent entity is dictated by a desire for rules which can lay claim to objective validity, i.e. a validity (and application) which is as far as possible independent of the concrete power situation in a concrete case, as is reflected in the advancement of the ban on taking law into one's own hands as a legal principle, even in inter-state relations. The unrest over the significance and function of international law may be more spectacular than that over the significance and function of law in general and national law in particular, because in international law it is precisely in critical circumstances that its maintenance is left to the interested partics themselves and the autonomy of parties, as in private law, is in the forefront. The unrest, how-

[11] The various theories are surveyed by A. TRUYOL in "Doctrines contemporaines du Droit des Gens", *R.G.D.I.P.*, 1950, pp. 369-413 and 1951, pp. 22-40 and 199-236.

[12] Cf., in Dutch literature on international law, B.V.A. RÖLING, *International Law in an Expanded World*, 1960; G.H.J. VAN DER MOLEN, "The Present Crisis in the Law of Nations", *Symbolae Verzijl*, 1958, pp. 238-255; A.M. STUYT, "Op de grens van het volkenrecht", *Volkenrechtelijke Opstellen, presented to B.M. Telders, F.M. Baron van Asbeck and J.H.W. Verzijl*, 1957, pp. 186-204; H. J. ROETHOF, *De norm in het volkenrecht*, 1962, pp. 151 et seq.; and H.F. VAN PANHUYS, "Regional or General International Law? A misleading dilemma", *N.T.I.R.*, 1961, pp. 146-165.

ever, affects law — and society — in general. It can be seen in the context of — and in interaction with — a line of thought that concentrates on the individual himself.

After a period in which man, as it were, has been able to lose himself in scientific practice which appeared exact, he is now again feeling thrown back on himself, on his 'self' which cannot be objectivised. He is learning that he can only pronounce on his self from the point of view of that self, in other words, that in his objectivising he always has his self in the background. The unique quality of each 'self' is irreconcilable with the attempt of law to level it out into an average type, into an 'individual' whose behaviour can be expressed in rules. This tendency of law to eliminate the 'self' has found an epitome in international law in the doctrine of the sovereignty of the state and the view that the state is the only original subject in international law.[13] As TAMMES states in *Het universele rechtsstelsel beschreven aan de hand van een classificatie.* (The universal legal system described with the aid of a classification) the natural person, however, has, precisely in contrast to artificial persons 'in the absence of national legal hindrances due to the legal system to which he belongs, sufficient properties to act in any quality which may be recognised by international practice, such as participation in creation of law, by, among other things, concluding agreements with foreign states on an equal footing, as the upholder of his own laws, as subject of international liability, etc.'[14] These national legal hindrances due to the legal system to which he belongs and the recognition by international practice of the qualities in which he can act, can be felt by the individual to be extraneous circumstances which are such that they — and thereby law — apply to him as an external power : the community, which imposes its will on him. The individual, however, is himself a part of the community; the community consists of individuals.

The usual contrast between autonomous and heteronomous behavioural rules separates the individual from the world to which he belongs, whereas on the one hand the individual can in no way regard morality as wholly his own — here too he is influenced by his environment — and on the other hand the prevailing ideas on what law and morals require of him

[13] This view is hardly put forward any more. Cf. H. MOSLER, "Die Erweiterung des Kreises der Völkerrechtssubjekte", *Z.f.a.ö.R.V.*, 1962, pp. 1-48. The publication of the Academy of Sciences of the U.S.S.R., Institute of State and Law, entitled *International Law; a textbook for use in Law Schools*, (c. 1960), says on this however : "As a rule, only a State can be such a subject under present-day International Law" (p. 89).

[14] Mededelingen der Koninklijke Nederlandse Akademie van Wetenschappen, Literature Section, New Series, part 32, No. 2, 1969, p. 45. Cf. also MOSLER, *op. cit.*, pp. 7 and 30-31.

are not so completely strange to him that he feels he cannot influence them. The dividing line between morality on the one hand and law and morals on the other is not so sharp as the terms 'autonomous' and 'heteronomous' would lead us to expect. Another objection to this distinction is that it emphasises the existence of norms — as if regulations are independent entities — and then subdivides them into those which the individual has to deal with if he wants to, and those with which he has to deal whether he wants to or not. The distinction ignores the emergence of norms which requires our attention at this very time when the freedom of the person and the personal responsibility inherent in it are also being emphasised in international discussions.

In his study '*Norm en handeling*' (Norm and Action) GLASTRA VAN LOON argued that the individual is not a subject who also has to deal with norms in the sense of objective occurrences outside him. In his view, law does not derive its normative power from objective facts outside the individual, nor from subjective inclination, but from actions which are never without commitment but without exception are our own responsibility.[15]

In his actions, as in his language, the individual expresses himself in a way recognisable to his fellow-men, i.e. in a way which can have a certain significance for them. The individual must take account of this significance in his actions. The significance of a certain action may be accepted between two persons and in larger groups, varying from a private club to mankind as a whole. GLASTRA VAN LOON attributes normative power to actions because they create precedents, because, unless denied in the sense of being rejected, they are valid as demonstrations of 'the done thing'. Norms are not prescriptive or descriptive but regulate relationships between actions. By indicating the normative power of actions, says this writer, we reach the limit of what may be explained, a limit which cannot in principle be transgressed, not a coincidental limitation of our knowledge. In his inaugural speech *Recht en menselijke natuur* (Law and human nature, 1959), GLASTRA VAN LOON seems nevertheless to transgress the limit himself by not confining himself to actions, but by taking as his basis the essential equality of individuals as subjects.[16] Admittedly, he is consistent in saying that this essential equality cannot be determined positively, but he maintains it nevertheless

[15] J.F. GLASTRA VAN LOON, *Norm en handeling* (Norm and Action, Contribution to an epistemological foundation of the social sciences), 1957, pp. 202 and 218. See also *Norms and Actions, National Reports on Sociology of Law*, edited by R. TREVES and F.F. GLASTRA VAN LOON, 1968.

[16] *Loc. cit.*, p. 9 : "Essential equality of individuals as subjects must be assumed if any word is to have any meaning, and any rule to be laid down meaningfully".

as a norm, although it is an assumption and not an action, by seeing in essential equality the basis of an objectively rejecting judgment. In his opinion equality places limits on the actions of men with each other, without providing a positive criterion for them. He maintains that the course of the development of law is not determined in other words by a pole star twinkling in the distance, but by continually repeated adjustments of existing law (...) in which each adjustment remains capable of re-adjustment, because in applying an adjusted rule cases may arise in which the rule has consequences which we reject as unjustified.[17]

Functional doctrine of law concentrates also on actions as *utterances* by the individual, because it feels that the essence of man himself cannot be known. It thus, as it were, again detaches the individual from his actions and seeks the normative character in actions according to plan, in the expectation of a suitable reply which one individual may have with regard to another, given the concrete rules and the concrete situation.[18]

It may not be deduced from individuals' actions that all are essentially equal as subjects — in Glastra van Loon's view this equality is therefore also an assumption — while this equality in itself contains no indication on the inclination of the individual.[19] This very problem is receiving the attention of the existentialist-phenomenologist tendency in the philosophy of law. In his introduction for the Netherlands Association for the Philosophy of Law *Existentiële fenomenologie van het recht* (The existential phenomenology of law) published in 1966, A.N. Kotting concludes that, although ideas of philosophers of law who are following in the wake of phenomenology are still highly varied, some findings are gradually being made regarding law which are nevertheless common coin among existentialists. Among the examples of this he mentions 'that the essence, including that of law, is not to be sought outside the individual, but only by looking at the individual in his world' and 'that the problem of the relation between norm and fact, insoluble in the isolating, intellectualistic approach to positive

[17] The assumption of essential equality indicates, however, not only that laying down of rules can be a matter of correcting faults which have arisen in the past, but also that the experiment of laying down rules as such must be permitted. The acceptability of the experiment is also determined by whether any wrong *results* of the rules laid down can be put right, and that presupposes an estimate of what the future has in store.

[18] J. ter Heide, *Vrijheid, over de zin van de straf*, (Freedom, the sense of punishment, with summary in English), 1965, pp. 34 et seq.

[19] It will be realised that personal responsibility and freedom are not reflected in equality. Here love could bring a result which does not have a formal character, but a personal content, which can give an answer for everyone to the question "how should *I* behave?".

law, becomes clear and the link between norm and fact becomes obvious if we base ourselves on the realisation that in his existence the individual is continually involved with a world which is given at the same time as him' (p. 61). This clarity in the link between norm and fact is seen by considering individual *action* and rejecting the idea of a norm that exists independently. Each action is the responsibility of the individual who performs it. The reaction to it can be acceptance or rejection. By this, however, the area of law is not demarcated vis-à-vis other areas of human behaviour.

The specific nature of the area of law is now sought in the above ideas in the presence of an order of authority (power) and/or judicial settlement. If the community did not have bodies which again and again definitively decided on conflicts arising from ambiguities, a chaos of actions or meanings would inevitably develop and intercourse would be completely impossible. 'All forms of human society require the existence of a structure of authority. Authority and the exercise of authority are essential ingredients of human society, not convertible into certain acts of intercourse, because they are assumed by every society'.[20]

The humanising — demythologising — of the norm, which is behind the above tendencies thus contains the danger of too much emphasis on authority or power, detached from the norm which it assumes. The individual then threatens to become a subject who is concerned, it is true, not with norms but with authority (power) in the sense of objective occurrences outside him. The remarkable phenomenon occurs, in other words, that a relativising — normalising — of the significance of legal norms can be linked with an absolutising — de-humanising — of authority. This difference in approach to authority and to law can be called typical of the jurist who knows the relative value of the law by training and experience, but who needs authority in order to be able to work.

Glastra van Loon only wants to speak of legal norms if the decision on the application and interpretation of norms rests with a body created especially for the purpose by the community and furnished with guarantees of independent operation. In the functional doctrine of law he defends Ter Heide argues that the legal sense is the court's answer to parties who are in dispute about the normative sense, it is the legal sense that it expresses in the given situation. The court's role is thus exaggerated at the expense of that of the legislature to which the legal subjects between whom a dispute has arisen themselves belong. The legal sense of the relationship between legal subjects is determined in the first instance by the legislature in the abstract and made concrete by the judiciary in a specific relation between specific legal subjects together with these legal subjects.

[20] Glastra van Loon, *Norm en handeling*, p. 233.

The operation of the legislature makes the borderline between law and politics a fluid one. The interest groups involved will have to find some common ground in order to do their job. In a society which functions satisfactorily there is no more mystique in this. This does not affect the fact that giving a phenomenon the label of 'law' is seldom an action for the individual of pure recognition or description, but is at the same time an expression of the desire that the phenomenon be accepted as a norm.[21] In a legal order force may be needed to maintain that order, but the regulated character of force in that order can guarantee the link between means and end. The legal subjects are involved in regulating force, as it is part of the creation of law.[22] To a large extent, creation of laws is in the hands of the legislature. By concentrating attention too much on the importance of judicial settlement, as is done in the views of law mentioned above and as many a jurist is inclined to do because of his legal training, the function of the legislature is neglected. This very function, however, creates the possibility of making the significance of authority, power and force clear in a democratic society. In the legislature the individual already has an excellent opportunity, while negotiating, to exercise influence as a legal subject on the weighing of interests as between the individual and the community. Via the influence of the legal subjects which is exercised through the legislature that they have created for themselves, the way is clear for a functional approach to law, authority and force. The individual is unique, but this applies to *every* individual. Doing justice as much as possible to what is unique in each individual is the function of creation of law in the abstract (legislating) and in concrete (judicial settlement), and in the upholding of law (exercise of authority). When the individual subjects his feeling and action to criteria of evaluation, three tendencies can clearly be distinguished : a striving for harmony with other individuals, a striving for

[21] G.E. LANGEMEIJER, *Inleiding tot de studie van de wijsbegeerte des rechts* (Introduction to the study of the philosophy of Law), 1970, p. 334. The author adds that this desire can alter the phenomenon itself. As an example he mentions international law, which he considers as one of the most imperfect areas of law. Taking human desire as a basis, we can in my opinion only speak of 'law'. The sub-division of law into private and public, and public into constitutional, criminal, international, etc., is valueless in itself and is a matter of classification. Assuming that law as such is a social phenomenon, we can ask from the classification point of view whether there is any point in grouping certain legal relationships and studying them separately. The handbooks on international law and the many monographs on parts of the system indicate that, as far as international law is concerned, the question can be answered in the affirmative. Cf. H.L.A. HART, *The Concept of Law*, Chapter X, "International Law", (1961).

[22] Regulatory force is therefore not anti-existential.

harmony with oneself, and a striving for harmony with that which is transcendent.[23]

In creation of law all these motive forces can be asserted : in the legislature during debates on bills, in everyday life in the emergence of customs, and in the legal suit during discussion between parties and the court. The result of this creation of law — the Act of Parliament, the custom, the court judgment — has the importance of a signpost in a period of rapid change, which is followed as long as the direction indicated seems sensible.

To sum up, law is autonomous in the sense that norms emerge by the actions of *individuals*, acting as individuals or together, as an action or reaction and these actions create a pattern that arouses expectations. The expectations can be enshrined in abstract in custom and/or law and within the legal framework thus created in concerete, i.e. in a specific relation between specific parties, in the judicial settlement. The actions cannot however be seen as independent entities, but as the result of negotiations between individuals — if they still have to come to mutual understanding — or of joint actions, if the mutual understanding already exists.

As a society is less able to order things, the need for a 'mystic' norm will be stronger. The jurist who concerns himself with international law must not however let himself be led astray by seeking such a norm in an attempt to obtain a grip on international relations via law.[24] Nor is there any point in these circumstances in his trying to make the function of judicial settlement independent of the connection with that of the legislature. He would be doing his fellow-men more of a service by showing them clearly that the law gives rules which they can or must follow, but which, however binding they may be, are always drawn up by individuals for individuals, in other words, by emphasising their own responsibility for the origin and survival of the legal order. Law is not so much an entity in itself as the product of a community in which each legal partner is empowered and able to influence the laying down of the law. Law pre-supposes communication between individuals in both its creation and its implementation.

[23] LANGEMEIJER, *op. cit.*, p. 337.

[24] HART, *op. cit.*, p. 270 "Again once we emancipate ourselves from the assumption that international law *must* contain a basic rule, the question to be faced is one of fact".

Part 3.

The significance of mutual agreement between legal subjects in the formation of legal rules

For a long time the international community was restricted to fifty or so nations. In a small circle of this nature, certainly according to the earlier view that only states are subjects in international law, the impression can be confirmed and maintained that international law is the result of an agreement 'between ourselves', with the opinion of the country which is the most influential in a particular field being decisive. François argues, for example, that in order to be regarded as valid a rule of law requires the consent of the community of states, but not of each state individually. It can happen, says this writer, that the refusal of one state to accept a norm can prevent it being recognised as valid international law, as for example if Great Britain does not recognise a rule of maritime law.[25] The new states have not always proved willing to put up with such positions of power, an example of which, they feel, is the idea that any expropriation must always and directly be covered by compensation.[26]

The idea that international law only applies to states may be considered outmoded. International law too demonstrates the concentration of legal thinking on the individual. An illustration of this is provided by the discussion of the individual's constitutional rights. The text of the Covenant of the League of Nations limited consideration of the individual to 'fair and humane conditions of labour for men, women and children' and 'just treatment of the native inhabitants of territories' over which League members had control (Art. 23, League of Nations Covenant). This interest in satisfactory working conditions, which even before the Covenant came into force had led to the setting up of the International Labour Organisation in 1919, developed in the United Nations Charter into a 'respect for human rights and for fundamental freedoms for all without any distinction as to race, sex, language or religion' (Art. 1, Charter). This objective was elaborated in Chapter IX of the Charter, devoted to International Economic and Social Cooperation, while an Economic and Social Council was formed (ECOSOC) — Chapter X — to bring it about. Since 1945 the humanising

[25] J.P.A. François, *Grondlijnen van het volkenrecht,* (Outline of International Law) 3rd. ed., 1967, p. 29.

[26] R. Bystrický, "On the Principle of Obligatory Co-operation of States", in the WFUNA publication *The Legal Principles governing Friendly Relations and Co-operation among States in the spirit of the United Nations Charter*, 1966, pp. 99 et seq. Discussion of expropriation was given particular impetus by the process of decolonisation.

tendency of international law has been reinforced, despite all the tensions to which the world is subject. Reference may be made here to the Declaration of Human Rights accepted by the UN General Assembly in 1948 (Resolution 217 (III) of 10 December 1948) and — even more characteristic because the new countries were involved — to the Covenants on Human Rights accepted by the General Assembly on 16 December 1966, viz. the International Covenant on Economic, Social and Cultural Rights and the International Covenant on Civil and Political Rights.[27]

A further striking example of the humanising of international life as a whole is provided by development aid, the very aim of which is to create economic and social structures in developing countries within which they can progress by their own efforts to a worthy level of prosperity. This 'humanisation' of international law means that it can more and more be regarded as a normal part of law as a whole. Yet international law still feels, because of its origin as law between sovereign states, the consequences of legal philosophical attempts to base national law as an independent entity. With regard to international law jurists are rather inclined to see the basis in a 'pactum' between states, even though in the basis of their national legal systems they are trying to get away from the idea of mutual agreement between legal subjects. Thus international law — in the most favourable case — is labelled from the philosophical point of view as weak and incomplete law.

An example of a juridical basis for national law is offered by FRIEDRICH, who in a consideration of peace as a world legal order mentions the struggle to arrange law itself juridically as 'the contribution of Western constitutional law to the history of the world'. This is in a plea for the drawing up of a world constitution which on the basis of a decision of all participating nations would expressly have to establish in a positive law the most important legal rules for general international law. He finally describes law as a system of reasonable rules based on human experience, aiming at the realisation of justice, achieved by the participation of legal subjects *on the basis of a constitution* and based on the continually-changing and self-renewing community of legal subjects.[28]

[27] W. KOREY, "The Key to Human Rights - Implementation", *International Conciliation*, 1968, No. 570; M. SLUSNY, "Quelques observations sur les systèmes de protection internationale des Droits de l'homme", *Mélanges Rolin*, pp. 374-397.

[28] C.J. FRIEDRICH, *Die Philosophie des Rechts in historischer Perspektive*, 1955, p. 143. FRIEDRICH points out that both out of philosophical objections and because of discomfort at the practice of international law, people have wished to deny that it is real law : "Denn da das Völkerrecht nicht auf einer Verfassung beruhe, so könne es auch nicht wirkliches Recht sein", (p. 140).

Now a constitution is in no way a *juridical foundation* of law. The actual political situation at the time the written constitution is drafted is too influential for that. Constitutional law therefore develops to a great extent outside the constitution. Written constitutions have not succeeded in really mastering constitutional law. Nor can any 'juridically-based arrangement' of law be seen in constitutional law outside the constitution, for, with regard both to the structure of authority and the relations between authority and its subjects the element of the actual situation is important. Until now the written constitution has thus preserved something of the character of an agreement, because in it actual elements — conflicting interests — have to be reconciled.[29] Treaty theory cannot satisfy the jurist from the standpoint of his specialist knowledge; the idea of which it is the basis, viz. the mutual agreement of the legal subjects as the basis of a legal order, comes again and again to the fore, and this in greater relief the less developed is the legal order.

This comes out in international law, where the idea of a 'pactum' between states is still the basis of many a theory.

In both the Dutch handbooks on international law that have been published since 1945 the principle 'pacta sunt servanda' is called an inadequate explanation.[30] But each rule of international law, says FRANÇOIS, in order to be regarded favourably, needs the approval of the community of states, albeit not that of each state individually.[31] Although FRANÇOIS rejects the construction of a 'pactum' in the juridical sense, he introduces consensus and thereby the element of negotiation into the formation of law. TAMMES does the same. He contests the validity of 'pacta sunt servanda' as a basic norm but considers that a repeated explanation of the creation of a new legal situation lies in the *expectation* aroused in a subject in international law (p. 237). From the juridical point of view this is more of a refinement of the norm 'pacta sunt servanda' than a rejection, just as the idea of the attributable expectation in private law is not an undermining but a refinement of the law of contract.[32] The idea of a 'pactum' comes to the fore

[29] Cf. J. VAN DER HOEVEN, *De plaats van de grondwet in het constitutionele recht*, (The position of the constitution in constitutional law) dissertation, 1958 (with summary in English).

[30] FRANÇOIS, *op. cit.*, pp. 27-28, TAMMES, *op. cit.*, See also HART, *loc. cit.*, p. 228.

[31] *Op. cit.*, p. 29. In this view there is no place for formation of law by other subjects in international law than states, and the legislative influence of non-governmental organisations (NGOs) is ignored. Cf. LADOR-LEDERER, *op. cit.*, pp. 82-89. The legislative function of NGOs can be inferred from Art. 38 of the ICJ Statute.

[32] See on this H.C.F. SCHOORDIJK, *Beschouwingen over drie-partijenverhoudingen van*

again in fact with TAMMES when he asserts that legal intercourse is based on the expressed will, not the actually-thought will.

Even less in international law than in national legal systems will the doctrine of the 'contrat social' be able to offer a satisfactory solution to jurists as specialists. This however is not to deny the idea of mutual agreement as a basis of law. TAMMES points out rightly that behaviour and immaterial actions can lead to directives which are considered binding within a community and are therefore called binding. If it is objected to this that something which is *known to be binding* is not the same as *being* binding, he says, it can be pointed out that this is all a question of point of view. If one stands outside the legal system this directive is a socio-psychological fact, that, seen from the point of view of the legal system and particularly for the bodies which apply it, is a binding norm. For the organ there is nothing but law, apart from that organ's freedom of decision, the limits of which are determined in turn by law. For the subject there is law as a social value in addition to other social and ethical values, which are capable of being weighed against each other.[33]

In the national legal system this weighing takes place in the legislature. One representative will see in a draft law the confirmation of the existing legal situation, another will see in it a change thereof. The former will urge acceptance on the basis of his juridical arguments, the latter will urge rejection. Both however will find that juridical arguments alone will not be decisive in the debate. Both will find allies and opponents on economic, social, cultural, philosophical and other grounds. All these grounds together finally determine the lot of a given draft law, just as they determine custom and the idea that custom can have the force of law. TAMMES rightly notes (p. 239) that in many cases the international legislator will merely be an embodiment of the practice of *negotiation* between states. In this however international law is no different from other areas of law. The legislator is always a personification of the practice of negotiation between men, individually or within the framework of their institutions.

If the jurist, from within his specialist field, wants to look for a yardstick by which to evaluate the interplay of negotiation, he will come out of it just as cheated as the medical specialist and the economist — to name only two — who wish to establish foundations for their subject as a value in itself. If he objects that he knows whether it is soundly based or not, he

obligatoire aard, (A consideration of tripartite relationships of a compulsory nature) dissertation, 1958 (with summary in French).

[33] *Op. cit.*, p. 21. See also HART, *loc. cit.*, p. 96 and Chapter VI : "The foundations of a legal system", pp. 97 et seq.

knows this not as a jurist, etc., but as a person. It may be hard for the jurist to have to admit that from within his field he cannot achieve a hold on reality which regulates matters so inexorably that a good and justified society will arise. He will have to accept the fact that *as a jurist* he cannot solve the puzzle of man.

In national law, negotiation on the creation of law — apart from custom law and case law — takes place in a specific legislative body. In international law there is still no such body.[34] Negotiation usually takes place on an ad hoc basis, apart from the start made on institutionalising legislation at regional level. Creation of law via the settlement of disputes plays an important part in this. If a dispute breaks out or threatens to do so between subjects in international law, particularly states, there is seldom agreement on the content and applicability of the rules advanced by both states as law. Just like parliamentary representatives during preparation of a new law in a national legislature, the parties in a dispute in international law see their own point of view as 'jus constitutum' and each other's as 'jus constituendum'. What one sees as a legal dispute, the other will describe as a political dispute. In all proceedings — also in litigation before the national court — can parties thus confront each other. The difference between judicial settlement by the national court and by the international court however, is that the former does not normally have to do more than form law within the limits laid down by the legislature. In drawing those limits all possible motives have already played their part. The international court however is not always accompanied by an international legislature which has already attended to all weighing of interests in creating the law. It is then faced with a task which its function does not call upon it to perform, because it has no political accountability.

S.D. METZGER referred to this in his article 'The Settlement of International Disputes by Non-Judicial Methods'. He argues : 'The legislative process of compromise, rather than the judicial process of victory-defeat, is considered more suitable to the resolution of disputes in these relatively

[34] In their book *World peace through world law*, 1962, G. CLARK and L.B. SOHN experiment with the idea of a world organisation with legislative, judicial and executive organs, the accent being however on the judicial function. An important position in the experiment is allotted to a "World Equity Tribunal" of 15 members which would settle non-legal disputes, and in normal circumstances would not be able to take binding decisions, unless the parties consented, but whose recommendations could, in exceptional circumstances constituting a threat to peace, have legal force (pp. xxxiv, xxxv, 176-178 and Annex III), after having been sanctioned by the legislative organ : the UN General Assembly.

new and uncharted paths of economic cooperation between nations'.[35] In this situation it is not surprising that states frequently prefer direct negotiations in settling disputes and that this preference has been maintained as a principle by a number of countries, particularly Czechoslovakia.

Part 4.

THE FUNCTION OF JUDICIAL SETTLEMENT IN THE IMPLEMENTATION OF LAW

Art. 38, 1 (d) of the ICJ Statute states that the Court, in performing its duty of settling, in accordance with international law, the disputes submitted to it, must apply, subject to the provisions of Art. 59 (the decision only binds parties), *judicial decisions* and the teachings of the most highly qualified publicists of the various nations, *as subsidiary means* for the determination of rules of law.[36] Judicial decisions are therefore regarded here as aids in determining rules of law. We may wonder whether rules of law will ever be formulated so clearly that the aids do not need to be used or whether judicial decisions will ever take on a more independent significance than the description 'aid' may lead us to expect. TAMMES considers a possible system of clearly formulated international public law to be so crucial that he includes disputes on compliance with it among what is called the pathology of international law.[37]

Disputes on the observance of rules of law are also occasionally described as the pathology of law within national legal systems.[38] However, those who are prepared to recognise law as a product of negotiation and interaction between individuals as subjects should not see anything pathological in

[35] *A.J.I.L.*, 1954, pp. 408-421. Although METZGER's remark was prompted by disputes with an economic background, it also applies to other disputes, e.g. those with a social or cultural background.

[36] Author's italics.

[37] *Internationaal Publiekrecht*, pp. 178 and 236. HART understands the pathology of a legal system to be a situation in which the official sector and the private sector have grown so far apart that there is no longer general obedience to the rules which are valid according to the criteria of validity in use in the courts (*loc. cit.*, p. 114).

[38] As far as the Dutch legal system is concerned, cf. the speech entitled "De betrekkelijke waarde der wet" made by M.H. BREGSTEIN on the 320th anniversary of the University of Amsterdam and included in his *Verzameld Werk* (Collected Works), 1960, part 1, pp. 1 et seq. BREGSTEIN identifies private law with the social order and maintains that this order should fulfil itself without procedural law being involved. He calls this area of law the pathology of law (p. 9). In his opinion law has failed to achieve its primary aim if legal proceedings become necessary.

legal proceedings as a means of settling disputes arising from the application of law to concrete relationships between parties. If it is wished to use the term pathological in this context, it should be applied at the most to the parties in the proceedings — not to the procedural *law* — and then not by any means in every case. A normal action in which parties have not broken off communication with each other is in all respects acceptable. The fact that parties cannot always reach agreement is no more pathological than parliamentary debates, which certainly do not always lead to a bill being which cannot weigh the pros and cons of each other's position to have recourse to the court.

Rules of law emerge, exist and die in and through intercourse between individuals as subjects. They can take shape in everyday practice, through the work of a legislature that has been set up by a community for that purpose, through the work of a judicial body of that community and also through the work of the executive. All these methods of creation of law continually influence each other. Legal science as such cannot put them in any order, any more than the legislature or judiciary can. There is therefore nothing inferior about legal proceedings.

When creating law in the abstract (Acts of Parliament) the legislature cannot be expected always to keep in view the application of rules between specific legal subjects — creation of law in concrete — in such a way that concrete justice is not affected. Failure to do so can be a reason for parties which cannot weigh the pros and cons of each other's position to have recourse to the court.

The pathological character, not of the legal action as a means of solving a dispute or of procedural law, but of the parties concerned, is clear where communication between parties has ceased and where the way would be clear for use of naked force if there were no body which was not only empowered but also able to take a decision to end the conflict.

If legal subjects have recourse to legal proceedings, it cannot be concluded that the primary aim of law has not been achieved. Law is not a closed system which everyone can know and which any proceedings between legal subjects can affect. Judicial settlement itself is an important means of creating law, not only in the 'case law' countries but also in the 'civil law' countries. This is largely due to the fact that procedural *law* enables parties to communicate with each other and with the court. The interplay between subjects and the court is not pathological at all, precisely because it leaves room open for communication.[39] If legal subjects had been able to deter-

[39] This is made clear in J. EGGENS' view that in a legal procedure it is the material legal relation between parties themselves that develops under the guidance and influence o

mine their legal relationship themselves — which is usually the case in interstate relations — the court's decision, from the legal point of view, would not have been of a higher order than the solution the parties might have been able to find by direct negotiation.

The method of solution which is the most efficient and will be most frequently used depends on the parties and the legal order in which they live. From the theoretical abstract point of view it is impossible to state what good interpretation of law involves. The most that can be said is that the judge's pronouncement has social significance, i.e. that he holds a 'regulatory dialogue' with society, as TER HEIDE says.[40] This dialogue can only bear fruit within a society which is already regulated. FRANÇOIS rightly states, in a consideration of *L'Avenir de la Cour Internationale de Justice* :

> "La juridiction ne peut faire de progrès que si un certain nombre d'éléments se trouvent être réunis, tels qu'une idéologie commune, des notions de droit concordantes, un esprit de solidarité et la conviction que les intérêts d'État seront finalement mieux servis par le respect du droit que par quelque autre moyen".[41]

The less regulated a society is, the less support the judicature will receive from the legislature and the executive, and the less will the court, when approached, be able to help taking over some of the work of the legislature, to the detriment of its own function.[42]

The fact that the international judge encounters great vagueness in his concrete creation of law and is thus tempted to assume general rules on his own is *not* disturbing because his job is only to interpret law, not to create it, but rather because he is still unable to harmonise his law-creating task with that of an international legislature.

That the law-creating task is not new to the court, that the legislature even assumes this, is clear from the fact that

the court (LAND-EGGENS, *Verklaring van het Burgerlijk Wetboek* (Explanation of the Civil Code) part 6, 1933, p. 7, in Dutch).

[40] TER HEIDE, *Rechtsvinding*, (Interpretation of Law) introduction for the Netherlands Association for the Philosophy of Law, 1965, pp. 33 and 34. This means that the court juridicizes general legal ideas (principles of society) within the framework of its statutory room for manœuvre.

[41] *Volkenrechtelijke Opstellen*, Gesina van der Molen, 1962, p. 76. Cf. also C.W. JENKS, *The Prospects of International Adjudication*, 1964, in particular pp. 757 et seq.

[42] Report of a Study Group on the Peaceful Settlement of International Disputes, David Davies Memorial Institute of International Studies, 1966, para. 5, p. 3 : "In short, owing to the nature of international law and the consensual basis of international jurisdiction, arbitral and judicial decisions may sometimes have the appearance of a substitute for the legislative process in much the same way as conciliation". The report was produced by a study group under the chairmanship of H. WALDOCK, who also acted as rapporteur.

"one of the fundamental tenets of all legal systems is that no court may refrain from giving judgment on the ground that the law is silent or obscure".[43]

The significance and scope of this 'non liquet' can only be understood if it is realised that the court also creates law and that judicial settlement is not the only or the best means of resolving a conflict. It does not follow from this that parties, by choosing to submit their dispute to a court instead of, for example, to a political body, intend and may reasonably expect the court to decide only on the basis of law without taking into consideration

"the point of view of humanity, moral obligation, convenience, reasonableness and similar considerations..."

because such considerations would be inappropriate to a court but are the responsibility of political and legislative bodies and of the parties themselves.[44] This takes no account of the fact that the case partly determines the decision. In a national legal system these considerations will rightly influence decisions of the court, which can use the 'safety valves' — material illegality in criminal law, good faith, attributable expectation, obligation of morals and decency in civil law. This will never be explicitly stated in the court's decision. It creates law in concrete, and in doing so it will not line up against the legal subjects and the legislature they have created — in the style of 'you are wrong, I say that it must be different' — but in fact alongside them.

The court has its own responsibility in creating law in concrete. Those who fail to recognise this easily start splitting hairs over what should or should not be called interpretation. It is not harder for the legal subjects to recognise the court's responsibility in creating law than to accept majority decision-making in the legislature. In the relation between legislature and judicature there is only a demarcation of powers which need provide no more difficulties than other demarcations, such as those between State and local authority or between the Ministries themselves, difficulties which are considerable but never insurmountable. The distribution of powers between the community bodies is a question of expediency.

The court's own responsibility, from the juridical point of view as well, is reflected in the fact that its judgment binds parties and their assigns under

[43] Judgment No. 11 of 12 August 1953 of the ILO Administrative Court, quoted by H. LAUTERPACHT in his contribution to *Symbolae Verzijl*, 1958, entitled "Some Observations on the Prohibition of 'Non Liquet' and the Completeness of the Law", p. 196. It should be borne in mind, however, that the parties, by submitting a dispute, help to determine the Court's ability to pronounce.

[44] LAUTERPACHT does indeed draw this conclusion on p. 217 of the article referred to in note 43.

general and special title. It is clear from this contrast with the work of the legislature, which after all binds *all* members of the community and also non-members who are involved with that community, that the legislature is not out to regulate in concrete the relations between legal subjects in all circumstances.[45] This is not affected by the fact that court pronouncements, as experience shows, often take on considerable authority which extends far beyond the concrete relations which they have helped to determine. This authority is reflected in a more or less constant jurisprudence on comparable case positions, which has provided food for the 'doctrine of precedent' or 'doctrine of stare decisis'. This does not prejudice the rule that court pronouncements only bind parties and their assigns, even if a constitutional court pronounces on a dispute in which the constitutionality of an Act is disputed.

"One of the cardinal limitations on the Court's power of judicial review of federal and state legislation on constitutional grounds is that it will decide only a ripened controversy in which the results are of immediate consequence to the parties and will not render advisory opinions or entertain non-adversary proceedings".[46]

The parties' own responsibility is clear from the fact that they help to determine their legal relation by the way in which they represent their interests. The fact that in an ordered society taking the law into one's own hands is not accepted does not imply that the parties themselves do not have and keep the prime responsibility for the solution of the dispute. The ban only prevents the strongest one from being able to impose his solution on the weakest one by force and thus excludes physical power from deciding who is right. In other words, the ban underlines the very need for communication between legal subjects as the cornerstone of the legal system, even if a dispute arises between them. The ban, however, does not make the court into the protector of the physically weakest party. The court does not prevent parties taking the law into their own hands, nor does it do so itself. Its work only gives it a form worthy of man by the 'regulatory dialogue'. In inter-state relations in particular the tendency can be detected, as witness discussions at international peace conferences, to overestimate the role of the court as a result of a misapprehension of the connection between

[45] Otherwise the law, and not the court's decision, would bind the parties. Cf. Art. 59 of the ICJ Statute : "The decision of the Court has no binding force except between the parties and in respect of that particular case". EGGENS' pronouncement that a case produces not the absolute truth, but a legal truth, should be borne in mind (see LAND-EGGENS, *op. cit.*, p. 10).

[46] E.A. FARNSWORTH, *An Introduction to the Legal System of the United States*, 1963, p. 145 and pp. 49-58. The author draws attention to the fact that the 'stare decisis' is only relative.

this role and the whole legal, economic, social, cultural, in short public order.

In the non-functioning or faulty functioning of the international legislature the explanation can be found of the obstinacy with which international law literature and treaty practice on the pacific settlement of disputes between states maintain the distinction between legal and political disputes.[47] The distinction emphasises the fact that rules of law are not yet always felt in the inter-state community to be a framework that is adequate for the judge to solve disputes. It illustrates states' freedom of choice in arriving at a method for pacific settlement of disputes and in other words confirms that judicial settlement is not the only way of pacific settlement. States which limit judicial settlement to legal disputes do no more than indicate that they will not subject all disputes to judicial settlement. This distinction is more political than legal.

The division into legal and political disputes can also be traced back to the fact that in inter-state relations a search is going on for a guarantee that some disputes at least will reach the court. This became clear again recently during the sessions of the Special Committee on Principles of International Law concerning Friendly Relations and Co-operation among States held in 1961 in Mexico City and in 1966 in New York. By on the one hand expecting more of the international court than it can by its functions provide — the creation of a legal order, even if an international legislature is more or less absent, in other words, in a situation in which the legal subjects will not themselves show proof of this responsibility for the legal order — and by on the other hand veiling the court's own responsibility and that of the parties for the development of the process, we curtail the international court's opportunities of fulfilling its function.

The basis of the functioning of the international court, and of the emergence of international law, is mutual agreement between legal subjects. This applies both to the involvement and the content of the court's function. Judicial settlement is a form of institutionalising negotiations between parties on how their mutual relations in a concrete case can legally be interpreted, i.e. on the legal consequences of a specific set of circumstances.

Those who value law as an independent supra-human factor in society may have no difficulty in always allocating pride of place to judicial settlement among methods of pacific settlement of disputes, because denying

[47] For a definition of legal disputes in various treaty texts, see *Survey I*, p. 60, where the fatal statement for this legal classification is made : "If there is a difference of opinion whether a dispute is of a legal nature, this preliminary question may usually be submitted to the Court, or, if the Parties agree to set up an arbitral tribunal, to that tribunal".

mutual agreement between legal subjects as the basis of law implies a restriction of the freedom of legal subjects to resolve disputes in the peaceful way they prefer. The only limitation of this freedom, however, if there is to be an ordered society, is the ban on force, because force disturbs the communication needed for the process of mutual agreement as the basis of the legal order by reducing the person at whom it is directed to the level of an object. In the struggle to formulate the principle that disputes must be settled peacefully, at the conferences of the Special Committee on Principles of International Law concerning Friendly Relations and Co-operation among States the choice fell upon freedom of choice instead of on special emphasis of direct negotiations or judicial settlement as the most suitable methods. An analysis of the treaty pattern of states in respect of the pacific settlement of disputes, including the Western countries, (Chapter II) and their practical application (Chapter III) confirms that there is indeed a codification, an inventarisation of what exists.

In a dynamic legal situation legislation and judicial settlement complement each other in the creation of law. In the common law countries there may be a certain preference for case *law* and a certain restraint with regard to codification, and in the civil law countries, which means most countries — including most of the new nations — the reverse may be true. There is a technical nuance here, assuming mutual agreement between legal subjects to be the basis of creation of law — and no difference in principle.[48] Judicial settlement is one of the ways in which the members of a community can settle disputes peacefully — this is without the use of unregulated compulsion which degrades the other party to object status. The criteria for the degree of development (humanity) of a social order are the possibility and willingness of people to communicate, even when there are disputes or they threaten to arise. This possibility and willingness, as experience shows, are not only determined by the presence of a judiciary.[49]

If the jurist can and will recognise that in his capacity — i.e. from education and experience — he cannot assert himself as a formulator and applier

[48] Cf. E. McWhinney, "The 'New' Countries and the 'New' International Law: The United Nations Special Conference on Friendly Relations and Co-operation Among States", *A.J.I.L.*, 1966, pp. 1-33.

[49] Cf. A. Gros, "Peaceful Settlement of International Disputes - Mediation and Conciliation, in *International Law in a Changing World*, 1963, p. 49 : "For every dispute which becomes known to the general public, probably ten have been settled by the quiet intervention of diplomats and governmental legal advisers. Direct negotiation is the commonest means for settling such disputes and, thanks to its influence, the daily rhythm of international life is very much more peaceful than would seem to be the case from a reading of headlines".

of supra-human norms and cannot in that way put the world to rights, his contribution to the world order will be all the more effective. By seeing the dynamic character of law, he will be more open for his specific task,which is to help the community, which for once has come to realise that disputes must be settled peacefully, to achieve satisfactory procedure, an implementation of law which recognises the responsibility of all those involved, judge and parties, in resolving the conflict.

CHAPTER II

PACIFIC SETTLEMENT OF DISPUTES BETWEEN STATES — CREATION OF LAW

Part 1.

THE PRINCIPLE THAT DISPUTES MUST BE SETTLED PEACEFULLY

The terms of reference and the name of the Special Committee on Principles of International Law Concerning Friendly Relations and Co-operation among States indicate that the pacific settlement of disputes is regarded as a principle of international law. In para. 1 of the relevant resolution the Committee was asked to prepare a report

"containing, for the purpose of the progressive development and codification of the four principles so as to secure their more effective applications, the conclusions of its study and its recommendations, ..."

A codification means rules, not principles, and these rules are the application in practice — effective or otherwise — of principles. Discussion in the Committee was concerned not with principles but with methods of pacific settlement. The Special Committee's reports do not reveal any differences of opinion on the principle itself.

"The principle ... was generally recognized by the representatives who took part in the debate as a legal obligation which contemporary international law imposed on all States members of the international community".[1]

This general recognition emphasises the remarkable character of the pacific settlement of disputes as a principle, for it is a recognition of the pacific character of the settlement, not the fact that all disputes must be settled. A standpoint that all disputes must be settled, for example because all disputes harm international relations, could be posited as a principle. No general recognition can then be expected, however. The sessions of the Special Committee support this impression. In 1964 a member of the Committee drew attention to the fact that

"it would be lawful for two States parties to a dispute which did not endanger peace to maintain the *status quo* without violating the Charter".[2]

[1] Doc. A/5746, paras. 5 and 138.

[2] Doc. A/5746, para. 146. Cf. P.-H. Houben, "Principles of International Law concerning Friendly Relations and Co-operation among States", *A.J.I.L.*, 1967, pp. 710-716.

In contrast to this it was suggested by another delegate that Art. 2, para. 3 of the Charter applies to all disputes, including those which do not endanger peace. He judged the existence of disputes to be in conflict with the preamble of the Charter, in which the states declare that they will "live together in peace with one another as good neighbours". Similar remarks could be heard in 1966 when the Special Committee met in New York.[3]

A principle that all disputes must be settled cannot in any event be seen as a principle of *law*. A legal system aims to objectivise relations between individuals, and to do this it gives rules for the settlement of disputes. However, the function of law does not imply that all disputes which may arise in a legal community must always be settled via the organs of that community. The fact that there is agreement that disputes must be settled *peacefully* implies that a declaration of such agreement relates to the methods of settlement. The principle of this pronouncement lies in the ban on force; the legal principle lies in the ban on force that is not imposed by a regulated and competent authority that has to maintain order — for example by backing with force judicial decisions, which if necessary are implemented against the will of the losing party by the arm of the law — but that is based on one of the parties or others interested taking the law into their own hands. It can be politically relevant to emphasise the principle of pacific settlement as a positively formulated variant of the ban on force if a legal community is lacking or being built up, if in other words, the principles of peaceful relations and cooperation still have to be inventarised. From the academic legal point of view the pacific settlement of disputes derives logically from the function of law : the pacific regulation of society, the promotion and maintenance of a minimum of communication between legal subjects.

The peaceful nature of the settlement of disputes was indeed regarded as the logical corollary of the ban on force during the Special Committee's discussions.[4] The ban on force in a community underlines the need for communication between legal subjects as a cornerstone of law. It imposes on the community the task of designing adequate methods to maintain and promote this communication, in those very situations in which disputes threaten to disturb it. Discussions in the Special Committee contributed little to this. The general declarations on the pacific settlement of disputes on which the Committee managed to reach agreement in 1966 and which were contained in the 1970 Declaration on Principles of International Law concerning Friendly Relations and Co-operation among States in accordance

[3] Doc. A/6230. paras. 175 et seq.

[4] Doc. A/5746, para. 139.

with the Charter of the United Nations hardly go any further than those already contained in the Charter itself.[5] The main new feature is that the many new nations created since 1945 have proved able to underwrite the ideas of the Charter.[6]

The inclination in inter-state discussions on the organisation of the world community to make pacific settlement into an independent legal principle may be explained by the fact that the function of judicial settlement is usually regarded as too independent, particularly in legal systems which are not yet fully developed. Attempts to have the jurisdiction of the ICJ accepted illustrate this.[7]

While the Western countries felt that the principles of international law could be properly applied by strengthening international organisation, in particular by effective settlement of disputes, the East European and Afro-Asian countries put the emphasis on codification.[8] The attempts to give a new stimulus to judicial settlement by the ICJ again came to nothing in the Special Committee's meetings in 1964, 1966 and 1967. The 1970 Declaration merely included judicial settlement in the list of methods, as does Art. 33 of the UN Charter. There is no reference to the compulsory jurisdiction of the ICJ, in fact the Court is not even referred to.

In the series of Principles of International Law concerning Friendly Relations and Co-operation among States in accordance with the Charter of the United Nations the pacific settlement of disputes is out of place as a principle of law. That the discussions have concentrated upon the method of solving disputes shows that this is seen as the application of the principle of law and therefore confirms the above conclusion. In the discussions the political solution of disputes, for which the legislature bears the responsibility in the last resort in national legal systems, was only considered in passing. The delegates then concentrated on the distinction between legal and political disputes and aimed to encourage the submission of legal disputes to the ICJ.[9] Furthermore, the Special Committee's reports hardly dwell on the fact that treaties have been and are being concluded in inter-state relations, in which parties undertake to settle peacefully disputes which

[5] Res. 2625 (XXV).

[6] See on this C.G. FENWICK, "International Law : The Old and the New, *A.J.I.L.*, 1966, pp. 475 et seq.; MCWHINNEY, *A.J.I.L.*, 1966, pp. 1 et seq., particularly p. 7.

[7] Cf. Docs. A/5746, A/6230 and A/6799, in particular the paragraphs on judicial settlement.

[8] *International Conciliation* No. 554, p. 180.

[9] Docs. A/5746, paras. 145 and 166 et seq.; A/6230, paras. 193 and 210 et seq. and A/6799, paras. 384 et seq.

arise between them. The 1966 report only touches on this when mention is made of the remark of a delegate

"... that in the present state of international law it was necessary that their (i.e. the states') consent should be declared in some form or other".[10]

The 1970 Declaration says on this

"Recourse to, or acceptance of, a settlement procedure freely agreed to by States with regard to existing or future disputes to which they are parties shall not be regarded as incompatible with sovereign equality".[11]

This marks the situation in the inter-state community and goes sharply to the hub of the matter : the consent of states is still needed in the present situation for the application of any method of pacific settlement.

Part 2.

The system of pacific settlement

2.1. *Sovereign equality of states as the organisational basis*

Art. 2, para. 1 of the UN Charter lays down that "The Organization is based on the principle of the sovereign equality of all its Members". This declaration is a guide to understanding that part of currently valid international public law that regulates relations between states. It is so directly obvious for this day and age that it forms the only legal principle on the content of which the Special Committee on Principles of International Law concerning Friendly Relations and Co-operation among States managed to reach any measure of agreement during its first meeting in Mexico City in 1964. The fact that these points constitute no more than a repetition of the definition of the implications of sovereign equality which were accepted at the 1945 San Francisco Conference does not affect the importance of this agreement, for it is striking that the 1945 agreement has been confirmed by the many new nations which have been created since then.[12]

The juridical equality of states is a formal matter, an organisational fact, about whose effects various opinions are held, as the discussions in the Special Committee illustrate.[13]

[10] Doc. A/6230, para. 192. Only a few treaties are mentioned in Doc. A/5746, para. 141.

[11] Doc. A/L. 600, p. 13.

[12] Doc. A/5746, para. 339.

[13] Cf. Tammes' speech in Committee VI on 12 November 1965, published in the Report on the 20th General Assembly of the United Nations, publ. Ministry of Foreign Affairs, The Hague, No. 81, pp. 459 et seq. : "The contrast is well illustrated by the reference

From the organisational point of view the sovereign equality of states implies that the construction of the organisation of states, i.e. the formation of organs for states in common, which can act for them and in their name, rests on the voluntary cooperation of states. This is of great importance for the settlement of disputes between states, particularly as soon as those who are not parties to the dispute are involved in settlement. When a dispute arises between states regarding their mutual relations, the principle of sovereign equality offers no opportunity for third parties to help in settling it, other than by maintaining or opening communication between the states which are parties to the dispute, unless these states have themselves created wider possibilities by organising their mutual relations. An independent agreement to settle disputes peacefully, as contained in many general treaties and special provisions, does not rank as a demarcation of competences between the treaty partners which offers third parties an adequate basis, although the phenomenon of sovereignty clauses in such treaties creates the opposite impression.[14]

A treaty on the pacific settlement of disputes between states is as such an inadequate framework for the proper functioning of the commissions of enquiry, mediation or conciliation or arbitral or judicial settlement tribunals set up or to be set up by the treaty partners, for the consent of states to the creation of such commissions or tribunals does not automatically imply, in view of the principle of sovereign equality, that they regard themselves as part of an organisation of which the commissions or tribunals are organs.

2.2. *Classification of methods*

Most treaties and treaty provisions on the pacific settlement of inter-state disputes aim to fill the gap which arises when direct diplomatic negotiations fail.[15] They do this by providing for the intervention of bodies belonging to the parties themselves which specialise in the field in which the dispute arises and/or of third parties : states, organisations or persons who are accepted by the parties as impartial. This is intended to help the point at issue to be removed as far as possible from the influence of political

to the postulate of equal rights of man which is a matter of essence to be fought for while juridical equality of states is rather a matter of form".

[14] *Survey I*, pp. 23-39. From the organisational point of view these sovereignty clauses are, however, a logical outcome of an international public law that regulates inter-state relations on the basis of the sovereign equality of *all* states.

[15] *Survey I*, p. 13.

emotions which could hinder a more rational approach to the problem. The provisions concerned may be divided into two main groups :

I. those in which the parties reserve to themselves the decision which can end the dispute;

II. those in which parties entrust this decision to third parties.

In provisions in class I the parties themselves in the last resort bear sole responsibility for the decision which ends the dispute. In the second class a third party is involved in the decision which, by virtue of its function in the community to which the parties belong, bears its own responsibility for the regulating of the dialogue between parties. In the classification of the treaties, all provisions in class I have been grouped as conciliation, and all those in class II as arbitration or judicial settlement. Conciliation thus also includes, in addition to the work of conciliation commissions, enquiry, mediation and good offices, direct negotiations which are carried on at technical rather than diplomatic level. By analogy with the administrative appeal procedure, such negotiations can be designated as administrative conciliation.

Art. 33 of the UN Charter lists the traditional means of settling interstate disputes. Apart from the fact that good offices are not mentioned by name, the list is complete.[16] The seven methods of pacific settlement — negotiation, inquiry, good offices, mediation, conciliation, arbitration and judicial settlement — have no fixed form and content. They do not perform different functions, but are all aimed at the same objective : the pacific settlement of the dispute by promoting and maintaining communication between the parties. They may be regarded as variations of real negotiations between the parties themselves, i.e. aids therein — good offices, mediation, conciliation or enquiry — or attempts to institutionalise the willingness of states to negotiate when a dispute arises : arbitration and judicial settlement. The role of the third party or parties in establishing the relationship between the parties — investigator, mediator, conciliator or judge — is always to bring about a dialogue between the parties and/or keep it going.

The idea that conciliation differs from arbitration and judicial settlement in that its opinions are not binding, in other words that the court imposes while the mediator or conciliator proposes, renders too independent the court's function vis-à-vis the parties.[17] Both the conciliator and the arbi-

[16] KELSEN, *op. cit.*, pp. 376-377.

[17] Cf. VAN ASBECK, "La tâche et l'action d'une commission de conciliation", *N.T.I.R.*, 1956, p. 3, in which he describes this view as a 'communis opinio'. Also J. EFREMOFF, "Organe Central de Conciliation", *Conciliation Internationale*, 1933, Na 1-2, p. 90 and M. HABICHT, *The Power of the International Judge to give a Decision 'Ex Aequo et Bono'*,

trator or judge function within the framework of party relationships and, in conjunction with the parties, determine this relationship. The conciliator does not represent the parties any more than the judge does. The members of the conciliation commission who are citizens of party-states do not have to put forward points of view of governments. The government's agents do that.[18] The job of the conciliation commissions, like that of the courts, is to investigate the case which the parties have submitted. Treaties on the pacific settlement of disputes usually instruct conciliation commissions 'to elucidate the questions in dispute' and 'to collect with that object all necessary (or relevant) information by means of enquiry or otherwise'.[19] Many treaties lay down that the conciliation commission shall take decisions by majority vote.[20] The procedure of a conciliation commission is no different from that of a court : the parties state their case, they are then heard, along with witnesses and experts, and there is even the possibility that one of the parties can set the conciliation machinery in motion.

Most treaties lay down that parties agree

"to facilitate the work of the Commission and to supply it to the greatest possible extent with all relevant documents and information" [21].

A number of treaties emphasise that the conciliation commission's report is not binding as to fact-finding and/or legal considerations. This reservation confirms the great similarity in procedure between conciliation and judicial settlement, a similarity which is felt to be so great by the parties that, as it were, they wish to protect themselves against its consequences, an understandable reaction when an inclination is seen to over-emphasise the independent nature of judicial settlement.[22]

The conciliation commission, like a court, will have to give reasons for its decision, as the frame of reference shown above indicates. The significance and function of conciliation in the wide sense — including in particular any intervention of impartial third parties other than in the form of arbitra-

1935, p. 69; C. VULCAN, *La conciliation dans le droit international actuel*, 1932, pp. 9 et seq.; J.-P. COT, *La Conciliation Internationale*, 1968, pp. 10 et seq.

[18] VAN ASBECK, *loc. cit.*, and *Survey I*, p. 213.

[19] *Survey I*, p. 243.

[20] *Survey I*, p. 233.

[21] *Survey I*, pp. 194 and 213.

[22] *Survey I*, pp. 251 et seq. It is striking that many internationally-renowned jurists have belonged to the conciliation commissions that have functioned so far. Cf. H. WEHBERG, "Die Vergleichskommissionen im modernen Völkerrecht", *Z.f.a.ö.R.V.*, 1958, pp. 586-587. Also GROS in "Remarques sur la conciliation internationale", *l'Evolution du Droit Public; mélanges Achille Mestre*, 1956, p. 280.

tion or judicial settlement — in addition to that of judicial settlement is seen in the basis on which conciliation commissions and courts construct their reasoning. The latter should be bound by existing rules of law, the former can create new rules, which is considered important in a situation in which the legislature's function is inadequately performed.

"La conciliation peut remplir la fonction d'une législation internationale ne possédant pas encore d'organisation suffisante, elle peut concilier les droits respectifs des Parties avec les nécessités politiques de la situation de fait, avec leurs besoins vitaux incontestables. Elle peut créer le droit international nouveau consacré par la libre acceptation de ses solutions par les États souverains",

as EFREMOFF said in 1933.[23] A viewpoint that, as is shown by recent discussions at the meetings of the Special Committee on Principles of International Law concerning Friendly Relations and Co-operation among States over thirty years later, is still popular.[24]

In his 1959 report 'La Conciliation Internationale' ROLIN notes, with regard to the position defended by STONE, that the Institut de Droit International must establish the kinds of dispute for which conciliation is the most suitable method :

"Dans l'état actuel des relations internationales, l'opportunité d'un recours à la conciliation ne dépend pas seulement de circonstances propres à la nature du différend, mais tout autant de l'orientation politique des États Parties aux différends, de leur disposition à l'égard d'autres modes de règlement".

GUGGENHEIM adds :

"A ce sujet il est important de constater que lorsqu'on examine les différents litiges soumis aux commissions de conciliation, il s'agit en général et à peu d'exceptions près de conflits d'ordre juridique qui auraient pu être soumis aussi bien à un tribunal arbitral ou à une cour de justice".[25]

The fact that the treaty texts offer no support for a demarcation of the fields of operation in which the various means of pacific settlement are employed confirms this viewpoint.[26] Despite their different names, the means

[23] EFREMOFF, in *Conciliation Internationale,* 1933, No. 1-2, p. 136. Cf. also HABICHT, *op. cit.*, pp. 81-82.

[24] Doc. A/6230, para. 207 : 'During the discussion, mediation and conciliation were mentioned as being especially appropriate for the settlement of non-legal disputes'. Also BLIX, *op. cit.*, p. 63, and J. STONE, *Annuaire* 1959, p. 91.

[25] *Annuaire* 1959, pp. 9 and 76. Cf. also : CH. DE VISSCHER, *Théories et réalités en droit international public*, 1960, p. 429.

[26] A distinction is made in many treaties between legal disputes and political disputes. It will suffice here to say that the kinds of dispute mentioned in Art. 36, para. 2 of the ICJ Statute in particular belong to the former category.

of solving disputes peacefully do not each have a 'domaine naturel'.[27] They are all a continuation and a variation of negotiations between parties. The powers obtained by third parties to whom parties have recourse as impartial entities depend on the stage of development reached by relations between the states concerned, on the extent to which in these relations the communal functions of legislature, judiciary and executive have developed. The preference of parties for a specific method, or more exactly for the name of the method, is more an illustration of the state of the mutual relationship between the states which are parties to the dispute.[28]

In the classification of provisions on settlement of disputes according to whether they aim at conciliation, arbitration or judicial settlement, diplomatic negotiation has not been included in the conciliation group, and it has been disregarded in making up the tables contained in this section. It should be regarded as a prelude to settlement in the form of conciliation, arbitration or judicial settlement. It is not dealt with in the treaties and treaty provisions. If states have recourse to it, they may arrive at a solution which is accepted by the community of all states or a number of states, provided that they remain within the room for manoeuvre which they have as members of this community. The margin available is connected with the extent of development of this community as a legal community in the field in which the conflict arises. The larger it is, and the less the community is able to find a solution within the existing legal framework, the nearer the process of diplomatic negotiation to that of legislation than that of judicial settlement.

Inquiry is not mentioned separately in addition to conciliation, arbitration and judicial settlement, because it is an essential feature of any method of settling a dispute.

The UN Secretary General's report on methods of fact-finding, in which attention is paid to the importance of enquiry as a method of pacific settlement of disputes, notes for example that

"as the procedure of inquiry evolved, particularly within the framework of treaties, it gave rise to the procedure of conciliation with which it is still usually linked. The commissions originally established with an exclusively fact-finding mission were later envisaged differently, being given new functions and an additional power of conciliation".[29]

[27] VAN ASBECK, *Annuaire* 1959, p. 48 and FRANÇOIS, *ibid.*, p. 66. COT, on the other hand (*op. cit.*) tries to introduce a clear distinction between conciliation as the means of the wise and mediation as the means of the sovereign (pp. 1 et seq.).

[28] Cf. L.M. GOODRICH and A.P. SIMONS, *The United Nations and the Maintenance of International Peace and Security*, 1955, p. 294.

[29] Doc. A/5694, paras. 5 and 6.

The Dutch initiative at the UN General Assembly in 1963 to set up an international fact-finding centre did not take sufficient account of the fact that inquiry as a method of settling disputes needs a community sense on the part of the parties to the dispute and presupposes a willingness to negotiate. SCHURMANN's remark

> "It may be that this blurring of the lines between fact-finding in a dispute and endeavors to bring the parties to a settlement has made governments wary of agreeing to the former because of fear to the latter"

seems too much dictated by the desire to gain acceptance for the proposal for a fact-finding centre.[30]

With regard to the methods of mediation or good offices, which also are not shown separately in the classification, it is important to remember that during both Hague Peace Conferences it was expressly laid down that states are entitled to offer mediation or good offices to other states between whom a dispute has arisen without parties being able to consider the exercise of that right as an unfriendly act.[31] In this right of states which are not parties to the dispute the beginning can be seen of the idea of an inter-state *legal* community. Since then it is no longer disputed and has obviously been so fully accepted that it is no longer formulated in later treaty provisions on pacific settlement. During the discussions of the Special Committee on Principles of International Law concerning Friendly Relations and Co-operation among States as well, this right was not discussed either during treatment of the principle of pacific settlement or of that of non-intervention. The recognition of the right of states to offer mediation or good offices pre-supposes that the idea has matured in the inter-state community that a conflict is not only a matter for the parties themselves. It paves the way for the involvement of an impartial element in the negotiations. States have proved willing to follow this path. The declaration by the states of their willingness, preferably in joint consultation, to invite third parties to suggest solutions when a dispute arises between them, can be seen as a modest further step. Whether this third party is a state, an IGO or a private individual is hardly relevant in this situation, given the right of states to offer their services — nobody disputes the right of individuals and IGOs to do so — as a distinction forming the basis of a system of methods of pacific settlement. Hence the fact that a distinction between good offices,

[30] C.W.A. SCHURMANN, *A Center for International Fact-Finding: A Review and a Proposal*, 1963, p. 26.

[31] Convention for the Pacific Settlement of International Disputes, 1907, Art. 3.

mediation and conciliation cannot be linked with the nature of the third party.[32]

The offer of or the invitation to the third party can be limited to seeing whether there are ways, or to suggesting ways, in which direct negotiations can be resumed. In such situations it is usual to speak of good offices. The offer or invitation is not usually limited in this way, however, but the third parties are also expected to suggest solutions. In these cases mediation is an obvious description. A next step is that parties decide to set up a commission, of which they each nominate one or more members, who do not however sit as their representatives, and in which, in one way or another, provision is made for the joint appointment of one or more other members. The commision may itself determine the procedure to be followed in formulating proposed solutions to the dispute to the parties. In the classification followed in this book, this method of settlement, which is normally called conciliation, is called 'conciliation commission', not only to distinguish it from the previously-mentioned methods of negotiations at the technical level (enquiry, mediation and good offices), which all come under conciliation, but also because the name better describes this method, for the special nature of the procedure of the conciliation commission does not lie in conciliation, but in the commission's activities.

The beginnings of institutionalising the settlement of disputes can clearly be seen in the procedure of the conciliation commission. Once states reach the stage at which they wish to establish in a treaty their willingness to settle all their disputes peacefully, they will easily give this willingness forms which resemble judicial settlement. The treaties show this. Not only do they usually provide for the setting up of conciliation commissions whose procedure is analogous to that of judicial settlement, but in many cases they also link the conciliation commission as a method of pacific settlement with the long-standing institutions of arbitration and judicial settlement.

[32] HOYER (*op. cit.*, pp. 26 and 31) and OPPENHEIM-LAUTERPACHT (*op. cit.*, p. 9, para. 7) confine the descriptions good offices and mediation to activities by states. Oppenheim-Lauterpacht adds, however, that a private individual can also offer to mediate or provide good offices (*loc. cit.*, note 1). BLIX automatically assumes that good offices and mediation can be provided by states, IGO's and private individuals (*op. cit.*, pp. 54-55). COT makes a sharp distinction between conciliation and mediation (*op. cit.*, pp. 1 et seq.). Literature on the subject does not provide any basis for a distinction of these methods according to the legal persons who act as 'third parties'. Nor do treaty texts. The Inter-American Treaty on Good Offices and Mediation of 23 December 1936 provides for 'good offices or mediation of an eminent citizen of any of the other American countries, preferably chosen from a general list made up in accordance with the following Article'. (Art. 1, *Survey I*, p. 1108).

When states conclude treaties which deal solely with pacific settlement they seldom content themselves with agreements on conciliation (commissions). The share that jurists have in the preparation and drawing up of treaties comes out here. The attention received by the conciliation (commission) as a method of pacific settlement in specialist literature and at conferences is obviously more politically than legally based.

The treaties indicate that the many states which are parties to the treaties mentioned in Table I — about 70 from all over the world — are realistic enough from the legal point of view to see coming the moment at which direct negotiations via diplomatic channels and in the form of conciliation (commissions) reach deadlock and the deadlock has to be broken with the aid of third parties if use of force is to be avoided. This is borne out by the fact, for example, that treaties providing for arbitration on the one hand choose a special agreement as a basis for the referral of the dispute and on the other hand take measures, albeit not always effective ones, in case no special agreement is made.[33]

2.3. *Classification of general treaties and special provisions*

In the tables below conciliation, arbitration and judicial settlement have been called C, A and J respectively, and the various combinations indicated by combinations of these letters, e.g. CAJ [34]. The categories all disputes, legal disputes and political disputes have been designated by figures I, II and III respectively. In the first table the *general treaties* have been broken down according to whether they provide for conciliation, arbitration, judicial settlement or a combination of these for all disputes, legal disputes or political disputes.

[33] *Survey I*, pp. 70-89.

[34] See also Annex I, in which the treaties are mentioned in accordance with the numbering in the respective publications. The treaties mentioned therein with 'P' do no more than state the obligation to settle disputes peacefully without elaborating in any way.

TABLE I

Classification of general treaties according to whether they provide for conciliation (C), arbitration (A) and/or judicial settlement (J) for all disputes (I), legal disputes (II) or political disputes (III).[35]

I	II	III	1918-1928	1928-1949	1949-1962	1918-1962
A			10	8	4	22
J			1	2	6	9
AJ			1	1		2
CA			7	8	3	18
CJ			5	8	3	16
CAJ			7	13		20
CA	J		11	51		62
C	J	A	2	2	1	5
	J	CA	4	3		7
	J	A				
C	AJ		14	34		48
C	A		3	31		34
C	J		3	3		6
	J	C			1	1
	CA			13		13
	CJ					
	CAJ			2		2
	A		2	2	2	6
	J		1	1	5	7
	AJ		1			1
C			11	11		22
Total			83	193	25	301

A similar classification of *special provisions* produces the following, depending on the subject of the treaty :[36]

[35] Of the 301 general treaties 15 are multilateral. Nos. 22-27 from *Post-War Treaties* have not been included because they were added to in later treaties — Nos. 51, 54-57 and 59. When Table II in *Survey I*, pp. 1189-1201, was being drawn up, only the titles of bilateral treaties were apparently taken into account when classifying them, and not their content.

[36] This table includes, along with the treaties mentioned in *Survey II*, the Convention on the Law of Treaties of 22 May 1969 (Doc. A/Conf. 39/27 of 23 May 1969) classified as CJ, and the treaties setting up IGO's with special provisions, if they were not included in *Survey II*. In these cases the texts have been taken from PEASLEE or *International Organisation and Integration*, and from WIONCZEK, *op. cit.*, cf. Annex II. It should also be pointed out that disputes on the interpretation and application of treaties are counted as legal disputes, so that in this case all disputes are legal disputes. There is therefore no point in breaking them down according to the kind of dispute, as is done in Table I.

TABLE II

Classification of special provisions by treaty subject, according to whether they provide for conciliation (C), arbitration (A) and /or judicial settlement (J).

Treaties on \ Kind of arrangement	A	J	AJ	CA	CJ	CAJ	C	Total
Alliance, mutual security and military assistance	1	4	–	–	–	–	3	8
Regional cooperation (multilateral)	4	2	1	1	4	–	3	15
Communications & transport	42	1	5	4	–	–	9	61
Economic matters (multilateral)	6	1	–	2	–	–	6	15
Commodities (multilateral)	3	–	–	1	2	1	–	7
Social & humanitarian interest (multilateral)	–	10	2	4	–	–	1	17
Economic matters (bilateral)	5	–	–	3	–	–	16	24
Treaties on behalf of nationals :								
a. Commerce & navigation	9	6	2	–	–	1	–	18
b. Consular agreements	–	5	1	–	–	1	–	7
c. Establishment & emigration	–	1	1	2	–	1	–	5
d. Social security	4	–	–	18	–	–	1	23
e. Property & investment	11	–	19	–	–	–	–	30
Regime in frontier areas	–	–	–	4	–	–	13	17
Miscellaneous (multilateral)	1	6	2	–	1	–	1	11
Total	86	36	33	39	7	4	53	258

Apart from the combination of arbitration or judicial settlement with conciliation, negotiation plays an important part in the institution of these procedures on the basis of a general treaty or special provision on the settlement of disputes. This is reflected both in the appointment of the arbitrators and in the fact that the parties to these treaties cannot usually submit a dispute unilaterally to the body for arbitration or judicial settlement, but cannot do without the cooperation of the other party in this.

The treaty texts show that the following possibilities arise :[37]

[37] *Survey I*, Chapter II, para. 3 (special agreements) pp. 70-78, para. 4 (procedure in cases where the parties fail to agree upon the terms of the special agreement) pp. 78-89, and para. 5 (appointment of arbitrators) pp. 89-107.

1. The arbitral tribunal cannot be constituted and a dispute cannot be submitted to it or to the body responsible for judicial settlement without the cooperation of both parties, and no special measures have been taken to bring about this cooperation and parties are dependent for this on direct negotiations.
2. As 1, except that special measures have been taken to ensure the cooperation of parties in appointing arbitrators or concluding agreements to submit the dispute to arbitration or judicial settlement. These measures relate to the involvement of third parties in the appointment procedure and the making of the agreement, in which the decision, however, remains reserved to the parties themselves, as in the case with conciliation procedure.
3. If a party refuses to cooperate in constituting the arbitral tribunal, a third party may nominate the arbitrator(s) at the request of the other party.

If the parties cannot agree, a dispute may be referred to the arbitral tribunal or the body responsible for judicial settlement by one of the parties.

In the table below the *general treaties* providing for arbitration and/or judicial settlement contained in Table I have been broken down in accordance with the three possibilities above, the first being indicated by —, the second by :·: and the third by +.

TABLE III

Sub-division of arbitration (A), and judicial settlement (J), as contained in general treaties, according to whether their application is dependent (—) or not (+) on the cooperation of all parties, or whether parties have taken special measures to ensure this cooperation (:⁛:).[38]

—	:⁛:	+	1918-1928	1928-1949	1949-1962	1918-1962
IA			9	8	2	19
	IA		–	–	1	1
		IA	1	–	1	2
IJ			–	1	6	7
		IJ	1	1	–	2
IAJ			1	–	–	1
		IAJ	–	1	–	1
ICA			7	8	3	18
ICJ			–	1	–	1
		ICJ	5	7	3	15
	ICAJ		–	1	–	1
		ICAJ	7	12	–	19
*ICA IIJ			1	1	–	2
*ICA	IIJ		–	1	–	1
*ICA		IIJ	9	30	–	39
	*ICA	IIJ	1	16	–	17
		*ICA IIJ	–	3	–	3
*IC IIIA		IIJ	2	2	–	4
		*IC IIJ IIIA	–	–	1	1
*IIICA		IIJ	4	3	–	7
IC		IIAJ	14	34	–	48
IC IIA			–	30	–	30
IC	IIA		3	1	–	4
IC IIJ			–	1	–	1
IC		IIJ	3	2	–	5
IICA			–	10	–	10
		IICA	–	3	–	3
		IICAJ	–	2	–	2
IIIC		IIJ	–	–	1	1
IIA			2	2	2	6
IIJ			–	1	1	2
		IIJ	1	–	4	5
IIAJ			1	–	–	1
Total			72	182	25	279

[38] The figure-letter combinations in this and subsequent tables indicate the group of disputes to which the method applies. For example, IC IIJ indicates : conciliation for all disputes and judicial settlement for legal disputes. See also Annex I and the explanation given there.

With this information we can compile the following :

TABLE IV

Sub-division of the general treaties according to whether they provide for arbitration (A), judicial settlement (J) or a combination of the two for all disputes (I), legal disputes (II) or political disputes (III), dependent (—) or not (+) on the cooperation of all parties, or in which special measures have been taken to ensure this cooperation (:·:).[39]

Class	Total	—	:·:	+
I A	102	79	18	5
II A	53	46	4	3
III A	12	11	-	1
I J	25	8	-	17
II J	88	5	1	82
I AJ	22	1	1	20
II AJ	51	1	-	50
Total	353	151	24	178

This table shows that in most cases the method of arbitration under the general treaty cannot be used if parties refuse to cooperate. With treaties which provide for judicial settlement, in addition to arbitration or not, the cooperation of parties plays a noticeably less significant part, particularly if the use of judicial settlement is limited to legal disputes.

Breaking down the classification of *special provisions* in Table II according to the extent of cooperation required for the use of arbitration and judicial settlement gives the following result :

TABLE V (page 44)

Sub-division of arbitration (A) and judicial settlement (J) contained in special provisions, according to whether the use of these methods is dependent (—) or not (+) on the cooperation of all parties.[40]

[39] Limitation of judicial settlement to political disputes (III) to the exclusion of legal disputes (II) is unlikely. This is borne out in practice. None of the treaties confines judicial settlement to political disputes, so classes IIIJ and IIIAJ do not occur in the table. The difference between the totals in Tables III and IV lies in the fact that in Table III the combinations indicated by * have been counted twice, because arbitration and judicial settlement do not relate to the same categories of dispute.

[40] The intermediate group of arrangements for whose application the cooperation of parties is crucial, although special provisions may have been taken to obtain it (indicated as :·:) does not occur in the special provisions contained in this table.

TABLE V

Treaties on :	Kind of arrangement	Total —	Total +
Alliance, mutual security and military assistance	A	–	1
	J	4	–
Regional cooperation (multilateral)	A	–	4
	J	1	1
	AJ	1	–
	CA	–	1
	CJ	2	2
Communications & transport	A	22	20
	J	–	1
	AJ	1	4
	CA	4	–
Economic matters (multilateral)	A	–	6
	J	1	–
	CA	2	–
Commodities (multilateral)	A	–	3
	CA	–	1
	CJ	2	–
	CAJ	–	1
Social & humanitarian interest (multilateral)	J	4	6
	AJ	2	–
	CA	4	–
Economic matters (bilateral)	A	4	1
	CA	2	1
Treaties on behalf of nationals :			
a. Commerce & navigation	A	9	–
	J	3	3
	AJ	2	–
	CAJ	1	–
b. Consular agreements	J	–	5
	AJ	–	1
	CAJ	–	1
c. Establishment & emigration	J	–	1
	AJ	1	–
	CA	2	–
	CAJ	–	1
d. Social security	A	–	4
	CA	3	15
e. Property & investment	A	–	11
	AJ	–	19
Regime in frontier areas	CA	2	2
Miscellaneous (multilateral)	A	1	–
	J	3	3
	AJ	2	–
	CJ	1	–
Total		86	119

With this information, we can compile the following :

TABLE VI

Sub-division of the special provisions according to whether the use of arbitration (A) or judicial settlement (J) or a combination of the two is dependent (—) or not (+) on the cooperation of all parties.

Kind of arrangement	—	+
A	55	70
J	21	22
AJ	10	27
Total	86	119

This table shows that, unlike in general treaties, arbitration can be used in most special provisions if parties refuse to cooperate.

Part 3.

Conciliation

3.1. *General treaties*

In general treaties conciliation is usually regulated in conjunction with the other methods of pacific settlement : arbitration and judicial settlement, either as a prelude to them, or as a separate method for the group of all disputes or political disputes, with arbitration or judicial settlement being confined to legal disputes.

In all the combinations mentioned in Tables I and III in which disputes are submitted to both the procedure of conciliation and that of arbitration or judicial settlement, conciliation is part of the jurisdictional function in the inter-state community.

The general treaties providing for conciliation for all disputes or political disputes in combination with arbitration and/or judicial settlement for legal disputes bring out more sharply than the first group of treaties the fact that in the inter-state community in which rules of law are not always found to be a framework within which a solution can be found, a heavy demand is made on the parties' own responsibility for the solution of the dispute. They assume that legal and political disputes form two clearly distinguished groups and that the latter should not lend themselves, or should lend themselves less, to arbitration or judicial settlement. In political disputes, the decision which must end the dispute should rather be reserved to the parties themselves. As far as the organisation of pacific settlement is concerned, the distinction between legal and political disputes, however, only forms a shaky basis. The distinction, as asserted earlier, is more relevant politically than legally. Treaty practice confirms this insofar as states which are parties to general treaties in which the distinction between legal and political disputes plays a part have, with one exception — the former German Reich — also concluded general treaties which make arbitration or judicial settlement possible for all disputes.

That conciliation is nevertheless also regarded in the second group of treaties as part of the jurisdictional function in the inter-state community is clear from the fact that most general treaties work this method out in the form of a permanent conciliation commission which follows a procedure in line with that of arbitration and judicial settlement. The main exceptions to this are the conciliation treaties to which the USSR is a party. As far as procedure is concerned, these treaties are clearly in line with the method of direct negotiation. They also belong to the relatively small number that provide solely for conciliation. The other treaties in this group follow the method of the conciliation commission.

As all the treaties which go no further than conciliation cover the range of possibilities in this area, we shall do no more than discuss them, it being understood that, if relevant, attention will be paid to special characteristics of the organisation of the conciliation commission in treaties in which this procedure is combined with that of arbitration or judicial settlement.

3.1.1. Bilateral treaties

All general treaties that contain conciliation only are bilateral. They can be divided into two groups on the basis of the organisation of settlement of disputes. One group covers the 15 conciliation treaties to which Latin American and/or European countries, except the Soviet Union, are parties. The second group covers the other 7 conciliation treaties concluded by the Soviet Union with the same number of European countries. The first and larger group clearly organises the conciliation procedure by analogy with that of arbitration or judicial settlement. The process of direct negotiation clearly served as a basis for the second group.

℩.1.1.1. *Conciliation procedure by analogy with the procedure of arbitration and judicial settlement*

The following characteristics indicate that the procedure of arbitration ınd judicial settlement served as a model for the first group.[41]

ı. Conciliation is entrusted to permanent commissions, normally of five nembers, two of whom are of the same nationality as the parties to the lispute. These two members are not considered to represent the respective positions of the parties.

b. Either party can submit a dispute to the commission.

Ad b : the position of the group in question is somewhat clearer in this

Treaty number and parties / ription and e	PT″ 2 Chile - UK	PT 5 Chile - Sweden	PT 11 Sweden - Uruguay	PT 17 Sweden - Switzerland	PT 18 Denmark - Switzerland	PT 30 Austria - Switzerland	PT 37 Latvia - Sweden	PT 40 Estonia - Sweden	PT 41 Lithuania - Sweden	PT 75 Denmark - Estonia	PT 87 Colombia - Sweden	SI″ 106 Chile - Poland	SI 164 Chile - Denmark	SI 181 Brazil - Poland	SI 206 Chile - Norway
ımposition of mmission, Art. :	2	2	3	2	2	3	4	4	3	4	4	3	3	3	4/5
ıilateral submission of ;pute, Art. :	–	5	6	5	5	4	8	8	7	8	6	6	6	6	7
;presentation of parties, 't. :	–	9	10	7	7	–	11	11	10	11	12	8	8	8	11
ı-spot enquiry (* denotes ference to Chap. III of 07 Hague Convention), :t. :	3	8	8/ 10*	8/ 10*	8/ 10*	6/ 8*	10/ 13*	10/ 13*	9/ 12*	10/ 13*	8/ 9*	6/ 8*	6/ 8*	6/ 8*	11/ 13*
ıorum, Art. :	–	–	–	11	11	–	14	14	13	14	13	9	9	9	12
Majority view, Art. :	–	14	12	11	11	–	14	14	13	14	13	9	9	9	12
Reasoned minority view, Art. :	–	14	13	12	12	–	15	15	14	15	8	11	11	11	14
ɔmmission's decisions not nding, Art. :	3	13	15	12	12	6	–	–	–	–	8	11	11	11	14
ɔcal legal remedies :hausted, Art. :	–	–	–	–	–	–	3	3	–	3	3	2	2	2	2
omestic jurisdiction served, Art. :	–	–	–	–	–	–	–	–	–	–	–	1	1	–	1

″ PT = *Post-War Treaties*; SI = *Survey I.*

respect than that of treaties in which conciliation is combined with arbitration or judicial settlement for all disputes, legal disputes or political disputes. The group of American treaties in the classification IC— IIA for example confines itself to laying down that, if parties do not succeed in solving the dispute through diplomatic channels and do not have recourse to arbitration 'they shall at once refer it to the International Commission for investigation and report'. The Commission may, however, 'spontaneously by unanimous agreement offer its services to that effect ...'. It is worthy of note that a group of treaties which, with one exception (class IC + IIAJ) belongs to the classification —ICA + IIJ expressly state that only legal disputes need be submitted jointly to the conciliation commission. If joint action proves out of the question, one of the parties may submit the dispute to the International Court. With regard to political disputes, it has been laid down that, if parties cannot submit the dispute to the commission jointly, each party

"shall, after giving one month's notice, be entitled to submit the question direct to the said Commission."[42]

c. The parties may have themselves represented at the commission by agents (see a).
d. The commission may carry out investigations on the spot and hear persons. In many treaties it is laid down that the procedure unless agreed otherwise shall be regulated by the provisions in Part III (International Commissions of Enquiry) of the Hague Convention of 1907 for the Pacific Settlement of International Disputes.
e. The majority (11) of the treaties in the group in question contain a provision on the quorum. Eight of these provisions make decision-taking possible if all members have been properly convened and at least the jointly chosen members or the jointly chosen member and two other members are present. The other 3 treaties require that all members be present for decisions of substance [43].
Ad e : of the 88 treaties from the classifications IC IIAJ, IC IIA and IC IIJ in which conciliation also has an independent role in respect of the settlement of all political disputes, 31 contain a quorum provision, only 5 of which also explicitly make decision-taking in substance possible only when all members are present.[44] The other treaties do not contain a quorum provision. In these cases it must be assumed, in view of the function of conciliation, that in

[42] *Survey I*, p. 194.

[43] *Survey I*, Nos. 106, 164 and 181.

[44] The presence of all members for decisions of substance is required in treaties *Survey I*, Nos. *86*, Art. 19, p. 617, *105*, Art. 19, p. 695, *122*, Art. 19, p. 767, *125*, Art. 17, p. 784 and *216*, Art. 14, p. 1115, all classed as IC IIAJ.

any case all members must be present when decisions of substance are taken.[45]

f. The commission's decisions usually represent a majority view, and it is usually expressly laid down that the reasoned minority view must be included in the final report. This forms an indication that under treaty practice the conciliation method does not neccessarily imply that the commission does not pronounce on the positions of the parties and that, on the contrary, a reasoned point of view may be required.

Ad f : the treaties do not form a cross-section of all treaties in which conciliation is given an independent role. Of the 88 treaties mentioned in e, 7 contain a provision that a reasoned minority view must be included in the final report, at the request or otherwise of the members concerned.[46] Five treaties, however, lay down expressly that the report or minutes may not express any majority or minority view.[47].

An interesting feature in this connection is the discussion which developed on this in the Institute of International Law, on behalf of which ROLIN brought out in 1959 the report 'La Conciliation Internationale', mentioned above. ROLIN asked his fellow members of the Commission :

"Êtes-vous d'avis qu'il y a lieu pour les conciliateurs de s'abstenir de tenter de dégager de leurs échanges de vues l'opinion de la majorité de la Commission quant aux points contestés et davantage encore de s'abstenir de faire connaître l'avis de la Commission à ce sujet?".[48]

The majority replied in the affirmative, with STONE quoting WEHBERG :

"... Empfehlenswert ist es wenn die Parteien von der Vergleichskommission kein Gutachten über Rechtsfragen verlangen. Es könnte sonst dahin kommen, dass die Vergleichskommission ihren eigentlichen Charakter als Vergleichskommission verliert".

[45] The draft conciliation arrangement in the 1959 *Annuaire* laid down in this regard (Art. 10) : "Sauf convention contraire, les décisions de la Commission de conciliation seront prises à la majorité des voix, sans qu'il soit fait mention du nombre de voix recueilli. La Commission ne peut formuler des termes d'arrangement que si tous les membres sont présents" (p. 20). The version finally accepted by the Institute, however, says : "Si la Commission ne parvient pas à un accord général, elle peut prendre ses décisions à la majorité des voix, sans qu'il soit fait mention du nombre des voix recueillies". (*Annuaire* 1961, p. 245.)

[46] *Post-War Treaties*, Nos. *28*, Art. 21, p. 158, *36*, Art. 18, p. 214, *42*, Art. 18, p. 266, *52*, Art. 13, p. 341, *68*, Art. 17, p. 465, *82*, Art. 13, p. 583; *Survey I*, No. *18*, Art. 13, p. 393.

[47] *Survey I*, Nos. *86*, Art. 22, p. 618, *105*, Art. 22, p. 695, *122*, Art. 22, p. 768, *182*, Art. 12, p. 1008, *185*, Art. 14, p. 1027.

[48] *Annuaire* 1959, p. 43.

The minority included Van Asbeck and François, and, with reservations, Bastid, Guggenheim and McNair. GUGGENHEIM pointed out in the above yearbook in illustration that the will of the parties is decisive in this :

"Dans les trois litiges que le Gouvernement suisse a porté ces dernières années devant une Commission de conciliation, il a toujours désiré connaître l'opinion des conciliateurs sur les thèses juridiques défendues par les agents des deux Parties".

VAN ASBECK defended the need for an impartial recommendation.[49]

Most general treaties, including, with one exception, the 88 treaties mentioned above, lay down explicitly that the commission shall decide by majority vote, with a quorum present.[50] It seems important for parties to know whether a decision is taken by majority vote or with the largest possible or simple majority of votes, and what the viewpoint of the impartial element in the commission is. It must be assumed that unless laid down otherwise — as in the cases discussed here — the minutes and the report of the commission on this clear up the question. The views of GUGGENHEIM, VAN ASBECK and others are more in tune with treaty practice — as is clear in particular from the general treaties which only contain conciliation — than that of the majority mentioned above, which obviously thinks too much in terms of conciliation procedure in accordance with the method of direct negotiation.

g. In a relatively high number of treaties it has been laid down that the commission's decision does not have the character of a final judgment or arbitral award.

Ad g : it should be mentioned in this connection that the treaties in class IC — IIA, to which the USA is a party, although they have none of the above characteristics, lay down :

"The High Contracting Parties reserve the right to act independently on the subject matter of the dispute after the report of the Commission has been submitted" [51]

h. In a relatively high number of treaties a provision has been included to the effect that local legal remedies need to be exhausted before recourse is had to the conciliation commission.

i. Some treaties include a provision to the effect that matters belonging to 'domestic jurisdiction' are not within the commission's province.

With one exception all general treaties that are confined to conciliation contain provision for the appointment of the impartial chairman if the parties themselves are unable to agree on the choice. Four treaties extend the

[49] *Annuaire* 1959, pp. 91 et seq. (Stone), 77 (Guggenheim) and 50 (van Asbeck).

[50] The major exceptions are the treaties in class IC— IIA to which the USA is a party.

[51] *Survey I*, p. 253, under XXVII.

provision in this kind of situation to all three members to be appointed jointly by the parties.[52]

That the conciliation procedure must be regarded as part of the jurisdictional function in inter-state relations, rather than as part of the legislative function, is emphasised by the fact, already mentioned, that the treaty partners set limits to the commission's powers. The treaties concluded by *Chile* with *Poland*, *Denmark* and *Norway* respectively remove from the conciliation procedure, and thus reserve to the procedure of direct negotiation

"questions which, according to international law, fall within the exclusive competence of one Party ... or (to) disputes relating to the territorial status of the High Contracting Parties".

Against the same background the provision that, if a dispute, under the national legislation of one of the treaty partners, comes under the jurisdiction of a national court, the state concerned may refuse to call in the conciliation commission until the competent national authorities have pronounced in the last resort, is fully understandable. This provision only relates to disputes between citizens of one of the treaty states and the other treaty state, or between both partners themselves in disputes which arise through their dealings with each other as private persons, as only in such disputes can the national courts of one of the treaty partners be competent. The acceptance of international jurisdiction normally depends in such cases on the fact that the national legal remedies of the state concerned have been exhausted.

The fact that this condition has also been declared applicable in the above treaties to the acceptance by the treaty partners of the competence of the permanent conciliation commission points to the fact that the function of this commission has been approached from the point of view of that of an international judicial appeal body.

The parties to the above conciliation treaties were members of the League of Nations. According to their preamble the treaties between *Sweden* and *Latvia*, *Estonia* and *Lithuania* respectively, and between *Denmark* and *Estonia* were concluded at the exhortation of the League of Nations Assembly, laid down in various resolutions, to set up conciliation commissions.[53] In the League of Nations Covenant the Council was given the function of reconciliation centre. Art. 15 of the Covenant laid down that

[52] *Post-War Treaties*, Nos. *17*, Art. 2, p. 86, *18*, Art. 2, p. 93, *87*, Art. 5, p. 618 and *Survey I*, No. *206*, Art. 6, p. 1101.

[53] Doc. A/5694, paras. 83 and 119.

any dispute that would lead to a breach and was not subject to arbitration or judicial settlement should be submitted to the Council and that the Council would endeavour to settle the dispute. The Scandinavian countries in particular took initiatives in the 1920s to make League members set up in pairs permanent commissions for conciliation and arbitration with, if the conciliation attempts proved abortive, an 'appeal' to the Council or the Assembly. These attempts finally led to the General Act for the Pacific Settlement of International Disputes of 1928, that was revised in 1949 in the light of the UN Charter.[54]

3.1.1.2. *Conciliation procedure by analogy with the procedure of direct negotiation*

That the direct negotiation method served as the basis for the second group of conciliation treaties concluded by the USSR with seven countries is clear from the following characteristics :

a. The conciliation commission is constituted on a basis of parity of members who have the nationality of the respective treaty partners, therefore without third parties being involved. The impartial element, in other words, is absent.

b. Parties are not represented by agents, but may appoint experts to assist the commission members.

c. Decisions may only be taken if all members are present and unanimously.[55]

With the exception of the Italo-Soviet Union friendship treaty that only mentions conciliation without further details, the conciliation treaties to

[54] *International Organisation and Integration*, p. 194.

[55]

Treaty number and parties / Description and article	SI'' 58 Germany - USSR	SI 173 Finland - USSR	SI 174 Estonia - USSR	SI 175 Latvia - USSR	SI 176 Poland - USSR	SI 177 France - USSR	SI 189 Italy - USSR
a. Parity basis, Art. :	3	2	3	3	2	II	no special features
b. Appointment of experts, Art. :	3	2	3	3	2	II	"
c. Presence of all members and unanimous decisions, Art. :	–	7/9	–	8/9	7/9	IV	"

''SI = *Survey I*

which the USSR is a party provide for a special commission of which the treaty partners designate two members of their own nationality for each meeting — the commission does not normally meet more than once a year. The commission has to consider points of dispute which are notified by the treaty partners at least 15 (14) days before it meets. It can only take decisions if all members are present. If no agreement is reached, the Finnish and the Polish treaties lay down that the dispute may be submitted again to the commission at the request of either of the parties, if it is not settled within a reasonable time. The German, Estonian, Latvian and French treaties lay down in each case that either party is entitled to ask the commission for an extraordinary meeting, which must be held within 4 months. If still no agreement is reached, the German treaty explicitly falls back on diplomatic negotiations. Art. 5, para. 3 says : 'Failing this, the question shall be dealt with through the diplomatic channel'.[56]

The conciliation treaties concluded with the Soviet Union are, according to their preamble, complementary to the non-aggression treaties concluded by that country with the above countries in the same period, and therefore to the legal form of exclusion of force in the respective mutual relations.

The organisation of the conciliation in these treaties is significantly different, as is clear from the foregoing, from that in the first group. The treaties are based on the idea of parity in consultation between the parties themselves without the intervention of third parties.[57] The commission members are regarded as delegates to whom the parties may attach experts as advisors. The intention of the treaties is only to call in the commissions on disputes which cannot in the first instance be settled by diplomatic negotiation. Borne particularly in mind in this are disputes relating to the interpretation and application of treaties. The significance of the treaties should be seen in the attempt to settle disputes on a technical level which cannot in the first instance be settled through diplomatic channels, or by taking the law into one's own hands, the latter being ruled out — at least juridically — by non-aggression treaties. The treaties create an administrative procedure for the settlement of disputes.

3.1.2. Multilateral treaties

Breaking down the general multilateral treaties of Tables I and II gives the following :

[56] *Survey I*, p. 521.

[57] *International Law*, Academy of Sciences of the USSR Institute of State and Law, pp. 381-384, in which conciliation commissions are shown as a part of Soviet diplomacy.

TABLE VII

Classification of general multilateral treaties, according to whether they provide for conciliation (C), arbitration (A) or judicial settlement (J) for all disputes (I), legal disputes (II) or political disputes (III), dependent (—) or not (+) on the cooperation of the parties or in which special provisions have been made to obtain this cooperation (:·:).

—	:·:	+	Total
IA			2
		IA	1
IJ			1
ICA			3
		ICAJ	1
	ICA	IIJ	2
		IC IIJ IIIA	1
IC IIA			1
IC IIJ			1
IIIC		IIJ	1
IIJ			1
Total			15

From this table it can be seen that none of the general multilateral treaties is confined to conciliation for all disputes or legal disputes.

3.1.2.1. *Conciliation procedure by analogy with the procedure of arbitration and judicial settlement*

Most general multilateral treaties which contain conciliation more or less attune this procedure to that of arbitration and judicial settlement. The organisation of the conciliation procedure does not differ in this from that contained in bilateral general treaties. In fact the general multilateral treaties also entrust conciliation to commissions which are constituted bilaterally between the treaty partners.[58] The Convention of Inter-American Conciliation, the American Treaty of Pacific Settlement (Pact of Bogota) and the Protocol of the Commission of Mediation, Conciliation and Arbitration, established by Art. XIX of the Charter of the Organization of African Unity (OAU), however, provide for the creation of permanent panels of conciliators from which, ad hoc or otherwise, candidates are selected for the bilateral commissions. Pending the constitution of these commissions, treaty organs can act as mediators.

In the *Convention of Inter-American Conciliation* the two permanent commissions of enquiry — one in Washington, one in Montevideo — provided for in the Gondra Convention act as conciliation commissions, either of their own volition or otherwise.[59] The *Pact of Bogota* (Art. 16) lays down that a Commission of Investigation and Conciliation will be formed, for

58

Treaty number and parties / Description and article	PT'' 34 Baltic States	SI'' 34 General Act	SI 51 Convention of Inter-American Conciliation	SI 79 Little Entente	SI 234 Pact of Bogota	SII'' Chap I 37 European Convention	SII Chap I 45/46 OAU with Protocol	SII Chap II 6 Western European Union
a. Composition of commission, Art. :	6	4	2	11	17/18	6	II/ XXIII	–
b. Unilateral submission of dispute, Art. :	7/10	7	3	14	16	9	XXII	–
c. Representation of parties, Art. :	13	11	II'	18	24	12	XXV	–
d. On-spot enquiry (* denotes reference to Chap. III of 1907 Hague Convention), Art. :	13*	13	I'	20	23	14	XXIV	–
e. Quorum, Art. :	14	12	–	19	–	13	–	–
f. 1) Majority view, Art. :	14	12	7	19	27	13	–	–
2) Reasoned minority view, Art. :	15	15	–	22	–	15	–	–
g. Commission's decisions not binding, Art. :	–	–	9	–	28	–	–	–
h. Local legal remedies exhausted, Art. :	3	31	–	3	–	29	–	–
i. Domestic jurisdiction reserved, Art. :	2	–	–	1	5	27	–	–

''PT = *Post-War Treaties*
SI = *Survey I*
SII = *Survey II*
'App. Gondra Convention (PT No. 15)
Cf. paras. 3.1.1.1. and Annex I.

[59] *Survey I*, p. 506, Art. 3. These treaties are no longer in force for the states which have ratified the Pact of Bogota. (Art. 58 of the Pact of Bogota).

which the treaty states, in mutual agreement, will each designate two members who together shall choose a fifth member as chairman. Pending the convening of the commission the Council of the OAS may make recommendations to the parties. The Pan American Union is also responsible for the constitution of a permanent panel of American conciliators, from which the parties may each select 2 members if a dispute arises before the Commission of Investigation and Conciliation has been formed.[60]

The *OAU Protocol* provides (Art. II) for the setting up of a commission of 21 members, elected by the Assembly of Heads of State and Government. This Commission has jurisdiction over disputes between states (Art. XII) which are submitted to it jointly or independently by the parties, the Council of Ministers or the Assembly of Heads of State and Government (Art. XIII). One or both parties may however refuse to recognise the Commission's jurisdiction, in which event the Bureau of the OAU submits the case to the Council of Ministers, which may adopt a resolution by a simple majority (Charter, Art. XIV), the significance of which is by no means clear. Within the framework of the OAU Charter, not much more can be seen in it than conciliation in the form of mediation or good offices. The preference of OAU members for the settlement of disputes by policy-making organs is also clear from Art. XXVII of the Charter, that entrusts typical legal disputes such as those concerning the interpretation of the Charter for settlement to the Assembly of Heads of State and Government, which has to decide on the matter by a two-thirds majority.

The protocol lays down that if a dispute is submitted by member-states for *mediation* to the Commission, the President shall nominate one or more mediators with the agreement of the parties (Art. XX). The procedure for the *conciliation commission* can only be set in motion by the parties themselves. The conciliation is entrusted in this event to a Board of Conciliators, of whom three shall be appointed by the President of the Commission from among the members of the Commission and one each by the parties.

Finally, the treaty setting up the *Western European Union* confines itself in Art. X (formerly VIII) to stating that the treaty partners will submit to conciliation all disputes that do not come under Art. 36, para. 2 of the Statute of the ICJ, without the method being elaborated. All original treaty partners, however, have ratified the General Act of Geneva of 1928. The Federal Republic of Germany and Italy, which acceded in 1954, have since then ratified the European Convention. Italy furthermore had ratified the Geneva Act in 1931. It may therefore be assumed that if a political dispute arises the conciliation methods elaborated in these treaties will be followed.

[60] *The Inter-American System*, pp. 389 and 390.

3.1.2.2. *Conciliation procedure by analogy with the procedure of direct negotiation*

According to Art. 2 of the UN Charter the Organisation and its members undertake to act in accordance with a number of principles, including

"All Members shall settle their international disputes by peaceful means in such a manner that international peace and security, and justice, are not endangered".[61]

The emphasis in this wording is upon the member-states. This line of thought is extended in Chapter 6 of the Charter, which is devoted to the pacific settlement of disputes.

The fact that the UN as an organisation leaves the responsibility for and initiative on the pacific settlement of disputes with the states is in accordance with its basic principle : the sovereign equality of states. The UN's organs can hardly have more than a mediating role. The Charter shows this too :

"The Charter system of peaceful settlement and adjustment consists of duties placed upon Members and of organs and procedures, which are intended *to aid Members* in performing their duties and serving the general purposes of the Organization".[62]

In view of this it is understandable that the *duty* is not imposed on member-states to bring a dispute to the attention of the General Assembly or Security Council. They *may* do so.[63] Only if they do not succeed in settling the dispute by the means mentioned in Art. 33 must they submit it to the Security Council.

The Council's role is limited to making recommendations, either on procedure or on conditions. The General Assembly as well may only make recommendations on pacific settlement.[64] Both organs may act on their own initiative. The General Assembly's recommendations require a two-thirds majority and parties to the dispute are not excluded from voting. This latter point is different in the Security Council whose recommendations require

"an affirmative vote of nine members including the concurring votes of the permanent members, provided that, in decisions under Chapter VI, and under paragraph 3 of Article 52, a party to a dispute shall abstain from voting".[65]

[61] *International Organisation and Integration*, p. 26.

[62] GOODRICH, *The United Nations*, p. 197, author's italics; cf. also F. VALLAT, "The Peaceful Settlement of Disputes", *Cambridge Essays in International Law; essays in honour of Lord McNair*, 1965, pp. 155-177.

[63] Art. 35 (*International Organisation and Integration*, p. 33).

[64] Art. 14, *ibid.*, p. 29.

[65] Art. 27, para. 3, *ibid.*, p. 31.

It is laid down that parties to a dispute which are not members of the Council, and of course without voting rights, may take part in the debates.[66]

The UN's function and that of its organs in the field of pacific settlement of disputes should thus be considered as conciliation. This is not altered by the fact that the Security Council, under Chapter VII of the Charter, may decide to take certain action in respect of threats and breaches of peace and acts of aggression. For the application of these measures it is wholly dependent on the cooperation of members. The extent to which this may be obtained is one of the factors which parties to a dispute may weigh in the balance. The possibility of sanctions does not deprive the system of pacific settlement contained in the Charter of its place in the main group of provisions in which parties may reserve for themselves the decision which can end the dispute.

The General Assembly's recommendations on the nomination of a rapporteur or conciliator in a dispute or situation which is submitted to the Security Council and the setting up of a Panel for Inquiry and Conciliation should be seen in this light.[67] The members of this panel, who may be both private individuals and civil servants, will, if they are appointed to a commission, request or accept no instructions from Governments. The recommendation gives no indication of the procedure of enquiry or conciliation, except to lay down that the commission members are not government representatives, so that it cannot be established whether it is attuned to the method of direct negotiation, or that of arbitration or judicial settlement. This is not surprising, now that the recommendation has been made in the UN that covers both Communist and non-Communist countries. Indications can be found in the Charter in Art. 36 already mentioned, however, that legal disputes should preferably be submitted to the ICJ for settlement, in Art. 96, that empowers the General Assembly and the Security Council to advise the Court on legal questions, and in Art. 92, that makes the Statute of the Court an integral part of the Charter. In view of this the system of pacific settlement of disputes in the Charter has been classified as IC IIJ.

Finally, Art. 5 of the *Pact of the League of Arab States* aims to ban force between member-states as a means of settling disputes.[68]

The reservations made with regard to independence, sovereign and territorial integrity and the condition that both states must appeal to the Council,

[66] Art. 31, *ibid.*, p. 32.

[67] GA Res. 268 (III) B and D of 28 April 1949, *International Organisation and Integration*, pp. 201-204.

[68] *International Organisation and Integration*, p. 1104. G. MOUSSA DIB, *The Arab Bloc in the United Nations*, dissertation, 1956, pp. 27 et seq.

stamp the Council's function as one of mediation. Only if the above condition is met and no recourse is had to reservations may its role be called one of arbitration. The Article recognises this by stating at the end : 'The decisions relating to arbitration and mediation shall be taken by a majority vote'. Taking into account the fact that, according to Art. 7, decisions must be unanimous and majority decisions only bind the members who accept them and furthermore that, according to Art. 3, the Council consists of representatives of the member-states, it must be concluded that conciliation is in line with the procedure of direct negotiation. It may also be said that hardly any other general multilateral or bilateral treaties have been concluded between the 13 Arab members of the League, nor have they signed mutual treaties in specific sectors with special provisions, so that, apart from the membership of the UN and the specialised agencies, there is practically no regional treaty pattern on the settlement of disputes outside the Pact of the League of Arab States. This indicates that hardly any regional integration process has got under way in this sphere.

3.2. *Special provisions*

The Convention on the Law of Treaties of 22 May 1969 provides for a conciliation procedure for disputes on the interpretation and application of the provisions in Section V of the Convention (Invalidity, Termination and Suspension of the Operation of Treaties), excluding Arts. 53 and 64 and for judicial settlement *at the request of one of the parties* if a binding general international rule of law is at stake or a treaty is in conflict with such a rule (Arts. 53 and 64). By this is understood, according to Art. 53,

> "a norm *accepted and recognized by the international community of States as a whole* as a norm from which no derogation is permitted and which can be modified only by a subsequent norm of general international law having the same character".[69]

Since therefore there is only a peremptory norm if the parties to the dispute are agreed upon it — otherwise there is no recognition by the 'community of States as a whole' — the procedure before the Court has no significance de facto. In the relevant provision of the International Law Commission's 1966 draft — Art. 50 — there was no insertion regarding recognition by the whole community of States. In its explanatory note on this Article the report stated that the view that

[69] Doc. A/Conf. 39/27 of 23 May 1969, p. 699, author's italics.

"in the last analysis there is no rule of international law from which states cannot at their own free will contract out has become increasingly difficult to sustain".[70]

This view has prevailed again in the Convention. The settlement of disputes clauses in the Convention on the Law of Treaties came about after long and difficult discussions.[71] It was only possible to make them in any way binding in the case of the conciliation procedure which, however, as a compromise, was not laid down in the Convention, but in an annex, in which it is elaborated by analogy with the procedure of arbitration and judicial settlement, although the parties themselves do not submit the dispute to the conciliation commission, but this is done by the UN Secretary-General on being requested to do so by one of the parties under Art. 66 of the Convention, and the UN bears the cost of the procedure.

According to the annex the UN Secretary-General will draw up and maintain a list of conciliators consisting of qualified *jurists*, of whom each state that is a UN member or is a party to the present Convention will nominate two. If the Secretary-General receives a request for conciliation under Art. 66, the parties to the dispute must each nominate two conciliators, at least one of them from the list not having that country's nationality. The four conciliators together nominate the fifth.

"If the appointment of the chairman *or any of the other conciliators* has not been made within the period prescribed above for such appointment, it shall be made by the Secretary-General within sixty days following the expiry of that period. The appointment of the chairman may be made by the Secretary-General either from the list or from the membership of the International Law Commission".[72]

The commission's decisions are taken by a majority vote of the five members. This quorum requirement, which means that all members are deemed to be present, is a concession to the negotiating procedure. The 19 states which abstained from voting on the Convention include all the members of the Soviet bloc, which, in view of the treaty practice of these countries on the settlement of disputes, including the special provisions discussed below, is hardly surprising.[73]

The Convention is designed to be a framework treaty for all treaties between states — Art. 1 lays down : 'The present Convention applies to

[70] *A.J.I.L.*, 1967, p. 409.

[71] Doc. A/Conf. 39/27 of 23 May 1969, pp. 704, 712 and 713, classified in Tables II and IV as —CJ in the miscellaneous category. Cf. also note 70. The procedure indicated in the Annex is on the same lines as that outlined in this Chapter, para 3.1.1.1. Cf. R.D. KEARNEY and R. E. DALTON, "The Treaty on Treaties", *A.J.I.L.*, 1970, pp. 545-557.

[72] Doc. A/Conf. 39/27, p. 712, author's italics.

[73] Doc. A/Conf. 39/27, p. 679.

treaties between States' — so that there is reason to compare treaty practice on pacific settlement with it, all the more so as a comparison between Table I and Table II shows that conciliation in special provisions, mainly as an independent method, but also in combination with arbitration and judicial settlement, clearly plays a more important part than is the case in general treaties.[74]

3.2.1. Bilateral treaties

The direct negotiation method served as a basis for most of the special provisions occuring in bilateral treaties — 35 out of 39 — which are confined to conciliation. The same conclusion — 25 out of 29 — can be drawn with regard to special provisions in bilateral treaties in which conciliation is organised as consultation between administrative officials appointed for the purpose or mixed commissions. This situation does not therefore fit in with the form of settlement contained in the Convention on the Law of Treaties. In other words, the Convention in this respect contains no codification of treaty practice on the pacific settlement of inter-state disputes.

The 68 special provisions in Table II contained in bilateral treaties which provide for conciliation, with or without arbitration and/or judicial settlement, belong to alliance treaties (1), air transport agreements (10), trade agreements (19), treaties on behalf of nationals (21) and agreements on the regime in frontier areas (17).

3.2.1.1. *Conciliation procedure by analogy with the procedure of arbitration and judicial settlement*

Only in the areas of air transport and treaties on behalf of nationals regarding navigation and consular agreements have special provisions been

[74] According to Table II classes C, CA, CJ and CAJ occur 53, 39, 7 and 4 times respectively (103 times in all) in special provisions out of a total of 258.

Class	Multilateral		Bilateral		Total	
	—	+	—	+	—	+
C	14	–	39	–	53	–
CA	8	5	11	15	19	20
CJ	5	2	–	–	5	2
CAJ	–	1	1	2	1	3
Total	27	8	51	17	78	25

According to Table I classes IIC and IICJ do not occur in the general treaties and IICA and IICAJ occur 13 times and twice respectively in the total of 301.

made in which conciliation is regulated on the model of arbitration and judicial settlement.

A. The member-states of ICAO have two model texts available for *bilateral air transport agreements*, viz. the Standard Agreement for Provisional Air Routes, contained in recommendation VIII of the Final Communiqué of the Chicago Conference of 7 December 1944, and the Standard Clauses for Bilateral Agreements of 1953, drawn up by the European Civil Air Conference (ECAC).[75] The former leaves undecided whether member-states include a provision on the settlement of disputes in bilateral air transport agreements.[76] The European model, which is also used in agreements with countries in other parts of the world, contains a regulation in which the emphasis is on arbitration. It adds to this that the member-states will take steps to release themselves as soon as posssible from obligations which are inconsistent with the Convention on International Civil Aviation and which arise under agreements with non-member-states or with citizens of states, whether the latter are members or not. States belonging to ICAO thus aim to create a legal community in the field of civil aviation. Conciliation as an independent procedure plays a modest part in bilateral aviation agreements :

"With few exceptions all existing agreements — irrespective of whether direct negotiation or reference to ICAO-Council forms part of the agreed procedure — provide for arbitration either as an alternative to a decision by Council or as the principal means of settling disputes".[77]

Quite a lot of these exceptions — in view of conciliation provisions in other sectors — organise the conciliation procedure by analogy with that of arbitration and judicial settlement.[78]

B. If the special provisions in the *treaties on behalf of nationals* contain conciliation — 21 in all — they always combine this method with arbitration and occasionally with judicial settlement as well. Only 3 of them, however, also organise the conciliation procedure by analogy with that of these methods. They are the only treaty in the field of *commerce and naviga-*

[75] Handbook on Administrative Clauses in Bilateral Air Transport Agreements, ICAO Doc. 63-AT/6. Appendix I, p. 113 and Appendix II, p. 116.

[76] Point 9 of the standard text has the following in brackets : 'Where desired here insert provisions for arbitration, the details of which will be a matter for negotiation between the parties to each agreement'. (Doc. 63-AT/6, p. 115).

[77] Cf. Doc. 63-AT/6, p. 76, para. 4 and Table II. Of the 52 air transport agreements included in *Survey II*, 9 provide for conciliation alone. The majority (23) of the other 43 contain a provision ranking as +A, +J or +AJ. Cf. Annex II.

[78] *Survey II*, Chap. IV in the classification C : Nos. *16*, Art. 13, p. 369, *20*, Art. 13. p. 375, *22*, Art. 12, p. 378, *37*, Art. 12, p. 397 and in class —CA : No. *18*, Art. 17, p. 373,

tion, 1 of the *consular* agreements and the agreements on *establishment and emigration*, concluded in both groups between *France and Sweden*, in which reference is made to a bilateral general treaty between both countries dated 3 March 1928 which can be classified as —ICA + IIJ. Although under this treaty it would be possible to submit the dispute unilaterally to the ICJ (formerly the Permanent Court of International Justice), certainly as the treaty is referred to, and although both states have accepted the compulsory jurisdiction of the ICJ over legal disputes, both agreements lay down that, if a dispute cannot be settled through diplomatic channels or under the above general treaty, it may be submitted to the ICJ.[79] Both agreements thus illustrate the freedom which states feel with regard to agreements on the organisation of the settlement of disputes.

3.2.1.2. *Conciliation procedure by analogy with the procedure of direct negotiation*

Conciliation on the model of direct negotiation predominates in most treaty sectors in which conciliation occurs.

A. The bilateral *alliance treaty* that provides for conciliation concerns the settlement of the legal position of the Soviet troops in Hungary. A mixed Hungarian and Russian commission deals with disputes on the interpretation and application of the agreement. If no agreement is reached, the case has to be settled as quickly as possible through diplomatic channels.[80] This means that if agreement is reached, the question is settled by the commission itself, as an organ of the parties to the agreement.

B. Of the 10 bilateral *air transport agreements* which contain an organisation of the settlement of disputes in the form of conciliation, 5 are similar to the above agreement, although they do not provide for mixed commissions, but in the first instance entrust consultation, if a dispute arises on interpretation or application, to the aviation authorities of the countries concerned. If this proves fruitless, the matter is referred to diplomatic channels.[81] If it is successful, the agreement between the aviation authorities

[79] *Survey II*, Chap. IX No. *4*, Art. 33, pp. 625 and 626 (class —CAJ) and Chap. X, Nos. *6*, Art. 44, p. 655 and *10*, Art. 13, p. 662, with general treaty published in *Survey I* No. 5, p. 343 (class —ICA + IIJ). Both special provisions have been classed as +CAJ because failure of conciliation or arbitration does not prevent unilateral submission to the Court.

[80] Art. 17, *Survey II*, p. 155 (class C).

[81] *Survey II*, Chap. IV in class C : Nos. *45*, *46*, *47* and *53* and in class—CA : No. *49*. Cf. Doc. 63-AT/6, para. 3, in which it is pointed out that in a limited number of agreements direct negotiations between the competent aviation authorities — i.e. administrative conciliation — is the only form of dispute settlement.

means that the dispute is ended. With one exception, countries which are parties to the agreements which confine the special provision to this procedure belong to the Soviet bloc and are not ICAO members, the exception being Romania, which joined the organisation in 1965, 8 years after concluding its air transport agreement with the Netherlands.

C. In the field of *international trade* the preference in regulating the settlement of disputes in bilateral agreements also lies with the methods of direct negotiation and conciliation. The 19 trade agreements, all but 3 of which confine the special provision to a conciliation procedure, leave the settlement of disputes on interpretation and application to mixed commissions on which both parties are equally represented and which are responsible for supervision of the implementation of the agreement. There is no place in the conciliation procedure for an impartial third party. The significance of the mixed or joint commission is that in the first instance negotiations between the parties are not conducted through diplomatic channels, but by commissions which are constituted at the administrative level. It is therefore administrative conciliation.[82] The prevalence of this form of conciliation in the methods of settling disputes on interpretation and application of trade agreements is in line with the fact that the world-wide organisation of this sector is still in its early stages. The 3 remaining agreements provide for arbitration if the negotiations in the mixed commissions are unsuccessful.

D. All special provisions in the *social security* sector for citizens of either country contain consultation between the competent authorities — i.e. administrative conciliation — combined with arbitration (with one exception).[83] The agreements providing solely for conciliation (1) or a combination of conciliation with a form of arbitration classified as — (3) have been concluded between Soviet bloc countries themselves or between them and other countries. The latter kind confine themselves as regards arbitration to the statement that if consultation between the relevant competent authorities is fruitless, an arbitral tribunal will be formed in consultation between the parties. The other agreements concluded among Western European countries themselves contain the same arrangement with regard to arbitration. These countries, however, have elaborated the arbitration method in the European Interim Accords on social security, which can be applied even if one of the parties fails to cooperate.

[82] *Survey II*, p. 579 : "The settlement dispute provisions in the agreements relating to trade, payments, exchange or delivery of goods, reparations and economic co-operation in this section look to agreement between the parties rather than third party settlement as the chief mode of resolving differences." Cf. Annex II.

[83] *Survey II*, p. 645. Cf. Annex II.

E. The agreements on the *regime in frontier areas* contain negotiations between administrative officials and may therefore be described as administrative conciliation.[84] Implementation of the agreements is entrusted to officials nominated for the purpose in the agreements : frontier commissioners or authorities. The fact that the states have empowered the officials to take binding decisions on their behalf in certain cases does not alter the conciliatory nature of the procedure. In essence the parties have kept the decision which can end the dispute in their own hands by creating a procedure based on unanimity on decisions which bind the parties and by granting every official the right to submit a matter to his government for consultation at diplomatic level.

3.2.2. Multilateral treaties

Most special provisions in multilateral treaties organise settlement of disputes in the form of inter-state procedures on the initiative of the member-states. With the odd exception conciliation is entrusted to the competent authorities mentioned in the treaties — i.e. administrative conciliation — or to a body set up in the treaty on which all member-states are represented. This situation therefore is hardly in line with the method advocated by the Convention on the Law of Treaties. The impartial element, if present, is sought within the form of cooperation which is based on the treaty. In some cases the form of cooperation was created precisely to give form to consultation between the treaty partners in the sector concerned outside the normal diplomatic channels. In other cases the body — or one of the bodies — formed to implement the treaty has been given a mediating function if a dispute arises between the treaty partners on the interpretation of the treaty. The relevant special provisions are part of the multilateral treaties with a much wider scope than the organisation of consultation between the treaty partners. These multilateral treaties have a much clearer joint — usually economic — basis. The settlement of disputes arising from the interpretation and application of these treaties, however, has not usually become an internal matter for the international organisation. States remain free to settle disputes in the way they choose.[85] Nevertheless, the bodies set up under a treaty to implement it have been given a more active

[84] *Survey II*, pp. 476 et seq. Cf. Annex II and A.O. CUKWURAH, *The Settlement of Boundary Disputes in International Law*, 1968, particularly pp. 149 et seq.

[85] The EEC, EURATOM, and the European Convention on Human Rights and Fundamental Freedoms are definite exceptions. In Art. 219 of the EEC Treaty, Art. 193 of the EURATOM Treaty and Art. 62 of the Convention the member-states undertook only to settle disputes on interpretation and application in the manner indicated in the treaties.

role in the settlement of these disputes than those in the first group. This is reflected in the fact that the organs themselves may take initiatives in making recommendations; that one of the parties may submit the dispute to the competent organ; that this organ may make a recommendation by majority vote and/or that technical commissions are set up for investigation and advice.

In a number of treaties the organ has also been empowered to exempt a member-state or states from the obligations arising from the treaty vis-à-vis the member-state which is at fault. Without this arrangement the prejudiced party would also be able to ignore the obligations in such cases. This apart, this power does not lead to an ending of the dispute, but to an adjustment of the situation arising from the non-fulfilment, which implies a breaching of the treaty and is in conflict with the objectives of the treaty. The organs' power to grant exemption in certain cases cannot therefore be considered pacific settlement of the dispute. If parties wish to see that the treaty is complied with, with the aid of the organs appointed in the treaty, only the method of conciliation, whether or not in combination with arbitration or judicial settlement, is available.

The 35 special provisions in multilateral treaties contained in Table II which provide for conciliation, whether or not in combination with arbitration or judicial settlement, are part of treaties on alliance, mutual security and military assistance (2), regional cooperation (8), communications and transport (3), economic matters (8), commodity arrangements (4), social and humanitarian interest (5), social security (3) and miscellaneous (2).

3.2.2.1. *Conciliation procedure by analogy with the procedure of arbitration and judicial settlement*

As well as in the *Convention on the Law of Treaties* already discussed, arbitration and judicial settlement served as models for the conciliation procedures provided for in the European Convention on Human Rights, the treaties establishing the European Economic Community (EEC) and the European Atomic Energy Community (EURATOM) and the Protocol instituting a Conciliation and Good Offices Commission to be responsible for seeking the settlement of any disputes which may arise between States Parties to the Convention against Discrimination in Education.

The latter treaty is included in the sector of social and humanitarian interest, the others in regional cooperation (3) and miscellaneous (1).

The *European Convention for the Protection of Human Rights and Fundamental Freedoms* (Rome Convention) lays down (Art. 62) that the treaty partners will only settle disputes on the interpretation and application of the Convention in the way laid down therein. The Convention appoints the European Court of Human Rights to deal with disputes between the treaty partners on the interpretation or application of the Convention (Art. 45). The Court, however, may only deal with a matter after the European Commission of Human Rights has established, in a report to the Committee of Ministers and the parties concerned, that an amicable settlement has failed. The Commission therefore has a conciliatory function, to fulfil which it forms a seven-member sub-commission on which each party may nominate one member. This sub-commission hears the parties, carries out an investigation and decides by a majority vote. If no amicable settlement seems possible, the Commission, in its report to the Committee of Ministers, states whether it feels that a breach of the Convention has occurred. The opinions of the individual members may be communicated. The members of the Commission are chosen by the Committee of Ministers and sit as individuals.[86]

The treaties establishing the *EEC* and *EURATOM* lay down in Arts. 170 and 142 respectively that each member-state that feels that another member-state has failed to comply with its treaty obligations must refer the matter to the Commission of the European Communities before submitting it to the Court of Justice.

If the Commission feels that a member-state has indeed failed to meet its obligations, it may itself refer the matter to the Court, if the state concerned does not behave in accordance with its reasoned opinion. In view of the fact that the member-states' duty to submit the dispute first to the Commission is connected with the Commission's right to take initiatives on its own, the Commission's function vis-à-vis member-states between whom a dispute has arisen on the interpretation and application of the treaty may be considered one of conciliation. After all, if the Commission sees no reason to institute proceedings against a member-state because of failure to comply with treaty obligations, it may, partly because of its power to make recommendations and give advice (Art. 155 of EEC Treaty, Art. 124 of EURATOM Treaty), play a mediating role between the member-states concerned, without being able to prevent them from referring the matter

[86] *Survey II*, Chap. III, No. 2, p. 193 (C), Arts. 21, 23 and 28-34. In contrast to the procedure for written requests from individuals under Art. 25, the conciliatory function of the Committee predominates in the treatment of written requests from states under Art. 24, and not the jurisdictional function. The power to declare requests inadmissible, given under Art. 27, para. 3, if it feels that it is not in accordance with the Treaty only relates to requests from individuals, and not those from states.

to the Court themselves. This function of the Commission arises from the fact that it is responsible for the implementation of treaty provisions. The members of the Commission have to perform their duties in the general interests of the Community without accepting instructions from the respective governments. In relations between the member-states this activity of the Commission can therefore be compared with that of a conciliation commission : the hearing and re-hearing of sides, and the making of reasoned recommendations.[87]

Finally, the *UNESCO Protocol* provides for the setting up of a permanent Conciliation and Good Offices Commission, the task of which is to settle amicably disputes between states parties to the Convention against Discrimination in Education of 14 December 1960 on the interpretation and application of that Convention.[88] The Commission consists of eleven persons of high moral standing and acknowledged impartiality, who are appointed in view of their competence in the field of education and their judicial or legal experience particularly of an international character (Arts. 2 and 4).

The parties are entitled, if there is no member of the Commission possessing their nationality, to designate a member ad hoc. The Commission's decisions are taken by a majority of the votes of the permanent members and ad hoc members present. The chairman exercises a casting vote. A quorum is formed by two-thirds of the members, including any ad hoc members. The Commission may only handle a case if it is sure that all available domestic remedies have been invoked and exhausted, in accordance with generally recognised principles of international law (Art. 14). The final report contains either the solution reached with a brief statement of the facts, or, if conciliation fails, a survey of the facts and the majority view on the recommendations made. Each member, however, may add a separate opinion (Art. 17, paras. 2 and 3). The report is sent to the states concerned and forwarded to the Director-General of UNESCO for publication.

The resemblance to the pattern of arbitration and judicial settlement is strengthened by the provisions that the Commission does not consider

[87] *Survey II*, Nos. *8*, Arts. 155, 157, 169 and 170, pp. 232, 233 and 236 and *10*, Arts. 124, 126, 141 and 142, pp. 288, 289 and 292 (both +CJ) and Arts. 9 and 10 of the Merger Treaty of 8 April 1965, International Organisation and Integration, p. 891.

[88] Tractatenblad (Treaty Series) of the Kingdom of the Netherlands, 1964, No. 102, p. 18 (C). See S. Bastid, "Une nouvelle commission de conciliation?" *Mélanges Rolin*, pp. 1-12; Cot, *op. cit.*, pp. 277 and 316 et seq.; Report of a Study Group on the Peaceful Settlement of International Disputes, Annex IV : J.F. McMahon, *Settlement of Disputes in Special Fields*, paras. 30-32, pp. 200-201. The Protocol came into force under Art. 24 on 24 October 1968, three months after being ratified by at least 15 states.

matters it has already dealt with, if there are no new features (Art. 15); that the Commission may propose to the Executive Board or the General Conference of the UNESCO, if the latter is in session or will be within two months, that the International Court be requested to advise on any legal question connected with a matter submitted to the Commission (Art. 18) and that parties to the Protocol may declare, on a reciprocal basis, that matters which cannot be amicably settled by the Commission will be referred to the International Court. In view of all this it is not surprising that so far no Soviet state has ratified the Protocol.

3.2.2.2. *Conciliation procedure by analogy with the procedure of direct negotiation*

Most special provisions in this group make *permanent* treaty organs responsible for conciliation if disputes arise on the interpretation and application of the treaty. These are usually bodies on which all countries are represented.

The procedures to be followed by these bodies have not been elaborated, with the proviso that instructions are given on the quorum and voting. Apart from the sanction possibilities already mentioned, these organs' function cannot usually be considered as more than one of conciliation in line with the method of direct negotiation, even in cases in which most or all treaty partners are parties to general multilateral treaties and have concluded one or more bilateral treaties among themselves which provide for arbitration or judicial settlement.

A. The two special provisions in multilateral treaties in the *treaty of alliance* category which have been classed under C are Art. XVI of the Agreement between the Parties to the North Atlantic Treaty regarding the Status of their Forces, of 19 June 1951, and para. 4 of the Declaration on the Neutrality of Laos, of 23 July 1962 and Art. 14 of the annexed Protocol.

Art. XVI of the *NATO Status Agreement* states :

> "All differences between the Contracting Parties relating to the interpretation or application of this Agreement shall be settled by negotiation between them without recourse to any outside jurisdiction. Except where express provision is made to the contrary in this Agreement, differences which cannot be settled by direct negotiation, shall be referred to the North Atlantic Council."

Under Art. 9 of the North Atlantic Treaty the Council has a consultative function and it cannot be considered to make pronouncements which bind parties without their consent. Art. XVI of the NATO Status Agreement therefore boils down to the fact that, if negotiations are abortive, they are continued at another level, i.e. within the Council as a forum for political consultation.[89]

The 13 states which signed the *Declaration on the Neutrality of Laos* set up an International Commission for Supervision and Control in Laos, on which 3 states are represented, viz. Canada, Poland and India. This is contained in the Protocol which is in the form of an agreement between the 13 states and Laos. The commission is responsible for seeing that the neutrality of Laos is both realised and preserved.

The commission's decisions, except on procedural matters, conclusions and recommendations based on investigations, must be unanimous.[90] The arrangement is thus in line with the organisation pattern outlined above for the settlement of disputes between Western countries and the Soviet states.

B. In the *regional cooperation* category 3 special provisions are confined to conciliation and 2 combine this method with arbitration or judicial settlement.

The Charter of the *Council for Mutual Economic Assistance* (COMECON) aims to promote and organise economic, scientific and technical cooperation between members in accordance with the principle of sovereign equality of all member-states.

In view of the fact that, according to Art. IV (3), all recommendations and decisions require the consent of all members, except that of members which declare that they have no interest at stake — the recommendation/decision does not then apply to those members — COMECON is, from the organisational point of view, a permanent framework for bilateral negotiations outside the traditional diplomatic context in the field of economic, technical and scientific cooperation between the member-states.[91]

The cooperation agreement between Finland, Denmark, Iceland and Norway, who form the *Nordic Council,* lays down in Art. 35 that

> "With a view to achieving the aims set forth in this Agreement, the Contracting Parties should consult one another on a continuing basis and, when necessary, undertake concerted action."

This is in line with the Nordic Council's objective : to be a body within which the parliaments and governments of the member-states can cooperate,

[89] *Survey II,* Chap. II, No. 8, pp. 121 and 127; McMahon, *op. cit.,* paras. 181-184, pp. 236-238. In 1956 the NATO states adopted a resolution empowering the NATO Secretary-General to offer good offices in disputes between members.

[90] *Survey II,* Chap. II, No. 22, p. 163. Cf. A. Lall, *Modern International Negotiation,* 1966, in particular pp. 101, 102 and 117.

[91] *Survey II,* Chap. III, No. 14, p. 324 (C); A. Korbonski, "COMECON", *International Conciliation,* 1964, No. 549, pp. 15-29.

particularly in juridical, cultural, social and economic matters and in the field of communications.[92] Here, too, negotiations are being given a form outside the normal diplomatic channels.

The members of the *Organisation for Economic Cooperation and Development* (OECD) have, according to Art. 3 of the Convention, undertaken to

"(a) keep each other informed and furnish the Organisation with the information necessary for the accomplishment of its tasks;
(b) consult together on a continuing basis, carry out studies and participate in agreed projects; and
(c) co-operate closely and where appropriate take co-ordinated action."

Under Art. 5 the organisation may take decisions which bind the members, but under Art. 6, para. 1, only with their consent.

An abstention on the part of a member-state does not make the decision null and void vis-à-vis the other members.[93] The member abstaining is not, however, bound by the decision. The OECD is thus an organisation for consultation between member-states in the economic sector. The fact that an organisation for consultation between member-states by no means has to be without engagement is illustrated by the work of the OECD, particularly in the field of development cooperation. Under Art. 9 of the OECD Convention a development assistance committee (DAC) was formed which subjects members' efforts on development cooperation to a searching annual examination, the results of which are included in the DAC Annual Aid Review.

Art. XI of the treaty setting up the *European Organization for Nuclear Research* (CERN) dated 1 July 1951 charges the Council to provide good offices if a dispute arises between member-states on the interpretation or application of the treaty. The Council, on which each member-state is represented with one vote, decides by a simple majority vote of members present. A quorum is formed by a simple majority of the total number of members. Members may be accompanied by advisers. The conciliatory function has thus been entrusted to the representative organ of the member-states. If parties do not reach agreement, the dispute has to be submitted to the ICJ. It is not indicated, however, that this may be done by each of the parties independently of the other(s). If a member-state does not comply with its obligations, it may be deprived of membership (Art. XIII) by a decision of the Council that has been accepted by two-thirds of all members.

[92] *Survey II*, Chap. III, No. 15, p. 332 (C). LALL, *op. cit.*, p. 162, refers to the implications of the Nordic Council for the neutrality of Sweden and Finland, e.g. in negotiations on the composition of the Security Council.

[93] *International Organisation and Integration*, pp. 1019 and 1020 (C).

A state which has not paid its contribution for the current and previous financial years may not exercise its voting right unless the Council allows this by a two-thirds majority vote of all members.[94]

Finally, the *Convention of Association* between the EEC and the African and Malagasy States of 20 July 1963 (Convention of Yaounde) lays down that disputes on the interpretation and application of the Convention between one or more member-states of the Community on the one hand and one or more associated states on the other hand

"shall be submitted by one of the parties to the dispute to the Association Council which shall seek an amicable settlement at its next meeting. If this cannot be achieved and if the parties to the dispute fail to agree upon an appropriate solution, the dispute shall, at the request of the earliest petitioner, be submitted to the Court of Arbitration of the Association."

The Association Council is formed by the members of the EEC Council and Commission and government representatives of the associated states. The Council may only take legally valid decisions if half the members of the EEC Council, one member of the EEC Commission and half the government representatives of the associated states are present. Decisions must be unanimous. If the dispute is between the Community and the associated states, the Association Council's work involves a form of direct negotiation between both parties outside normal diplomatic channels, i.e. administrative conciliation. If the dispute is between an EEC member-state and one or more associated states, the Association Council may act more as a mediator.[95]

C. Of the 3 special provisions from the *communications and transport* group, one is confined to conciliation and 2 combine this method with arbitration, depending on the cooperation of the parties. Art. 55 of the convention on the *Intergovernmental Maritime Consultative Organisation* (IMCO) lays down that disputes on the interpretation and application of the convention

"shall be referred for settlement to the Assembly, or shall be settled in such other manner as the parties to the dispute agree. Nothing in this article shall preclude the Council or the Maritime Safety Committee from settling any such question or dispute that may arise among the exercise of their functions."

The Safety Committee may only make recommendations to the Assembly (Art. 30) via the Council, consisting of 18 government representatives elected

[94] *Survey II*, Chap. III, No. 5, pp. 213 et seq. Arts. V (Council), XI (Disputes) and XIII (Non-fulfilment of Obligations) (—CJ).

[95] *International Organisation and Integration*, Arts. 40 (composition of Association Council and quorum), 43 (decision-making) and 51 (disputes), pp. 884 and 885 (+CA).

by the Assembly. The Council may also only make recommendations to the Assembly, unless it is not in session, in which case the Council may address its recommendations to members (Art. 22). The Assembly's power under Art. 16 does not go further than to make recommendations to members. Decisions on them may be taken in the respective organs by simple majority of those present and voting (i.e. not abstaining). This does not alter the fact that the conciliatory functions are exercised by representative bodies in which negotiation is central to decision-making. The Assembly and the Council, with the Assembly's authorisation, are empowered to ask the International Court for juridical advice on any legal question within the framework of activities, other than questions concerning mutual relations of the organisation and the UN or other specialised organisations.[96]

The *International Convention concerning the Carriage of Goods by Rail* (CIM) and the *International Convention concerning the Carriage of Passengers and Luggage by Rail* (CIV) of 25 October 1952 provide for the setting up of a Central Office that may undertake conciliation at the request of a treaty party or a transport undertaking. The Central Office can also be asked for advice when such disputes arise and assist in settling by arbitration. With regard to arbitration on disputes between states, the conventions only lay down that the states are not bound by the arbitration arrangement appended to the convention and

"may freely determine the composition of the arbitration tribunal and the arbitration procedure".[97]

How the Central Office fulfils its conciliatory function is not elaborated. The description of the work as good offices and mediation and the possibility of giving advice on request imply that the office has more the job ofkeeping direct negotiations going between parties and facilitating them — the Office was set up

"in order to facilitate and ensure the operation of this convention"

(Art. 57) — than to act as a conciliation commission according to the pattern of the procedures of arbitration and judicial settlement.

D. The special provisions in the *economic matters* group containing conciliation are confined to that method, except for 2 which combine it with arbitration, depending on the cooperation of parties.

96 *International Organisation and Integration*, pp. 462-488 (C) and, with regard to advisory procedure, Art. 56 with Art. 9, para. 2 of the agreement between IMCO and the UN (PEASLEE, p. 918).

97 CIM and CIV Arts. 57 and 60 (PEASLEE, pp. 219 and 247) and *Survey II*, Chap. IV, Nos. 6a and 6b, pp, 355 and 358 (—CA) and Annex II.

The *Customs Cooperation Council*, set up on 15 December 1950 by 27 countries in Europe, Asia, Africa and the Middle East, along with Australia, aims, among other things, to promote cooperation between member-states in studying problems connected with the charging of import duties, to prepare draft agreements thereon, to promote the uniform interpretation of these agreements and

"to make recommendations, in a conciliatory capacity, for the settlement of disputes concerning the interpretation or application of the Conventions referred to in paragraph (d) above in accordance with the provisions of those Conventions".[98]

The conventions on the *Nomenclature for the Classification of Goods in Customs Tariffs* and the *Valuation of Goods for Customs Purposes* must be considered in connection with the setting up of the above Council.

Art. 9 of the nomenclature convention and Art. 11 of that on the valuation of goods mean that any dispute that cannot be settled by negotiation will be referred by the parties to the Nomenclature Committee or the Valuation Committee for recommendations. If these committees are unable to settle the dispute, they will refer the case to the Council, on which all members are represented.[99] The Council may also make recommendations on its own. It decides by a two-thirds majority of members present and entitled to vote, with a quorum being formed by more than half those entitled to vote on the matter. A member that is not party to a convention — concluded through the Council — the interpretation or application of which leads to a dispute, is excluded from the voting. The Council may also deprive a member of voting rights if it has not paid its contribution three months after receiving a reminder.[100]

The states parties to the *General Agreement on Tariffs and Trade* (GATT) have undertaken to hold consultations on trade and tariffs that may also be started by the general assembly, the Contracting Parties, at the request of one of the contracting parties.[101] If one of the parties feels that the advantages accruing directly or indirectly from the agreement are being

[98] *Survey II*, Chap. V, No. 3, Art. 3, p. 446 (C) and PEASLEE, pp. 371 et seq. Cf. Art. 3 (e) of the treaty, to which is added : 'the parties in dispute may agree in advance to accept the recommendations of the Council as binding'.

[99] *Survey II*, Chap. V, Nos. *4*, Art. 9 (b) and (c), p. 449, and *5*, Art. 11 (b) and (c), p. 450 (both C).

[100] *Survey II*, No. 3, Art. III (d), p. 446, Art. VIII (a) and (b), p. 447 and Art. XII (c), p. 448.

[101] *Survey II*, Chap. V, No. 1, Arts. XXII and XXIII, p. 438 (C) and *International Organisation and Integration*, p. 590. Cf. also Art. XXXVII of part IV on Trade and Development added in 1965; *op. cit.*, p. 599.

nullified or prejudiced and consultation — at first bilateral, later with the Contracting Parties — proves fruitless, Art. XXIII, para. 2 lays down, among other things, that the Contracting Parties may authorize a contracting party or parties to suspend the application to any other contracting party or parties of such concessions or other obligations under this Agreement as they determine to be appropriate in the circumstances.[102]

Under Art. XXV, para. 4 the Contracting Parties decide by majority vote or in exceptional circumstances by a two-thirds majority of the votes cast comprising more than half of the contracting parties.[103]

The exemption procedure can be instituted both by a state which is of the opinion that it cannot (yet) be required to comply with an obligation arising under the Agreement, and by a state which feels itself prejudiced by behaviour of another contracting party that in its opinion is against the Agreement. The first case is a request procedure by an interested party, and the second a dispute procedure. The request procedure can turn into a dispute procedure, however, if other states feel prejudiced by the exemption.

Although the starting point of the settlement of disputes is consultation between the contracting parties, and in this the Contracting Parties' function is confined to the making of recommendations, apart from the possibility of authorising one of the contracting parties to suspend application of the Agreement in respect of the contracting party who is in default, the Contracting Parties set up a Panel of Complaints in 1953. This Panel, which consists of states not involved in the dispute, examines the complaints and, if the dispute is not settled during the investigation, makes recommendations on it to the Contracting Parties.[104]

The extent to which investigation procedure in GATT is based on information from the countries concerned is clear from the agreement on the application of Art. VI of GATT — devoted to anti-dumping measures and countervailing duties — which was concluded during the negotiations on tariff reductions in Geneva, known as the Kennedy Round, on 30 June 1967. It is true that the agreement provides for investigation and adminis-

[102] *International Organisation and Integration*, p. 591.

[103] *Ibid.*, p. 593.

[104] *Ibid.*, p. 584, Art. XVIII (Governmental Assistance to Economic Development) section D, paragraph 22, and Art. XXIII (2); also *Survey II*, p. 422. Cf. Cot, *op. cit.*, pp. 273, 316 et seq.; J. H. Jackson, "GATT as an Instrument for the Settlement of Trade Disputes", Proc. ASIL, 1967, pp. 144-155; McMahon, *op. cit.*, paras. 267-275, pp. 254-256. He notes : 'The Panel operates almost as a arbitral tribunal... There is a high rate of compliance with these recommendations (i.e. the Panel's) and the Panel has now built up a valuable body of case law on the interpretation and application of the GATT Agreement'.

trative procedures relating to anti-dumping measures, but this is by and on the responsibility of the state concerned and not by an inter-state body.

The 'Review of the Contracting Parties through the last two decades and conclusions on their future work programme' accepted by the Contracting Parties on 24 November 1967 emphasises the element of negotiation in GATT, even in the settlement of disputes. In this survey the Contracting Parties reaffirm their confidence in GATT

"as the *contractual* basis for their trading relationships and their determination to co-operate in the trade field within the framework of the Agreement"

(author's italics).[105] They pointed out that when problems arose

"the established GATT consultation procedures were available to facilitate constructive co-operation between countries"

and underlined the fact that GATT's main aim remains to liberalise world trade by means of *negotiation*. The future programme contained in the Review mentions the setting up of a Committee on Trade in Industrial Products and an Agricultural Committee and in the latter case it is explicitly stated

"that the discussions should be conducted not in a spirit of confrontation, but as a means of arriving at mutually acceptable solutions".[106]

Although the area covered by the *European Free Trade Association* (EFTA) is not world-wide, like GATT, but regional, and the differences between members' economic levels of development are not as pronounced as in GATT, the settlement of disputes is confined to conciliation.

This is despite the fact that the Convention establishing the EFTA, as distinct from that of GATT, aims more clearly to create an international *organisation*.[107] The organisation of conciliation, however, is somewhat better than in GATT, particularly as it works out details of investigation. Under Art. 31 of the Convention, EFTA members can submit to the Council disputes arising from the interpretation or application of the convention which they cannot settle between themselves.[108] The Council, on which all members sit, can decide by a majority vote to refer the matter to Examining Committees consisting of

[105] GATT Doc. L./2943 of 28 November 1967, para. 2.

[106] *Ibid.*, par 10 B.

[107] Cf. Art. 1, para. 1, *International Organisation and Integration*, p. 998. See also *Survey II*, p. 422.

[108] *Survey II*, Chap. V, No. 8, Art. 32, p. 456 (C) and *International Organisation and Integration*, p. 1010.

"persons selected for their competence and integrity, who, in the performance of their duties, shall neither seek nor receive instructions from any State, or from any authority or organisation other than the Association."[109]

This referral must be made at the request of one of the parties to the dispute. Under Art. 31, para. 3, the Council can, partly on the basis of any report submitted by an examining committee, make recommendations by majority vote to the members concerned. If a member is unable to accept the recommendation and the Council is of the opinion that an obligation under the Convention has not been complied with, it may, also by majority vote, authorise any member-state to suspend the meeting of certain obligations vis-à-vis the defaulting member. This authorisation can be given at the request of any member-state as provisional measure anticipating the result of the investigation.[110]

Although suspension of compliance with an obligation vis-à-vis a defaulting member can be decided on by the Council by majority vote — it is therefore a decision which accepts as a starting point the failure of cooperation within the organisation — decisions binding member-states can only be taken unanimously.[111] In other words, the organisational form means that a member-state that does not observe the rules can itself be excluded, but cannot be directly compelled to comply.

The conciliation method in the *United Nations Conference on Trade and Development* (UNCTAD) is presented as part of the voting procedure and not as a method of settling disputes on the interpretation or application of the UNCTAD Statute. In essence, however, it is a dispute procedure. UNCTAD, just like other UN organisations, has inferred from the principle of the sovereign equality of states that each member-state's vote has the same value. During the first world trade conference, held in Geneva in 1964, it became clear that in the international organisation of inter-state economic relations this conclusion meets more difficulties than in that of other inter-state relations.[112] The solution to the deadlock was sought in the introduction of a conciliation procedure

"to take place before voting and to provide an adequate basis for the adoption of

[109] *Ibid.*, p. 1011, Art. 33.

[110] Art. 31, para. 4. The state failing to comply is not excluded from voting. On the other hand, the Council's decision does not have to be unanimous, as is usually the case (Art. 32, para. 5).

[111] Article 32, paras. 4 and 5 : cf. *International Organisation and Integration*, p. 1011.

[112] In the IBRD, IDA and IFC, ECSC, EEC and EURATOM and in the commodity agreements the economic position of member-states is therefore allowed for in the granting of the number of votes and in the voting procedure (the 'dual voting' system).

recommendations with regard to proposals of a specific nature for action substantially affecting the economic or financial interests of particular countries."[113]

It is applied if a request to that end has been submitted by a specific number of countries to the Chairman of the Conference or the Trade and Development Board and has the effect of suspending the voting procedure.[114]

The fact that proposals for action 'substantially affecting the economic or financial interests of particular countries' form the subject of conciliation confirms, just like the list of the various sectors to which they relate, the last point in particular : 'Rights and obligations under international agreements or treaties', the dispute-settling character of the procedure in question.[115] On the size and composition of the conciliation committee the resolution states :

"The conciliation committee shall, as a rule, be small in size. Its members shall include countries especially interested in the matter with respect to which such conciliation was initiated and shall be selected on an equitable geographical basis."[116]

The last condition is inherent in the structure of the conciliation; to ensure that the voting mechanism is operated in such a way that both the economically weaker majority and the economically stronger minority among the UNCTAD members can be satisfied with it. No further details are given on the committee's operating method. There is merely an announcement that the committee should start work as soon as possible and endeavour during the current meeting of the Conference or Board to reach agreement without a vote. Although the conciliation procedure in UNCTAD was mainly introduced as a method of and for states an active role was entrusted to UNCTAD organs, although a modest one. The procedure can be set in motion

"whenever the President of the Conference, the Chairman of the Board or the Chairman of the Committee concerned is satisfied that the required number of countries as specified in sub-paragraph (b) above are in favour of such conciliation ", while also "good offices of the Secretary-General of the Conference shall be utilized as fully as practicable in connexion with the process of conciliation".[117]

[113] *International Organisation and Integration*, GA Res. 1995 (XIX) of 30 December 1964, Art. 25, pp. 345-348 (C). Cf. on this point B. Gosovic, "UNCTAD :North-South Encounter", *International Conciliation*, 1968. No. 568; O. Schachter, "Conciliation Procedures in the United Nations Conference on Trade and Development", *Liber Amicorum Martin Domke*, pp. 268-274; Cot, *op. cit.*, p. 273, pp. 330, et seq.

[114] For a conciliation request in the Conference, the Council or a Committee the consent of 10, 5 or 3 members respectively is required.

[115] *International Organisation and Integration*, p. 346, para. 25 (2) sub (i).

[116] *Ibid.*, p. 346 under (g).

[117] *Ibid.*, pp. 345 and 347, para. 25 (c) and (m).

Other than in the above treaties in the category in question, the *Multilateral Treaty on Free Trade and Central American Economic Integration* of 10 June 1958 and the *Treaty on Economic Association between Guatemala, El Salvador and Honduras* of 6 February 1960 combine conciliation with arbitration. In both treaties conciliation is entrusted to organs in which all members are represented, viz. the Central American Trade Commission in the former treaty and the Executive Council in the latter, with appeal in the latter case to the Governing Board.[118] The former works on the basis of unanimity. The Executive Council decides by majority vote. Nothing has been laid down with regard to decision-making by the Governing Board, so it must be assumed — all the more so as this organ consists of the Ministers of Economic Affairs of the contracting parties — that unanimity is required.[119]

E. The 4 *commodity agreements* which provide for conciliation combine this method with arbitration and/or judicial settlement, although in one case this is not for all disputes on interpretation and application.

The treaties setting up the *International Rice Commission* of November 1948, as amended in November 1960, and the *Indo-Pacific Fisheries Council* of November 1948, as amended in November 1961 — on each occasion at the annual meetings of FAO — entrust conciliation to a special committee on which each party nominates a member. These members jointly choose an independent chairman.

If this procedure proves fruitless, the dispute has to be submitted to the ICJ in accordance with the Statute of the Court, unless parties agree on another method. It was not however laid down that each party may unilaterally submit a dispute to the Court.[120]

The *International Olive Oil Agreement* entrusts conciliation to the organ in which all member-states are represented and which has to implement the Agreement : the Olive Oil Council. The conciliatory function is performed by the Council, which otherwise decides by a majority — containing

[118] *Survey II*, Chap. V, Nos. *7*, Art. XXV, p. 454 and *10*, Art. XXIX, p. 461, (both —CA). Cf. J.S. Nye, "Central American Regional Integration", *International Conciliation*, 1967, No. 562, in particular pp. 20 and 29.

[119] Art. XVIII of the Free Trade Treaty and Art. XXIII of the Association Treaty. Art. XXI of the General Treaty for Central American Economic Integration of 13 December 1960, that — cf. Art. XXVII — takes precedence over the other treaties, lays down : 'Before coming to a decision, the Economic Council shall decide unanimously whether the matter shall be settled by the concurrent votes of all its members or by a majority vote' (Cf. *The Inter-American System*, pp. 476 and 478). This is the Central American Economic Council, consisting of the Ministers of Economic Affairs.

[120] *Survey II*, Chap. VI, Nos. *6*, Art. XI, p. 497 and *7*, Art. XIII, p. 498 (both —CJ).

at least 3 member-states — on disputes on the interpretation and application of the provisions of Chapter V of the Agreement : 'Designation and definitions of olive oil appellations of origin and indications of source in international trade'. In this the Council consults the International Federation of Olive Oil Growers, a competent professional organisation of a mainly importing country and if necessary the International Bureau for the Protection of Industrial Property, the International Chamber of Commerce and the Permanent Bureau for Analytical Chemistry. If conciliation proves unsuccessful, the governments can submit the case to the ICJ. In other disputes on application and interpretation the Council decides itself, if necessary after consulting an advisory committee 'the composition of which shall be fixed by the Council's rules of procedure'.[121]

The *International Coffee Agreement* of 1968 provides for the setting up of an independent conciliation committee by the Executive Director at the request of a party and with the consent of the other party (Art. 58). If a party does not consent to this, or if consultation is unsuccessful, the case can be submitted to the Council, in accordance with Art. 59 (disputes and complaints). If the consultation *is* successful, a report thereon is made to the Executive Director, who distributes it to all members.[122]

F. With one exception — the UNESCO Protocol dealt with above — the 5 *treaties in the humanitarian and social field* which provide for conciliation combine it with arbitration.

The 4 *Geneva Conventions* for the improvement of the condition of the sick, wounded and shipwrecked serving with armed forces, prisoners of war and civilians provide for conciliation in the form of inquiry and good offices by Protecting Powers, i.e. states or humanitarian organisations such as the International Red Cross. If a dispute arises between the parties to the dispute on the interpretation and application of the conventions, the Protecting Powers, at the request of one of the parties or of their own accord, may offer their good offices and propose to the parties that a conference be convened, on neutral territory if possible. 'The Parties to the dispute shall be bound to give effect to the proposals made to them for this purpose'. If one of the parties accuses another one of infringing the conventions — which also implies a dispute on interpretation and application — an investigation should be started in a manner agreed upon by the parties. If agreement has not been reached concerning the procedure for the enquiry,

[121] *Survey II*, Chap. VI, No. 9, Art. 12 (2) with 35, pp. 509 and 515 (+CAJ).

[122] *Survey II*, Chap. VI, No. 8 with Tractatenblad 1968, No. 52, pp. 82 and 93 (+CA).

the Parties should agree on the choice of an umpire, who will decide upon the procedure to be followed.

The investigation is therefore intended not only to establish the facts, but also to end the dispute. The parties undertake to make good an infringement if one is established. The 'umpire's' function too, although limited to laying down investigation procedure, indicates that the special provision aims at more than conciliation. A form of arbitration can be seen in it, the realisation of which depends wholly on the cooperation of the parties. The impression that the settlement of disputes in these treaties is the outcome of a compromise is reinforced by a resolution adopted during the diplomatic conference held in Geneva in 1949 to revise the conventions dating from 1929. It recommends that, if a dispute on the interpretation or application of the conventions cannot be settled in any other way,

"the High Contracting Parties concerned *endeavour to agree* between themselves to refer such dispute to the International Court of Justice".[123]

G. The 3 agreements in the *social security* field entrust conciliation in disputes on interpretation and application of these agreements to the competent authorities of the states which are parties thereto. This is therefore a form of administrative conciliation. If unsuccessful, it is followed by arbitration.[124]

H. The 2 treaties in the *miscellaneous* group which provide for conciliation are the Convention on the Law of Treaties discussed above and the agreement on the *European Commission for the Control of Foot and Mouth Disease*. The latter limits the settlement of disputes on interpretation or application of the agreement to investigation by a committee of experts.[125]

The agreement, however, makes not only the initiative for the investigation but also the adoption of the resulting recommendations the entire responsibility of the Committee members. It is therefore more a coordination of bilateral relations than an institution with its own responsibility.

[123] *Survey II*, Chap. VII, Nos. 2a, Art. 52, p. 532; 2b, Art. 53, p. 534; 2c, Art. 132, p. 536; 2d, Art. 149, p. 438 (all —CA).

[124] *Survey II*, Chap. X, Nos. *26*, Art. 11, p. 683; *27*, Art. 11, p. 692 and *28*, Art. 20, p. 701. These agreements have all been classified as +CA. Cf. part 5 below.

[125] *Survey II*, Chap. XII, No. 3, Art. XVII, p. 892.

Part. 4.

The relationship between special provisions and general treaties in the same inter-state link

As inter-state relations are organised at the present the freedom of states to choose a method of settling disputes is central. The text of the declaration on which the Committee on Principles of International Law concerning Friendly Relations and Co-operation among States was able to reach agreement underlines this :

"... 5. International disputes shall be settled on the basis of the sovereign equality of States and in accordance with the principle of free choice of means. Recourse to, or acceptance of, a settlement procedure freely agreed to *by States with regard to existing or future disputes to which they are parties* shall not be regarded as incompatible with sovereign equality; ..."[126]

The freedom of states to choose a method of peacefully settling disputes means that it cannot be assumed that unless otherwise laid down the states parties to a general treaty intend always to settle their disputes in the ways indicated in that treaty. The parties to general treaties retain the freedom to make special provisions in other treaties for the settlement of disputes arising from interpretation and application, even though it may not be expressly laid down. The states which are members of the UN have only undertaken to refrain from taking the law into their own hands and to settle their disputes peacefully, without declaring in favour of a specific method of settlement.[127] Most general treaties, including declarations on the acceptance of the compulsory jurisdiction of the ICJ, expressly keep open the possibility of settling by another method.[128]

In a number of general treaties it has also been laid down, however, that if the special provisions in other treaties only contain a conciliation procedure and under the general treaty the dispute could also be settled by arbitration or judicial settlement, these methods will be used if the special conciliation procedure is unsuccessful. These are the 1928 General Act for the Pacific Settlement of International Disputes, the 1929 general treaty between Czechoslovakia, Romania and Yugoslavia (the 'Little Entente') and 19 bilateral treaties attuned to the General Act, as well as the 1957 European Convention for the Peaceful Settlement of Disputes.[129] Art. 17 of

[126] Doc. A/6230, para. 248 — author's italics.

[127] L.M. Goodrich, *op. cit.*, pp. 199-200.

[128] *Survey I*, p. 39; ICJ Yearbooks.

[129] *Survey I*, pp. 39 and 42-43 under V and VI and Art. 28 of the European Convention (*Survey II*, p. 65).

the General Act stipulates as a minimum condition on ratification the acceptance of conciliation by the treaty partners. Most states have in fact accepted all chapters and thereby provide for conciliation and arbitration for all disputes and judicial settlement for legal disputes.[130] Under Art. 29 this is the minimum basis for these states for special arrangements for the settlement of disputes in other treaties between them.[131] The same applies to the European Convention (Art. 28).

Art. 34 of this Convention says that when ratifying, treaty states must accept at least Chapter I, devoted to judicial settlement for legal disputes. Under Arts. 1 and 34 with 28 however the treaty states can also provide for arbitration on legal disputes in other treaties that they have concluded or will conclude among themselves.

For the states which are parties to :

a. the (Revised) General Act, and when ratifying it have accepted not only the arrangement on conciliation but also that for arbitration or judicial settlement;

b. the 20 general treaties on settlement of disputes which are attuned to the General Act;

c. the European Convention for the Peaceful Settlement of Disputes,

these treaties are framework treaties for the special procedures in other treaties on the settlement of disputes arising from interpretation or application. If these special provisions are not above the level of conciliation, arbitration or judicial settlement still applies under the general treaty, unless expressly laid down otherwise.[132] After all, the disputes arising from the interpretation and application of the treaties of which the special provisions are part do belong to the category of legal disputes.

The extent to which special provisions appear in *bilateral* treaties alongside general treaties is shown by table VIII.

This table illustrates states' freedom to contract with regard also to pacific settlement of disputes.[133] It can be concluded from the figures that, if a + general treaty is in force between states, it is relatively likely that a special provision in another treaty between the same states will also rank as +.

[130] Except the Netherlands and Sweden with regard to Chapter III : Arbitration.

[131] *Survey I*, p. 440.

[132] In the General Act of 1928 and the 20 general treaties the jurisdiction of the PCIJ is mentioned, but under Art. 37 of the ICJ Statute the ICJ can be read for the PCIJ. Of the 20 general treaties attuned to the General Act, not one was concluded between states which have accepted the compulsory jurisdiction of the ICJ over legal disputes.

[133] Of the 39 special provisions classed as — which occur in addition to a general treaty, 12 were concluded in addition to a framework treaty.

TABLE VIII

Combinations of general treaties and special provisions in bilateral links, subdivided according to whether the application of the methods of settling disputes indicated in the general treaty (GT) and special provisions depends (—) or not (+) on the cooperation of all parties.[134]

Spec. provs.	Alongside GT of class +	Alongside GT of class —	Without GT	Tot.	Spec. provs.	Alongside GT of class +	Alongside GT of class —	Without GT	Tot.
— A	14	-	14	28	+ A	20	5	7	32
— J	1	-	6	7	+ J	7	1	-	8
— AJ	-	1	2	3	+ AJ	15	4	4	23
— CA	4	1	6	11	+ CA	13	-	2	15
— CAJ	-	-	1	1	+ CAJ	2	-	-	2
C	13	5	21	39					
Total	32	7	50	89	Total	57	10	13	80

It is significant that quite a few — 13 out of 39 — of the special provisions on conciliation which belong to bilateral treaties also occur in addition to general bilateral or multilateral treaties which allow arbitration or judicial settlement on the initiative of one of the parties. The treaties to which the provisions belong were concluded just after the Second World War, if non-Communist countries were involved, and in the 1950s and 1960s in inter-state relations when, after the general treaty was concluded, one or both parties joined the Communist bloc. Of the 13 special provisions on conciliation 5 occur in addition to bilateral or multilateral framework treaties. As these provisions do not expressly lay down otherwise, it must be assumed that arbitration or judicial settlement may be used under the framework treaties if conciliation is unsuccessful.[135]

[134] If states are parties to more general treaties which are not all classified as +, the relevant special provision has nevertheless been included in Table VIII in the +column of the general multilateral and/or bilateral treaties.

[135] Cf. in the economic matters sector : *Survey II*, Chap. VIII, Nos. *3*, Austria-Norway of 14 April 1947, Art. IV, p. 585, also parties to the bilateral general treaty of 1 Oct 1930 (:·: ICA+IIJ), *Survey I*, No. 144, p. 849 and to the European Convention; *8*, France-Norway of 11 June 1948, p. 602, also parties to the General Act; *10*, Czechoslovakia-

The special provisions on conciliation which occur in addition to general bilateral treaties classified as — belong to treaties to which at least one Communist country is a party.

Of the 50 special provisions in *multilateral* treaties which are classified as —, 11 belong to regional treaties concluded by states which between themselves are also parties to general treaties classified as + A or + J. With 4 exceptions they provide for arbitration or judicial settlement. Three of them were concluded in Central America.[136]

To these can be added the *Charter of the Organisation of Central American States* (ODECA) of 12 December 1962, which carries on the line on the pacific settlement of disputes contained in the previous treaties.

One of the organs of the ODECA is the Central American Court, which under Art. 14 of the Charter consists of 'Presidents of the Judicial Powers of each of the Member States'.[137] The Court's task is to prepare and render opinions on projects, for the unification of Central American legislation at the request of the Conference of Ministers of Foreign Affairs or the Executive Council and

"to decide the conflicts of a legal nature which arise among the Member States and which the latter *agree* to submit to it."[138]

The provision does not confine the Court's role to disputes arising out of the interpretation and application of the Charter, but contains a general provision : the mere settlement of legal disputes.[139]

Yugoslavia of 25 Feb. 1947, Art. 8, p. 583, also parties to the Little Entente of 21 May 1929 (:: ICA+IIJ), *Survey I*, No. 79, p. 572; it is unlikely that this framework treaty will be used, as the states concerned belong to the treaty pattern of the Soviet bloc. *11* Greece-Norway of 12 March 1949, p. 605, also parties to the General Act; *13* Greece-Turkey of 21 July 1949 Art. 7, p. 607, also parties to the General Act and bilateral general treaty of 30 Oct 1930 (+ICAJ).

[136] *Survey II*, Chap. IV, No. *51*, Convention establishing the Central American Air Navigation Services of 26 Feb. 1960 , Art. 25 (—A), p. 415; Chap. V, Nos. *7*, multilateral treaty on Free Trade and Central American Economic Integration of 10 June 1958 between Costa Rica, Guatemala, Honduras, Nicaragua and El Salvador, Art. XXV (—CA), p. 454; *10*, Central American Treaty of Economic Association of 6 Feb. 1960, Art. XXIX (—CA), p. 461.

[137] *The Inter-American System*, Appendix No. 22, p. 481, and *International Organisation and Integration*, pp. 1095 et seq. The Charter came into force on 30 March 1965. See S. ENGEL, "The New ODECA", *A.J.I.L.*, 1966, pp. 806-809.

[138] *The Inter-American System*, p. 482, author's italics.

[139] The Charter has therefore been included in class —IIJ in Tables I, III, IV, and VII, in which the general treaties have been broken down, and in Annex I.

Most Central American states have already ratified the compulsory jurisdiction of the ICJ and/or the Pact of Bogota.[140]

Four special provisions in multilateral treaties belong to treaties between members of the Council of Europe.[141]

Here, too, most treaty states have already proved willing to accept the compulsory jurisdiction of the ICJ and/or to ratify the (Revised) General Act or the European Convention — i.e. framework treaties. A number of these states have also concluded bilateral general (framework) treaties between themselves which make arbitration or judicial settlement possible on the initiative of one of the parties.[142]

Noticeable among these is the treaty establishing the Benelux Economic Union, Art. 42 of which provides for the setting up of a 'Collège arbitral', the composition of which depends on the cooperation of the parties to a dispute.[143] Belgium, the Netherlands and Luxembourg have accepted the compulsory jurisdiction of the ICJ and have signed the General Act. Belgium has not yet ratified the European Convention. Moreover, not all bilateral relations between these countries are yet governed by bilateral general treaties.[144]

In the 1965 *Treaty on the establishment and statute of a Benelux Court of Justice* as well, the competence of the Court, which can be adjudicatory and/or advisory, depends on agreement thereon between the treaty partners.[145]

This is all the more so as the Committee of Ministers may lay down by decree that either Chapter III (Legal Jurisdiction) and Chapter V (Board

140

Treaty / State	Pact of Bogota (+ICAJ)		ICJ (+IIJ)
	signed	ratified	
Costa Rica	×	×	–
El Salvador	×	×	×
Guatemala	×	–	–
Honduras	×	×	×
Nicaragua	×	×	×
Total	5	4	3

No bilateral general treaties have been concluded between the states.

141 *Survey II*, Chap. III, Nos. *2*, European Convention for the Protection of Human Rights and Fundamental Freedoms of 4 November 1950, Arts. 45, 46 and 48 (—CJ), p. 193; *5*, treaty establishing a European Organization for Nuclear Research (CERN) of 1 July 1953, Art. XI (—CJ), p. 215; *7*, treaty establishing Eurofima of 20 Oct 1955, Art. 14 (—J), p. 223; *13*, treaty establishing a Benelux Economic Union of 3 Feb. 1958, Arts. 41 with 51 (—A), pp. 319 and 321.

[142]

State \ Treaty	General Act	European Convention for the Peaceful Settlement of Disputes		ICJ	Bilateral general treaty *	
		signed	ratified		+	—
Austria	–	×	×	×	4	1
Belgium	×	×	–	×	7	–
Cyprus	–	–	–	–	–	–
Denmark	×	×	×	×	7	1
France	×	×	–	×	7	–
Germany (Federal Republic)	–	×	×	–	7	–
Greece	×	×	–	–	7	–
Iceland	–	×	–	–	4	1
Ireland	×	×	–	–	–	–
Italy	×	×	×	–	8	–
Luxembourg	×	×	×	×	7	–
Malta	–	×	×	–	–	–
Netherlands	×	×	×	×	7	–
Norway	×	×	×	×	9	–
Sweden	×	×	×	×	10	1
Switzerland	×	×	×	×	8	3
Turkey	×	×	–	×	10	–
UK	×	×	×	×	–	1
Total	13	17	11	11	102	8

* These are bilateral general treaties concluded by member-states of the Council of Europe. If they provide for arbitration or judicial settlement for legal disputes at least on the initiative of one of the parties, they are included in column +.

[143] Tractatenblad 1958, No. 18, pp. 22-25. The Committee of Ministers mentioned in Art. 42 para. 3 can only, under Art. 18, take decisions unanimously. Also, no measures have been taken for the contingency in which parties fail to nominate their arbitrators. Art. 44, laying down that either party may submit a dispute, is thus left rather in the air.

[144] Cf. note 142.

	Belgium	Luxembourg	Netherlands
Belgium		PT') 89 :·: ICA + IIJ	
Luxembourg	PT 89 :·: ICA + IIJ		SI'') 101 IC + IIAJ
Netherlands		SI 101 IC + IIAJ	

') PT = *Post-War Treaties* '') SI *Survey I*

[145] Art. 1, para. 1. Cf. Tractatenblad 1965, No. 71, pp. 3 and 5.

of Arbitrators) or Chapter IV (Recommendations) shall not apply. At the beginning of 1972 the competence of the Court had still not been regulated. Depending on further statements of position by the treaty partners — a draft decree was submitted to the Consultative Interparliamentary Benelux Council in October 1970 for recommendations — the Court will be able to pronounce under Chapter III or V of the treaty on the interpretation of the legal rules indicated therefore which are at stake for the national courts in the Benelux countries or for the Board of Arbitrators. The system followed is analogous to that of the European Community Treaties with regard to the Court of Justice of the European Communities. According to the Explanatory Memorandum to the Treaty the nucleus of the latter Court's function is quite different, however, from that of the Benelux Court. Whereas the disputes submitted to the European Court are mainly of an administrative nature, civil and criminal law will be the main types coming up before the Benelux Court. Furthermore, the Benelux Court, at the request of one of the three governments, may give its judgment in the form of a recommendation on a legal rule submitted under Art. 1 (Art. 10). It consists in principle of members of the highest courts of the 3 countries, with 3 judges being nominated from each country by decree of the Committee of Ministers, which under Art. 18 of the Treaty of Union decides by unanimous vote.[146]

Finally, in the other multilateral treaties, all 4 of which were concluded in Western Europe, the special provisions are limited to conciliation, although most or even all treaty partners are also parties to multilateral framework treaties and have concluded one or more bilateral general (framework) treaties among themselves which make use of arbitation or judicial settlement possible in legal disputes at least, on the initiative of one of the parties. These are the NATO Status Agreement and the treaties setting up the Nordic Council, the OECD and EFTA.[147] With the exception of the NATO Agreement, these do not aim to rule out the possibility of arbitration or judicial settlement, whether or not on the initiative of one of the parties, under other treaties between the member-states, so that the framework treaties remain applicable. Eleven of the 15 members of *NATO* have accepted the compulsory jurisdiction of the ICJ, 11 have ratified the General Act and 12 signed the European Convention, 7 of which have already ratified it. In addition 12 NATO partners have concluded 108 bilateral general treaties with each other — an average of 9 each — which make

[146] Tractatenblad 1965, No. 71, Art. 1, p. 3, Chap. III-V pp. 11-17 and Explanatory Memorandum pp. 22 et seq., in particular pp. 25 and 31; Tractatenblad 1966, No. 244 with Supplementary Protocol to the Treaty. The Treaty, that should be classed as —J, has not been included in the tables.

possible arbitration or judicial settlement on the initiative of one of the parties. These include 6 framework treaties.

The other partners — Canada, the UK and the USA — which are not parties to similar bilateral general treaties with other member-states, belong to the group of those who have accepted the compulsory jurisdiction of the ICJ. Although the bilateral general treaties, the accession to the General Act as a framework treaty and the acceptance of the compulsory jurisdiction of the ICJ are older in date, the NATO members, in the 1951

[147] This table below shows the treaty position of the states adhering to said treaties. Cf. Annexes I and II.

Treaty / State	NATO	Nordic Council	OECD	EFTA	ICJ	Eur. Conv. Peaceful Settlement		Gen. Act	Bilateral general treaty	
	membership					sign.	rat.		+	—
Austria			×	×	×	×	×	–	5	2
Belgium	×		×		×	×	–	×	10	1
Canada	×		×		×	–	–	×	–	–
Denmark	×	×	×	×	×	×	×	×	9	2
Finland		×		×	×	–	–	×	11	1
France	×		×		×	×	–	×	10	1
Germany (Fed. Rep.)	×		×		–	×	×	–	8	1
Greece	×		×		–	×	–	×	8	1
Iceland	×	×	×		–	×	–	–	5	2
Ireland			×		–	×	–	×	–	–
Italy	×		×		–	×	×	×	10	1
Luxembourg	×		×		×	×	×	×	9	1
Netherlands	×		×		×	×	×	×	9	1
Norway	×	×	×	×	×	×	×	×	12	1
Portugal	×		×	×	×	–	–	–	7	1
Spain			×		–	–	–	(×)''	15	–
Sweden		×	×	×	×	×	×	×	13	2
Switzerland			×	×	×	×	×	×	12	4
Turkey	×		×		×	×	–	×	11	–
UK	×		×	×	×	×	×	×	–	1
USA	×		×		×	–	–	–	–	15
Total	15	5	20	8	15	16	10	16	164	38

'' Spain denounced the General Act on 8 April 1939.

On average, therefore, each country is party to 8 general bilateral treaties that make arbitration or judicial settlement possible on the initiative of one of the parties and to 2 '—' general treaties. In the '+' category Spain is well above the average, as in the US in the '—' category.

Agreement between the Parties to the North Atlantic Treaty regarding the Status of their Forces, expressly limited the settlement of disputes on the interpretation and application of this agreement to negotiations to the exclusion of 'recourse to any outside jurisdiction'. Apart from the fact that both the nature of the subject — armed forces — and the timing of the treaty — shortly after the War in the full blast of the 'Cold War' — will not be unconnected with these special provisions, it clearly illustrates the absolute freedom of states in the present-day world to choose themselves the method of settling disputes.

In relation to legal cooperation in the context of the *Nordic Council* it should be pointed out that Denmark, Finland, Norway and Sweden have accepted the compulsory jursidiction of the ICJ and that, Finland excepted, they have ratified the European Convention as a framework treaty. Iceland has signed it but not yet ratified it. On 27 June 1930 Iceland concluded bilaterally a general treaty with Denmark, Finland, Norway and Sweden on the settlement of disputes that provides for conciliation for all disputes, judicial settlement for legal disputes and arbitration for political disputes (class —IC IIIA +IIJ). The other countries have also concluded treaties between themselves which make judicial settlement possible on the initiative of one of the parties, but presuppose the cooperation of all parties for arbitration.[148]

148

	Denmark	Finland	Iceland	Norway	Sweden
Denmark		PT') 22 with 57 —IC IIIA +IIJ	SI'') 134 —IC IIIA +IIJ	PT 23 with 55 —IIICA +IIJ	PT 24 with 54 —IIICA +IIJ
Finland	PT 22 with 57 —IC IIIA +IIJ		SI 135 —IIICA +IIJ	PT 25 with 59 —IIICA +IIJ	PT 26 with 56 —IC IIIA +IIJ
Iceland	SI 134 —IC IIIA +IIJ	SI 135 —IIICA +IIJ		SI 136 —IIICA +IIJ	SI 137 —IIICA +IIJ
Norway	PT 23 with 55 —IIICA +IIJ	PT 25 with 59 —IIICA +IIJ	SI 136 —IIICA +IIJ		PT 27 with 51 —IIICA +IIJ
Sweden	PT 24 with 54 —IIICA +IIJ	PT 26 with 56 —IC IIIA +IIJ	SI 137 —IIICA +IIJ	PT 27 wiht 51 —IIICA +IIJ	

') PT = *Post-War Treaties* '') SI = *Survey I*

This underlines the fact that the importance of the Nordic Council as a consultative body must be seen more in the light of the legislative than of the jurisdictional function, as is also clear from the composition of the Council and Arts. 2 to 7 of the treaty of cooperation, aiming at the achievement of uniformity in private, criminal and other branches of law. The *OECD* is in a comparable position. It too was set up as a consultative organ.

Finally, the Convention establishing the *EFTA* is the only one to lay down explicitly (Art. 37) that 'nothing in this Convention shall be regarded as exempting any Member State from obligations which it has undertaken by virtue of international agreements to which it is a Party'.[149]

It can be assumed in view of this that the above general multilateral and bilateral treaties between the EFTA countries remain in force if a dispute arises between them on the interpretation and application of the EFTA Convention. The role entrusted to the Council in the convention on which all members are represented and which, unless laid down to the contrary, can only decide by a unanimous vote, only allows the intervention of the ICJ with great reservations, however, all the more so as under Art. 34 of the ICJ Statute only states may be parties to the Court.[150]

Part 5.

Institutionalisation of the cooperation of states in applying methods of pacific settlement of disputes

The juridical equality of states implies that the success of each stage in the pacific settlement of inter-state disputes depends on the cooperation of the states. These stages are :

— the 'prelude', in which parties declare their willingness to settle a dispute peacefully;
— the choice of method;
— the composition of the organs;
— the determination of procedure;
— the acceptance of the judgment;
— its implementation.

[149] *International Organisation and Integration*, p. 1012.

[150] Art. 32 entrusts supervision of the application of the convention to the Council. Under Art. 31 the Council is the organ that member-states must approach with complaints. A state that, under Art. 31 (4), is authorised by the Council to suspend application of the convention vis-à-vis another member-state, does not put itself in default vis-à-vis that member, apart from errors or deceit vis-à-vis the Council. This member will not be able to summon the Council as a whole before the Court, but only those states that belong to it.

In this section we shall consider the measures states have taken to guarantee the success of these stages, to see, in other words, that, even if one of the parties to the dispute fails to cooperate, a specific method of pacific settlement can be used. Only arbitration and judicial settlement can be considered, as they aim to produce a judgment that ends the dispute. Conciliation differs from arbitration and judicial settlement in that it results in a recommendation to the parties. Even if a conciliation commission could be constituted without the cooperation of all parties, its work would be advisory in nature. The fact that one of the parties refuses to cooperate in the conciliation procedure robs the recommendation of its significance as a basis for further communication.[151] If states have undertaken in advance to accept the conciliation commission's decision, this is no longer conciliation, but arbitration.

The less the use of arbitration and judicial settlement depends on the cooperation of states parties to a dispute, the more the organisation of the inter-state relations in question assumes the nature of a legal community and the bodies responsible for arbitration or judicial settlement become community organs responsible for fulfilling the jurisdictional function. The agreements the states have made, bilaterally or in multilateral treaties, to guarantee the fulfilment of this function in their mutual relations imply an institutionalisation of their cooperation. The difference between bilateral and multilateral treaties lies in the fact that in the latter case a treaty partner ratifying the treaty makes the same agreement on settlement of disputes with other countries which have also ratified or still have to do so, although the relation of trust between these states need not have reached the same level. The difficulties which this can create are avoided in these treaties because the treaty partners need not accept all methods contained therein and/or can make reservations on ratifying which govern the mutual bilateral relations or can specify in further agreements their general willingness to settle a dispute via one of the methods mentioned in the treaty. These possibilities underline the bilateral nature given in multilateral treaties to the organisation of the pacific settlement of disputes.

[151] Cf., for example, the "International Covenant on Civil and Political Rights", (*UN Monthly Chronicle*, 1967, No. 2, pp. 51-69). This Covenant provides for a conciliation commission that can if necessary be constituted without the cooperation of parties. If it cannot settle the dispute, all it can do is summarise the situation in a report. In line with this is the stipulation that if necessary the UN Secretary-General can meet the costs of the commission which would normally be borne by the two parties.

5.1. *General treaties*

5.1.1. Multilateral treaties

Of the 5 general multilateral treaties which provide for arbitration and/or judicial settlement for all disputes or political disputes, if necessary without the cooperation of both parties or in which special measures were taken to encourage cooperation, one — the (Revised) General Act — is world-wide in scope and 4 are regional, 2 in Europe and 2 in Latin America.

Without the cooperation of parties an arbitral tribunal can indeed be constituted, as the contracting states each undertake to draw up a permanent list from which the parties' arbitrators are appointed — if necessary by lot — and a third country can be invited to draw up a permanent list of arbitrators who do not have the nationality of the treaty partners, or a third party can be called in at the request of one of the parties who can constitute the arbitral tribunal if the parties cannot agree.

On the other hand, the special measures to encourage the constitution of an arbitral tribunal with the cooperation of the parties involve the parties, if they fail to agree, each nominating a third country. The two countries thus appointed should organise the constitution of the tribunal in mutual agreement. If they fail to do so, the appointments may be made, at the request of one of the parties, by the ICJ.

1. The *Treaty of Arbitration between the Central American States* of 7 February 1923 provides for the drawing up of a permanent list of 30 jurists, 6 of whom are nominated by each country, viz. 4 of its own nationals and 2 chosen from a list of fifteen American jurists drawn up by the USA at the joint request of the Contracting Parties and a list containing the names of five of its jurists drawn up by a Latin American country at the invitation of the Central American country in question. Once the above permanent list has been drawn up, the convening of a three-member tribunal is ensured.[152]

Art. VIII lays down that if a dispute arises and the parties do not manage to agree on an arbitration procedure, one country may notify the other(s) of its intention to proceed to arbitration by indicating its arbitrator. If a party fails to nominate an arbitrator,

"the appointment shall be made by lot, at the request of the Party seeking the organization of the Tribunal, by any of the Presidents of the Contracting Republics,

[152] Arts. II and III, *Post-War Treaties*, No. 9, pp. 39-40. To come into force, the treaty has to be ratified by 3 Contracting Parties (Art. XXVI). Only Costa Rica and Nicaragua have done this. The treaty is mentioned, however, because of its complicated procedure, which illustrates clearly how states endeavour to create guarantees of the use of a certain method of pacific settlement.

who are not interested in the dispute, within thirty days subsequent to the date upon which the request was received and from the jurists included in the permanent list, who would be eligible for appointment by the Party itself, if it were to make such appointment."

A similar ballot applies if parties cannot agree on where the tribunal is to meet. If neither the parties nor the arbitrators nominated by them or on their behalf can agree on the choice of the third arbitrator, these arbitrators shall nominate the third arbitrator by lot.[153]

Each of these parties can pay the share of the costs and fees of one or more other parties — important in the event of nomination by lot — and it is laid down that:

"In this case, if said Power or Powers should fail to reimburse said sum within thirty days after the Tribunal, at the request of the interested Party, shall have requested them to do so, they shall not be heard until they have made said payment, and this action shall not delay the course of the trial nor its decision."

Finally, the treaty holds out the possibility of procedure by default — which is not surprising in view of the above.[154]

2. The *American Treaty on Pacific Settlement* (the Pact of Bogota) of 30 April 1948, that under Art. LVIII replaces 8 previous Inter-American treaties on the prevention and settlement of disputes, which can be regarded as cornerstones of the OAS, was concluded under Art. 23 of the OAS Charter.

The treaty was the outcome of an initiative taken during the 1940 Lima Conference of American States because

"the juridical measures to prevent war in America are scattered in numerous treaties, conventions, pacts and declarations, which it is necessary to coordinate into an organized and harmonious unified instrument".[155]

The system behind the treaty is not really clear. The treaty provides for conciliation, arbitration and judicial settlement. As regards the sequence of these methods in the treaty, Art. III lays down that this does not mean that

"the parties may not have recourse to the procedure which they consider most appropriate in each case, or that they should use all these procedures, or that any of them have preference over others except as expressly provided."

If one of these procedures is commenced it should, under Art. IV, be completed before a new one may be begun. Art. XXXII, after the compul-

[153] Art. VII under b, and Art. VIII, *Post-War Treaties*, p. 41-42.

[154] Art. XXIII, *ibid.*, p. 45 and Annex B, Art. 10, *ibid.*, pp. 47-48.

[155] *The Inter-American System*, pp. 69 et seq.

sory jursidiction of the ICJ on legal disputes has been established in the preceding article in accordance with the formula used in Art. 36 of the ICJ Statute, lays down :

"When the conciliation procedure previously established in the present Treaty or by agreement of the parties does not lead to a solution, and the said parties have not agreed upon an arbitral procedure, either of them shall be entitled to have recourse to the International Court of Justice in the manner prescribed in Article 40 of the Statute thereof. The Court shall have compulsory jurisdiction in accordance with Article 36, paragraph 1, of the said statute."[156]

In its 1966 publication 'The Inter-American System', the Inter-American Institute of International Studies explains this provision as a restriction of the acceptance of the compulsory jurisdiction of the ICJ for legal disputes.[157]

In this viewpoint the method of judicial settlement is reserved to legal disputes, provided that the conciliation procedure has not produced a solution and the parties have not agreed upon arbitration. If the Court declares itself non-competent on the grounds mentioned in Art. V (domestic jurisdiction), VI (res juridicata or the presence of other treaties in force) and VII (local legal remedies not exhausted) 'such controversy shall be declared ended'. If the Court declares itself non-competent for other reasons, the parties undertake to use arbitration.[158]

The treaty provisions are susceptible of another interpretation, however : parties are free to submit a dispute to conciliation, judicial settlement or arbitration, it being understood that legal disputes should be submitted to the ICJ. If conciliation does not settle a political dispute, the parties have a choice between judicial settlement and arbitration. If they choose the former, they must use the latter if the Court declares itself non-competent for reasons other than those mentioned in Arts. V to VII — what these may be is not clear.

This view means that Art. XXXII, instead of laying down the compulsory jurisdiction of the ICJ for legal disputes, extends its jurisdiction to all disputes. It is supported by the reference in Art. XXXII to Arts. 36, para. 1 (the Court has jurisdiction over all matters submitted to it) and 40 (submission to the Court by means of 'the notification of the special agreement or by a written application addressed to the Registrar') of the ICJ Statute. It also fits in with the freedom of choice of parties laid down in Art. III with regard to methods of pacific settlement of disputes and is confirmed in the reser-

[156] *Ibid.*, pp. 387 and 391.
[157] *Ibid.*, p. 79.
[158] Arts. XXXIV and XXXV, *ibid.*, p. 392.

vations made on signature and/or ratification. This is clear from the provision in the USA's reservation that

... "1. The United States does not undertake as the complainant State to submit to the International Court of Justice any controversy which is not considered to be properly within the jurisdiction of the Court" ...

In the interpretation of Art. XXXII put forward by the Inter-American Institute this provision would be superfluous. Of the 10 American States which have ratified the Pact of Bogota, 7 are parties to general multilateral treaties which make arbitration or judicial settlement possible on the initiative of one of the parties. Of the 11 states which have not yet ratified, only 4 are parties to such treaties.[159]

Arbitration procedure is regulated as follows in the Pact of Bogota. Each of the parties to a dispute appoints an arbitrator and also submits a list of ten jurists to the OAS Council who have been chosen from the panel of members of the Permanent Court of Arbitration, who are not its nationals and are prepared to sit on the tribunal. The Council constitutes the tribunal by adding to the two parties' arbitrators three more who appear on both lists. If more or less than three persons appear on both lists, the arbitrators are chosen by lot. The same applies if the parties have not given the same persons on their list, under Art. XL. Art. XLV provides that if a party fails to appoint its arbitrator, the Council is able to constitute a tribunal.

Art. L lays down, with regard to the judgment of the ICJ or the arbitral tribunal, that if one of the parties does not meet its obligations under the judgment, the other party (or parties), before approaching the UN Security Council, shall propose a

"Meeting of Consultation of Ministers of Foreign Affairs to agree upon appropriate measures to ensure the fulfilment of the judicial decision or arbitral award."[160]

The Pact of Bogota, although this is concluded in the OAS context,

[159] The treaty was signed by Argentina, Bolivia, *Brazil* *, Chile *, Columbia *, *Costa Rica* *, Cuba, *Dominican Republic*, Ecuador, *El Salvador* *, Guatemala *, *Haiti* *, *Honduras* *, *Mexico*, *Nicaragua* *, *Panama* *, Paraguay, Peru *, *Uruguay*, Venezuela, USA. The states marked with a * are parties to a general multilateral or bilateral treaty that allows for judicial settlement or arbitration on the initiative of one of the parties. The countries printed in italics have already ratified the Pact of Bogota. Peru is also a party to the General Act (:⁚:ICA+IIJ). Cf. Inter-American System, p. 511 and FENWICK, "The Organization of American States : the transition from an unwritten to a written constitution", *A.J.I.L.*, 1965, pp. 315-320.

[160] *The Inter-American System*, pp. 392, 394 and 395.

regulates the settlement of disputes on the basis of bilateral relations, as is shown by Art. LV (reservations).

Furthermore, the procedures mentioned in the treaty under Art. V do not apply to cases which 'by their nature, are within the domestic jurisdiction of the State', it being understood that the preliminary question whether a case belongs to 'domestic jurisdiction' may be submitted to the ICJ at the request of a party. With regard to the procedures of arbitration and judicial settlement provided for in the Pact of Bogota, reservations were made on signature by Argentina, the USA, Paraguay and Peru, all of which opposed an arbitration procedure without the cooperation of both parties. Nor do the other general treaties to which these countries, except Peru, are parties belong to the category which provides for arbitration or judicial settlement against the will of one of the parties.[161]

3. The *European Convention for the Peaceful Settlement of Disputes* of 29 April 1957 assumes that the compulsory jurisdiction of the ICJ over legal disputes is accepted and that arbitration is used for political disputes, if necessary without the cooperation of all parties to the dispute.

The jurisdiction of the ICJ over legal disputes is established in Art. 1. Although this article does not explicitly lay down that a dispute may be submitted unilaterally, the treaty pattern indicates that. With regard to conciliation (Art. 9) and arbitration (Art. 25) it is stipulated that if no agreement is reached on submitting a dispute, this can be done by one of the parties. Art. 2, para. 2, states that parties may agree that a dispute should first of all be submitted for conciliation and Art. 18 adds :

"In the case of a mixed dispute involving both questions for which conciliation is appropriate and other questions for which judicial settlement is appropriate, any party to the dispute shall have the right to insist that the judicial settlement of the legal questions shall precede conciliation."[162]

Under Art. 35 the application of Chapter 1 cannot be excluded, so that the obligation to have legal disputes settled by the ICJ is made a minimum precondition of ratification.

With 1 exception — Cyprus — all 18 member-states of the Council of Europe, in the context of which this European Convention was signed, have signed it. Of those states 11 have in the meantime ratified. Of these 11, 8 have accepted the compulsory jurisdiction of the ICJ.[163]

[161] *Ibid.*, pp. 396-398.

[162] *Survey II*, Chap. I, No. 37, pp. 60 and 63.

[163] Cf. notes 142 and 147. Because most of the treaty partners had accepted the compulsory jurisdiction of the ICJ, the Contracting Parties were able to take this as their basis

Arbitration on political disputes is regulated as follows in the European Convention. If such a dispute arises an arbitral tribunal is made up, consisting of five members, of whom each party nominates one. Together they appoint the other three. If the members of the tribunal have not been appointed within 3 months of one of the parties requesting the other one accordingly,

"the task of making the necessary nominations shall be entrusted to the Government of a third State, chosen by agreement between the parties, or, failing agreement within three months, to the President of the International Court of Justice."[164]

Of the 11 states that have ratified the European Convention, 3 — Italy, the Netherlands and Sweden — have excluded the application of Chapter III of the Convention, in which the arbitration procedure is regulated.

As far as these states are concerned, this is not a rejection in principle of arbitration for all disputes or political disputes, because they are parties to bilateral general treaties which make arbitration possible.[165]

4. The (*Revised*) *General Act for the Pacific Settlement of International Disputes* of 26 September 1928 (28 April 1949) provides for the acceptance of the compulsory jurisdiction of the Permanent Court of International Justice (PCIJ) — now the ICJ — for legal disputes and arbitration for all disputes, with special measures being taken if parties do not succeed in reaching agreement on the constitution of the arbitral tribunal. Acceptance of the compulsory jurisdiction of the ICJ is laid down in Art. 17. Under Art. 18 parties may also agree to submit legal disputes to arbitration. If however they do not succeed in concluding the relevant agreement or forming the arbitral tribunal, each party, within 3 months of informing the other party accordingly, may submit the dispute to the ICJ. If parties do not succeed in reaching agreement on the composition of the *arbitral tribunal*, Art. 23 of

for the European Convention. See H. WEHBERG, "La convention européenne pour le règlement pacifique des différends", *Varia Juris Gentium*, pp. 394-5.

[164] *Survey II*, Chap. I, No. 37, Art. 21, p. 64. This arrangement aims to avoid obvious flaws in the appointment procedure. It can reasonably be assumed that one of the parties can raise the appointment procedure with President of the Court. Cf. WEHBERG, *op. cit.*, p. 397 and ROLIN, "L'arbitrage obligatoire : une panacée illusoire", *Varia Juris Gentium*, pp. 254-262.

[165] Cf. Annex I. Italy and the Netherlands concluded a treaty classed as +IA on 20 November 1909 that came into force again on 16 August 1949 after the Netherlands, under Art. 44 of the Peace Treaty with Italy, had indicated its desire to do so. C. *Survey II*, Chap. II, No. 11, p. 24. Italy is also a party to four treaties in class +I CAJ. The Netherlands is also a party to a treaty with Spain — *Survey I*, No. 152, p. 884 — in class —ICA +IIJ. Sweden, finally, is a party to 11 treaties providing for arbitration or judicial settlement for all disputes or political disputes which, however, require the cooperation of all parties for the use of these methods.

the General Act allows all the arbitrators — including those of the parties — to be appointed by a third party, if parties cannot agree on the choice, but it makes its operation, unlike in the European Convention, dependent on the cooperation of both parties. The organisation of arbitration in the General Act has therefore been classified as :·: I.[166] Twenty-three states have acceded to the General Act and 7 to the Revised Act.[167] At the time the members of League of Nations and a few other countries — a total of 64 — could have acceded to the General Act, and in principle all UN members, 127 in all, can accede to the Revised Act. The conclusion must be that, relatively speaking, the Revised General Act with its world-wide scope has met with far less response than the regional general multilateral treaties mentioned above.

5. The *General Act of Conciliation, Arbitration and Judicial Settlement between the States of the Little Entente (Czechoslovakia, Romania and Yugoslavia)* of 21 May 1929 came about, according to its preamble, on the basis of the recommendation of the League of Nations Assembly in its resolution of 26 September 1928, in which the General Act was also accepted. The act is worded in almost the same way as the General Act, with the proviso that judicial settlement is mentioned first, then conciliation and arbitration.[168] Unlike the Geneva General Act, however, it does not allow parties to rule out the chapters on arbitration and/or judicial settlement. In view of the limited regional scope of the treaty this is not surprising.

5.1.2. Bilateral treaties

Most bilateral general treaties were concluded between European countries themselves or between them and countries from other regions. A breakdown by region of countries which are parties to the bilateral general treaties shown in Table III gives the following picture :

TABLE IX

Breakdown by region of bilateral general treaties according to whether they provide for arbitration or judicial settlement for all disputes (I),

[166] The European Convention has prevented this by providing that the making of the necessary appointments shall be entrusted to a third state, chosen for the purpose jointly by the parties, or 'failing agreement within three months, to the President of the International Court of Justice'. The organisation of procedure has therefore been classified as + I.

[167] Cf. note 147. In addition to the 16 countries mentioned therein which are members of NATO, OECD, EFTA or the Nordic Council, Ethiopia (Africa), Estonia and Latvia (Europa), Peru (Latin America) and Australia, India and New Zealand (Commonwealth) acceded at the time to the General Act. With 8 exceptions, these countries made reservations on accession. Spain denounced the General Act on 8 April 1939.

[168] *Survey I*, No. 79, pp. 572 et seq.

legal disputes (II) or political disputes (III) and whether application thereof depends (—) or not (+) on the cooperation of all parties or parties have taken special measures to obtain such cooperation (:⁞:).[169]

Region/country \ Class general treaty	—I	—II	—III	:⁞:I	:⁞:II	+I	+II	Total
Africa								
Ethiopia	1	1	–	–	–	–	–	2
Liberia	1	1	–	–	–	–	–	2
2 countries	2	2	–	–	–	–	–	4
Asia								
China (Taiwan)	2	1	–	–	–	–	–	3
India	1	–	–	–	–	–	–	1
Indonesia	1	1	–	–	–	–	–	2
Japan	–	1	–	–	–	–	1	2
Philippines	7	–	–	–	–	–	2	9
Thailand	2	–	–	1	–	1	2 (1)	6 (1)
6 countries	13	3	–	1	–	1	5 (1)	23 (1)
Europe (incl. USA)								
Albania	–	1	–	–	–	–	–	1
Austria	2 (2)	2	–	2	–	–	5 (2)	11 (4)
Belgium	– (8)	1	–	5	1	1	10 (6)	18 (14)
Bulgaria	1 (6)	1	–	–	–	1	7	10 (6)
Czechoslovakia	1 (2)	1	–	3	–	2	11 (4)	18 (6)
Denmark	1 (5)	2	– (4)	–	1	6	10 (1)	20 (10)
Estonia	–	3	–	–	1	–	2	6
Finland	– (3)	2	– (4)	–	–	2	11	15 (7)
France	– (5)	2	–	1	–	2	10 (1)	15 (6)
Germany (Fed. Rep.)	–	2	–	–	3	–	11	16
Greece	1 (1)	2	–	3	–	6	4 (6)	16 (7)
Hungary	1	1	–	–	1	–	10	13
Iceland	– (1)	2	– (4)	–	–	–	5	7 (5)
Italy	1	1	–	1	–	17	5	25
Latvia	–	1	–	–	–	4	2	7
Lithuania	–	2	–	1	–	3	2 (1)	8 (1)
Luxembourg	– (2)	1	–	4	–	4	4 (3)	13 (5)

[169] The figures in brackets show the number of treaties that provide for a combination of arbitration for all disputes or political disputes with judicial settlement for legal disputes. Because the emphasis in this part of the book is on institutionalisation, the treaties in the mixed classes —I/II(2), —I/:⁞:II(1), —I/+II(39) and —III/+II(11) in columns —II, :⁞:II and +II have been included and put in brackets in columns —I and —III. The treaties in mixed classes :⁞:I/+II(15) and +I/+II(3) have been included in columns :⁞:I and +I for the same reason and put in brackets in column +II. The figures given as grand totals in columns —I et seq. of course include some counted double (as each treaty has been included for both parties). Cf. Annex I.

(TABLE IX continued)

Class general treaty / Region/country	—I	—II	—III	⁘I	⁘II	+I	+II	Total
Netherlands	– (1)	2	–	–	1	1	16	20 (1)
Norway	– (3)	2	– (4)	4	–	2	10 (4)	18 (11)
Poland	7 (3)	3	–	3	2	–	3 (2)	18 (5)
Portugal	– (5)	1	– (1)	–	–	1	6	8 (6)
Romania	1	1	–	1	–	1	5 (1)	9 (1)
Spain	10 (13)	–	–	1	–	3	14 (1)	28 (14)
Sweden	– (6)	4	– (5)	–	–	–	14	18 (11)
Switzerland	2 (5)	2	–	–	–	8	12	24 (5)
UK	1	1	–	–	–	–	1	3
USA	1	30	–	–	–	–	–	31
Yugoslavia	1 (1)	1	–	2	–	–	4 (2)	8 (3)
28 countries	31 (72)	74	– (22)	31	10	64	194 (34)	404 (128)
Latin America								
Argentina	1	–	–	–	–	–	–	1
Bolivia	4	–	–	–	–	–	–	4
Brazil	1 (2)	1	–	–	–	2	1	5 (2)
Chile	1	–	–	–	–	1	–	2
Colombia	4 (2)	–	–	–	–	2	2	8 (2)
Costa Rica	1	–	–	1	–	1	–	3
Dominican Rep.	–	1	–	–	–	–	–	1
Ecuador	1	–	–	–	–	–	–	1
El Salvador	1	–	–	–	–	–	–	1
Guatemala	–	–	–	–	–	–	1	1
Haiti	–	1	–	–	–	1	–	2
Mexico	2	1	–	–	–	–	–	3
Panama	1	–	–	–	–	1	–	2
Paraguay	2	–	–	–	–	–	–	2
Peru	3	–	–	–	–	1	–	4
Uruguay	4 (1)	1	–	–	–	–	–	5 (1)
Venezuela	4 (2)	–	–	–	–	–	5	9 (2)
17 countries	30 (7)	5	–	1	–	9	9	54 (7)
Middle East								
Iran	–	9	–	–	–	1	4	14
Iraq	–	1	–	–	–	–	1	2
Jordan	–	1	–	–	–	–	–	1
Lebanon	1	–	–	–	–	1	–	2
Saudi Arabia	1	2	–	–	–	–	–	3
Turkey	1 (5)	–	–	1	–	4	13 (1)	19 (6)
UAR	–	1	–	–	–	–	–	1
Yemen	1	–	–	–	–	–	–	1
8 countries	4 (5)	14	–	1	–	6	18 (1)	43 (6)
Grand Total : 61 countries	80 (84)	98	– (22)	34	10	80	226 (36)	528 (142)

Institutionalisation has gone furthest in the treaties classified as +I. It is in these treaties, however, that the parties have explicitly reserved their freedom to make different arrangements in other treaties, without this being bound by any restrictions.

Of the 19 bilateral general framework treaties only 4 come under column +I. Of the other 36 treaties 29 contain a provision under which different arrangements may be made, while 2 contain a reservation in respect of disputes concerning independence and territoriality.

Of the 17 treaties in column ⁘I, 8 belong to the framework treaties mentioned above.

Table X shows the numbers of treaties from the respective mixed classes split according to whether they were concluded between countries belonging to the same region (intra-regional) or different regions (inter-regional).

TABLE X

Intra- and inter-regional breakdown of bilateral general treaties depending on whether they provide for arbitration or judicial settlement for all disputes (I), legal disputes (II) or political disputes (III) and whether their application depends (—) or not (+) on the cooperation of all parties or parties have taken special measures to obtain this cooperation (⁘).

Class general treaty / Region/country	—I	—II	—III	⁘I	⁘II	+I	+II	Total
Africa								
Intra-regional	–	–	–	–	–	–	–	–
Inter-regional :								
Europe	1	2	–	–	–	–	–	3
Middle East	1	–	–	–	–	–	–	1
	2	2	–	–	–	–	–	4
Asia								
Intra-regional	4	–	–	–	–	–	–	4
Inter-regional :								
Europe	4	3	–	1	–	1	5 (1)	14 (1)
Middle East	1	–	–	–	–	–	–	1
	9	3	–	1	–	1	5 (1)	19 (1)
Europe								
Intra-regional	8 (33)	29	– (11)	14	5	26	84 (16)	166 (60)
Inter-regional :								
Africa	1	2	–	–	–	–	–	3
Asia	4	3	–	1	–	1	5 (1)	14 (1)
Latin America	10 (1)	1	–	1	–	7	5	24 (1)
Middle East	– (5)	10	–	1	–	4	16 (1)	31 (6)
	23 (39)	45	– (11)	17	5	38	110 (18)	238 (68)

(TABLE X continued)

Class general treaty / Region/country	—I	—II	—III	::I	::II	+I	+II	Total
Latin America								
Intra-regional	10 (3)	2	–	–	–	1	2	15 (3)
Inter-regional:								
Europe	10 (1)	1	–	1	–	7	5	24 (1)
	20 (4)	3	–	1	–	8	7	39 (4)
Middle East								
Intra-regional	1	2	–	–	–	1	1	5
Inter-regional:								
Africa	1	–	–	–	–	–	–	1
Asia	1	–	–	–	–	–	–	1
Europe	– (5)	10	–	1	–	4	16 (1)	31 (6)
	3 (5)	12	–	1	–	5	17 (1)	38 (6)

5.1.2.1. *Special measures on the cooperation of all parties in arbitration on all disputes*

Of the 17 treaties in column ::I, 15 belong to classification ::ICA+IIJ, 1 to ::ICAJ and 1 to ::IA. The 15 treaties from ::ICA+IA mainly follow the pattern of the General Act as regards the organisation of arbitration procedure. With 3 exceptions, they were concluded between countries one of which has acceded to the General Act. The exceptions are treaties both parties to which acceded to the General Act at a later date.[170]

The general treaty classified as ::ICAJ concluded between *Luxembourg and Poland* on 29 October 1928 lays down that if one of the parties does not accept the proposals of the permanent conciliation commission or does not announce its decision on the matter within the period mentioned in the commission's report, the dispute, by mutual consent in a special agreement, shall be submitted to the PCIJ or an arbitral tribunal. If the agreement has not been drawn up within 3 months of one of the parties requesting submission of the dispute to judicial settlement or arbitration, it will be drawn up by a special 5-member committee, 2 of whom shall be nominated by each party. One of these at most shall be a national. These 4 members together choose the fifth member, who acts as the chairman.

"If, for any reason one or more of these appointments should not be made, the President of the Swiss Confederation shall be asked to make the necessary appointments."[171]

[170] Cf. Table IX and Annex I.

[171] *Survey I*, No. 41, Art. 17, p. 466.

The arbitration procedure is not elaborated in the treaty. There is merely a reference to the 1907 Hague Convention. The procedure it contains should be classified as —I, since the arbitral tribunal can only be constituted with the cooperation of parties. Special measures were only taken for the appointment of the jointly-nominated arbitrator. If a party does not nominate its two arbitrators, the tribunal cannot be formed.[172] Since all disputes can be submitted to the PCIJ and a special measure is taken if parties do not succeed in drawing up the special agreement for the calling in of the PCIJ, the treaty has been classified as ::ICAJ.

Finally, the treaty classified as ::IA was concluded on 8 January 1910 between Costa Rica and Italy, and was again declared in force by an exchange of Notes on 16 and 18 November 1949.[173] Under Art. 1 of the treaty the parties undertake to submit all disputes to arbitration except those relating to the independence and honour of the nation.[174] The arbitral tribunal is formed by three arbitrators of whom each party nominates one. Together the parties appoint the third arbitrator, who acts as chairman.

> "If an agreement on this point is not possible, the Parties will appeal to a third Powei to select the umpire, and failing an agreement on this point also, a request to this effect shall be addressed to Her Majesty the Queen of the Netherlands or to her successors."[175]

The Chairman is selected from the list of members of the Permanent Court of Arbitration. None of the arbitrators may be a citizen or resident of one of the parties. Art. V adds :

> "Should the Parties be unable to agree as to the constitution of the Tribunal, the duties of arbitrator shall be entrusted to a sole arbitrator, who, failing any stipulation to the contrary, shall be appointed in compliance with the rules laid down in the preceding Article for the appointment of the umpire."

It is not clear who, in the absence of agreement on the composition of the tribunal, can decide to appoint only one arbitrator: parties together, one of the parties, or the Queen of the Netherlands at the request of both parties or of one party. The absence of agreement becomes clear if one of the parties refuses to appoint its arbitrator and thereby blocks the arbitration method. Art. IV also leaves vague whether the Queen of the Netherlands is empowered to appoint the chairman at the request of one of the

[172] Art. 45, *International Organisation and Integration*, p. 6.

[173] *Survey II*, Chap. 1, No. 7, pp. 15 et seq. The Exchange of Notes took place under Art. 44 of the Peace Treaty with Italy.

[174] The reservation in question states : 'It is, however, open to either of the two states not to submit to arbitration such controversies as, in its estimation, affect the independence and the honour of the nation'. (*Survey II*, p. 15.)

[175] Art. IV, *Survey II*, p. 16.

parties. As this is not laid down in so many words, it must be assumed, in view of the general rule on settlement of disputes, which says that a dispute may not be submitted to arbitration or judicial settlement against the will of parties unless explicitly agreed otherwise, that the Queen cannot appoint the sole arbitrator who is empowered to take the decision in a procedure of default. The above reservation on disputes which in the opinion of one of the parties affect the independence and honour of the nation also leads one to this conclusion. The involvement of the Queen, in other words, should be regarded as a special measure to bring parties to cooperate and the treaty has therefore been classified as :.:IA.

5.1.2.2. *Arbitration or judicial settlement of all disputes without the cooperation of all parties*

Of the 40 treaties in column +I, 4 make arbitration possible for all disputes, even if one of the parties refuses to cooperate : 1 in class +IA and 3 in +ICA IIJ, which belong to the framework treaties. The other treaties provide for judicial settlement for all disputes on the initiative of one of the parties, whether combined or not with conciliation and/or arbitration. In all the treaties at least one of the parties also acceded to the 1928 General Act. The general treaty of arbitration between the *Netherlands and Italy* of 20 November 1909 has been classified as +IA. It was declared applicable again by an exchange of Notes on 16 August 1949.[176] As distinct from the above arbitration treaty between Costa Rica and Italy, it contains no reservation with regard to disputes which in the opinion of one of the parties affect the independence and honour of the nation. Under Art. 1 the parties undertake to submit all disputes to the Permanent Court of Arbitration. If parties cannot agree on the composition and powers of the arbitral tribunal, each party can request the PCA to draw up a 'compromis'. Under Art. 3, para. 2 this task is entrusted to a committee of five members in accordance with the procedure laid down in Art. 45 of the 1907 Hague Convention. Art. 4 adds :

> "If it should prove impossible to reach agreement for the purpose of the second paragraph of the preceding article, the appointment of a single arbitrator or of a tribunal of arbitration shall, *on the request of one or both* of the Parties, be referred to His Majesty the King of Sweden."[177]

The King of Sweden's task is not confined to nominating the single arbitrator. He can also be asked by one of the parties to constitute the tribunal, which under Art. 43 of the 1907 Hague Convention consists of five

[176] *Survey II*, Chap. I, No. 11, p. 24. Cf. note 165.

[177] *Survey II*, p. 25, author's italics.

arbitrators. Candidates for the function of arbitrator are taken from the list of members of the PCA 'other than Members designated by the Parties and not being nationals of either of the Parties.'[178]

The 3 bilateral general treaties from category +ICA IIJ were concluded between *Greece* and *Belgium*, *Czechoslovakia* and *Denmark* respectively. Their Art. 26 lays down that if parties cannot agree on the appointment of arbitrators, they must each select a Power which can then do so.

"If, within a period of three months, the Powers so chosen have been unable to reach an agreement, or if the designation of the Powers mentioned in paragraph 2 of the present Article is not made within that period, the necessary appointments shall be made by the President of the Permanent Court of International Justice, to whom the matter may be referred by means of a simple application made by one or other of the Parties ... etc."

If parties cannot conclude a special agreement to submit the dispute to the arbitral tribunal, one of the parties can do so.[179] The parties to these 3 treaties have reserved the right to provide for special procedures in other treaties, it being understood that the general treaty becomes applicable if these procedures are unsuccessful. The treaties also empower the tribunal to take a decision 'ex aequo et bono' if there are no legal rules applying to the dispute.

The treaties which make judicial settlement possible for all disputes on the initiative of one of the parties were mainly concluded, as Table IX shows, between or with European states. Italy has concluded most of them. If they provide for arbitration they contain a provision under which a dispute may be submitted by one of the parties to the PCIJ — now the ICJ — if parties do not succeed in constituting an arbitral tribunal.[180] The treaties which combine judicial settlement with conciliation lay down that the latter method must be used first. If conciliation is unsuccessful, the way is clear for judicial settlement, by mutual agreement between parties or, if no agreement is possible, unilaterally. These treaties have nevertheless been classified as +ICJ, because it cannot be assumed that a party which refuses to cooperate in conciliation by failing to appoint any commission

[178] Art. 4, para 2, *Survey II*, p. 25.

[179] *Survey I*, Nos. *82*, pp. 589-90; *85*, pp. 610-11; *184*, pp. 1021-22.

[180] Cf. Annex I. *Post-War Treaties* , No. *20* (+IJ) and *Survey I*, Nos. *156* (+IAJ), *166* (+ICAJ) and *200* (+IJ) contain no provision enabling different arrangements to be made elsewhere. *Survey I*, No. *84* in class +ICAJ is a framework treaty. *Post-War Treaties*, No. *58*, Art. 1, p. 374 and *Survey I*, No. *14*, Art. 3, p. 378 in class +ICAJ contain a reservation in respect of disputes affecting independence and territoriality or sovereignty. The other treaties explicitly allow for different arrangements to be made elsewhere.

members can block the access of the other party to the ICJ with the argument that the conciliation method has not yet been used.

As a case may be submitted unilaterally to the Court, Art. 53 of the Statute is important. It lays down :

"1. Whenever one of the parties does not appear before the Court, or fails to defend its case, the other party may call upon the Court to decide in favour of its claim.
2. The Court must, before doing so, satisfy itself, not only that it has jurisdiction in accordance with Articles 36 and 37, but also that the claim is well founded in fact and law."

This provision implies that, in the view of the drafters of the Statute, a default procedure is not possible in a *political dispute*, even though parties may in advance have granted the Court the power to make an 'ex aequo et bono' pronouncement and an exception may be seen in this power to Art. 38, para. 1 of the ICJ Statute.[181] After all, in a default procedure the Court should not only check whether it has jurisdiction under Arts. 36 and 37 of the Statute, but also whether the claim is well founded in fact and in law. It is incidentally inconceivable for two parties to be convinced that a political dispute has arisen between them and that one of them should approach the ICJ, while the other goes by default, as the first party knows that the Court will then reject its plea.

If one of the states parties to the above general treaties feels its claim well founded, however, and applies to the Court, there is hardly any point in the other state's keeping quiet, for under the general treaty the Court is empowered to take note of all disputes. The other party then runs the risk that the Court shall derive from its failure to appear and answer the claim an argument in favour of awarding the claim to the first party. It can be concluded that the condition on default procedure laid down in Art. 53 of the ICJ Statute does not really affect the possibility of judicial settlement for all disputes on the initiative of one of the parties. That in these +I treaties the states also recognise use of judicial settlement as a continuation of negotiations by other means is illustrated by the fact that most treaties — 24 of the 36 — contain a provision to the effect that parties undertake to comply with the Court's judgment in good faith.[182]

[181] The granting of this power is connected with whether arbitration or judicial settlement can be used in all disputes. Cf. *Survey I*, Chap. II, para. 7, Law to be applied by the Court or by an Arbitral Tribunal, pp. 119-122. Nos. X-XXX. Cf. M. HABICHT, *op. cit.*, and DEGAN, *op. cit.*, in particular para. 26, pp. 72 et seq. No use has yet been made of the 'ex aequo et bono' clause with regard to the jurisdiction of the Court.

[182] Cf. Annex I. The treaties mentioned in which there is no such provision are, in class +ICJ : *Survey I*, No. 9; in class + IAJ : *Survey I*, No. 156 and in class +ICAJ :

5.1.2.3. *Special measures on the cooperation of all parties in arbitration or judicial settlement of legal disputes*

Of the 5 treaties in column ::II, 4 contain arbitration for legal disputes — classification IC :: IIA — with special measures being taken for the constitution of the arbitral tribunal if parties do not agree on this among themselves. Under these measures the Permanent Conciliation Council or a special committee may be called upon at the request of one of the parties, if the other one has not designated its own arbitrator(s), if the parties cannot agree on the arbitrator(s) to be appointed jointly or if the special agreement to subject the dispute to arbitration cannot be reached.[183]

The fifth treaty, concluded between *Belgium* and *Poland* on 25 October 1928, has been classified as —ICA ::IIJ. Under Art. 1 it provides for judicial settlement for legal disputes. Art. 2 lays down that parties should conclude a special 'compromis'. If they do not do so within 3 months after one of the parties has received a request to submit a dispute to judicial settlement, the parties will form a special commission to draw up the 'compromis'.[184]

5.1.2.4. *Arbitration or judicial settlement for legal disputes without the cooperation of all parties*

Of the 113 treaties in column +II, 3 confine themselves to arbitration for legal disputes. The other treaties belong to the categories —ICA +IIJ(39), IC +IIJ—IIIA (4), —IIICA +IIJ (7), IC +IIJ (5), + IIJ (5), IC+IIAJ(48) and +IICAJ (2).[185] They provide for recourse to judicial settlement on the initiative of one of the parties.

Iran is a party to each of the 3 bilateral agreements in group +IICA, which lay down that if one of the states fails to appoint an arbitrator,

> "the said arbitrator shall be chosen, on application being made by the plaintiff State, from the nationals of the defendant State by the President of the Permanent Court of International Justice."

The third arbitrator is also appointed by the President, if necessary. If the parties do not succeed in concluding a special agreement on arbitration,

Post-War Treaties, Nos. 70, 74 and 90 and *Survey I*, Nos. 84, 121, 147, 155, 166, 167 and 186. See also Table IX.

[183] Cf. Annex I *Post-War Treaties*, Nos. *42*, pp. 256 and 261; *66*, pp. 432, 434 and 435; *68*, pp. 456, 458 and 460; *Survey I*, No. *45*, pp. 476 and 479. All treaties contain a provision under which parties can make different arrangements in other treaties. See also Table IX.

[184] *Survey I*, No. 38, pp. 454-55.

[185] Cf. Annex I and Table IX.

"the arbitral tribunal before which the plaintiff State has laid the matter shall be responsible for drawing up the submission."[186]

5.2. *Special provisions*

5.2.1. Multilateral treaties

Of the 89 special provisions in multilateral treaties dealt with in Table II, 39 make arbitration and/or judicial settlement possible on the initiative of one of the parties. Twenty-one of these treaties are world-wide in scope, and 18 regional.

TABLE XI

Special provisions in multilateral treaties which make arbitration (A) and/or judicial settlement (J) possible on the initiative of one of the parties (+).

Scope of treaty \ Class special provision	+A	+CA	+J	+CJ	+AJ	+CAJ	Total
World-wide	9	1	9	–	1	1	21
Regional							
Africa	1	–	–	–	–	–	1
Asia	1	–	–	–	–	–	1
Europe (incl. Canada and USA)	5	3	3	2	–	–	13
Latin America	1	–	–	–	–	–	1
Middle East	–	–	–	–	–	–	–
Inter-regional							
Europe/Africa	–	1	–	–	–	–	1
Europe/(Latin) America	1	–	–	–	–	–	1
Total	18	5	12	2	1	1	39

Arbitration at the request of one of the parties to a dispute on the interpretation or application of the treaty concerned which is performed by administrative organs vis-à-vis the member-states of international organisations, by one arbitrator or by an arbitral tribunal for the nomination or constitution of which guarantees have been given is, as the table shows, technically accepted by states from all regions.

States belonging to the Soviet bloc, however, have only accepted this method (classified as +) in the form of arbitration by administrative organs or by a tribunal. In both cases the parties participate in the body responsible for arbitration — the IGO organ or tribunal.

States from all regions also accept judicial settlement at the request of one of the parties to a dispute on the interpretation or application of the treaty concerned, even if they have not made the declaration accepting the compulsory jurisdiction of the ICJ under Art. 36, para. 2 of the ICJ Statute.

Soviet bloc countries, however, have only ratified multilateral treaties with special provisions classified as +J if their wording leaves open the possibility of choosing another method of settlement in mutual consultation.

5.2.1.1. *Arbitration*

The special provisions classified as +(C)A and +(C)AJ can be subdivided as follows according to the way they organise arbitration procedure.

a. Provisions in which arbitration is entrusted to administrative organs set up under the treaty in which all member-states are represented or member-states involved in a dispute but not represented in these organs can have themselves represented there; this method can be described as administrative arbitration.

b. Provisions which make it possible for the dispute, if the parties cannot agree on the composition of the ad hoc arbitral tribunal, to be submitted to one arbitrator who at the request of one of the parties is chosen by the UN Secretary-General or the President of the ICJ or, if the latter possesses the nationality of one of the parties, by the Vice-President or the senior judge who does not possess such nationality.

c. Provisions which entrust arbitration to tribunals constituted permanently or for a specific period or create guarantees for the constitution of ad hoc tribunals.

Ad a. Administrative arbitration is provided for by the Articles of Agreement of the International Monetary Fund (IMF), the World Bank group (IBRD, IDA, IFC) and regional development banks, the international commodity agreements and the Convention on International Civil Aviation (ICAO).

1. The Articles of Agreement of the above *international finance institutions* — classified as +A — entrust the handling of disputes between the member-states or between a state and the institution to the Executive Directors in the first instance. A member-state whose interests are involved and which is not represented on the Executive Directors can have itself represented thereon at the relevant meeting.[187] All members are represented on the

[186] *Survey I*, Nos. *80*, p. 581; *123*, pp. 770-1; *198*, pp. 1069-70. Under these treaties both arbitrators first try to settle disputes on the interpretation and application of treaties between parties. If this fails, the third (impartial) arbitrator is appointed. In the first instance, then, it is a conciliation procedure, and the treaties are therefore classified as +IICA.

[187] IMF, Art. 18, PEASLEE, p. 1280; IBRD, Art. 9, PEASLEE, p. 963; IFC, Art. 8, PEASLEE,

Board of Governors, which acts as an appeal body for the member-states. Both organs decide by a simple majority of votes cast. A quorum of Executive Directors consists of the majority of the total number of directors, who can cast at least half of the total number of votes. A quorum on the Board of Governors is a majority of members with two-thirds of the total number of votes.[188] Although the constitutions of the IMF, the World Bank and the regional development banks do not explicitly provide for unilateral submission of a dispute on their interpretation or application to the Executive Directors, the settlement procedure has nevertheless been classified as +, for if a member does not comply with his obligations, the majority of the Board of Governors, representing the majority of the total number of votes cast, can suspend that member.[189] This means that a member, in a dispute on the interpretation or application of the constitution concerned, cannot unilaterally suspend compliance with its obligations without running the risk of being suspended and — if the suspension lasts a year — of having its membership declared lapsed.[190]

2. As already mentioned, the regularly concluded or extended *international*

p. 1186; IDA, Art. 1, PEASLEE, p. 1154; AFDB, Art. 61 and ASDB, Art. 60. WIONCZEK, *op. cit.*, pp. 439 and 475; IADB, Art. 13, PEASLEE, p. 849. Cf. M. SINGH, "Regional Development Banks", *International Conciliation*, 1970, No. 576 and I. SEIDL-HOHENVELDERN "Arbitration by Organs of International Organizations", *Liber Amicorum Martin Domke*, pp. 322-337; BROCHES, "International Legal Aspects of the World Bank", *R.d.C.*, 1959, part III, pp. 297-409.

[188] IMF, Art. 12, paras. 5 with 2d and 3h; IBRD, Art. 5, paras. 3 with 2d and 4f; IDA, Art. 6, paras. 3 with 2f and 4e; IFC, Art. 4, paras. 3 with 2f and 4e; AFDB, Arts. 35 with 34 and 31; ASDB, Arts. 33 with 29; IADB, Art. 8, paras. 4 with 2e and 3f. The Executive Directors of the Regional Development Banks have the same quorum as the Board of Governors — the majority of Directors or Governors casting two-thirds of the total number of votes. Decisions have to be made by a majority of the total number of votes.

[189] IMF, Art. 15, para. 2; IBRD, Art. 6, para. 2; IDA, Art. 7, para. 2; IFC, Art. 5, para. 2; AFDB, Art. 44; ASDB, Art. 42; IADB, Art. 9, para. 2. The ASDB and the IADB require a decision by two-thirds of the number of members of the Board, between them casting three-quarters of the total number of votes.

[190] The IMF, IBRD, IDA and IFC are world-wide in scope. Most countries are members, except those in the Soviet bloc. Cf. table "Memberships of the UN and Related Agencies" in *International Organisation and Integration*, pp. 646-651. All OAS members except 1 (Dominican Republic) belong to the IADB. All African developing countries except the Central African Republic, Gabon, Libya and Madagascar belong to the AFDB and all Asian countries are in the ASDB except Burma, Mongolia and Iran. Non-Asian countries also belong to the ASDB on the grounds of their membership of the ECAFE (Articles of Agreement, Art. 3). Unlike the IADB, the AFDB and ASDB were set up in the context of the relevant UN Regional Economic Commissions : ECA and ECAFE.

commodity agreements on sugar, tin, wheat — all classified as +A — coffee (+CA) and olive oil (+CAJ), give the power to take note of disputes on the interpretation and application of the agreements to the general representative organs of the member-states: the International Sugar Council, the International Tin Council, the International Wheat Council, the International Coffee Council and the International Olive Oil Council respectively.[191] These organs decide by a two-thirds majority (Sugar Council), or simple majority of the votes cast by both importing and exporting countries — distributed majority — at meetings attended by at least two-thirds of the total number of votes of the importing and those of the exporting countries (Sugar Council, Tin Council, Coffee Council, Olive Oil Council) or a simple majority of the votes of the importing and exporting countries (Wheat Council). If there is no quorum at a first meeting, valid decisions on the same point may be made by a subsequent meeting if at least the majority of the total votes or a distributed simple majority (Sugar and Coffee Councils) is represented.[192]

The international commodity agreements are world-wide in scope. Soviet bloc countries have only ratified — or acceded to — the Sugar, Coffee and Tin Agreements.[193]

The *International Olive Oil Agreement* also provides for judicial settlement of disputes on 'International classification and labelling of olive oils'.[194]

3. Finally, the convention setting up the *ICAO*, classified as +AJ, entrusts

[191] Cf. Annex II (V).

[192] International Sugar Agreement 1968, Art. 18 (quorum) and Arts. 11, 2 and 57, para. 4 (decisions); International Tin Agreement 1965, Art. IV, para. 11 and 18; International Coffee Agreement 1968, Arts. 19 and 14; International Olive Oil Agreement 1963, Arts. 26 and 29; World Grains Arrangement 1967/Wheat Trade Convention, Art. 28, para. 4 and Art. 29.

[193] The geographical breakdown of members of commodity agreements at present in force is as follows (as at end 1971):

	Sugar 1968	Tin 1965	Wheat 1967	Coffee 1968	Olive Oil 1963
Africa	10	2	5	20	5
Asia (incl. Australia)	6	7	5	5	–
Europe (incl. Canada & USA)	10 [1])	11 [2])	20	16 [3])	8
Latin America	13	2	12	18	1
Middle East	1	1	5	2	3
Total	40	23	47	61	17

1) Including USSR, Hungary and Czechoslovakia

2) Including Czechoslovakia and Poland

3) Including Czechoslovakia

[194] *Survey II*, p. 510.

the Council in the first instance, as a permanent organ of 27 member-states, elected by the Assembly at which all 111 members are represented, with the settlement of disputes on the interpretation and application of the convention. A member-state whose interests are involved may participate in deliberations of the Council, but without being entitled to vote. No Council member may vote on a dispute to which it is a party. The Council decides by majority vote. Each party may appeal against a Council decision to an ad hoc tribunal composed in mutual consultation, or to the ICJ.[195]

Art. 85 of the convention, in which provisions were made for the constitution of an arbitral tribunal if one of the parties in a dispute does not accept the PCIJ Statute, has lost much of its significance since the UN was founded (for PCIJ, of course, we should now read ICJ). Unlike in the days of the League of Nations, when there was a distinction between membership of the League and being a party to the PCIJ Statute, nowadays all UN members are automatically parties to the ICJ Statute. If a state is an ICAO member, but does not belong to the UN and furthermore has not accepted the ICJ Statute, the following procedure applies to the constitution of an arbitral tribunal.[196] If parties cannot agree on the constitution of the tribunal, each one appoints an arbitrator, and the two thus appointed appoint a third. If one of the parties fails to appoint an arbitrator and/or the arbitrators do not manage to appoint a chairman, the arbitrator and/or chairman will be appointed by the chairman of the ICAO Council from a list of qualified and available persons which the Council has drawn up.

Ad b. Seven European agreements make it possible, if parties cannot agree on the constitution and procedure of an arbitral tribunal, for disputes on the interpretation and application of the agreements to be submitted to one arbitrator, who at the request of one of the parties is appointed by the UN Secretary-General in the two agreements concluded under ECE auspices or — in the other cases — by the President of the ICJ, or if he possesses the nationality of one of the parties, the Vice-President or the senior judge not possessing such nationality. Three of these agreements were concluded on 11 December 1953 in the context of the Council of Europe, viz. the +CA

[195] Arts. 50, 52, 53 and 84, *International Organisation and Integration*, pp. 450, 451 and 456.

[196] The following non-UN members belong to the ICAO : Federal Republic of Germany, Republics of Korea and Vietnam, and Switzerland. Cf. table in *Internation Organisation and Integration*, pp. 646-651. Switzerland has accepted the compulsory jurisdiction of the ICJ. The USSR and some of the countries within its sphere of influence do not yet belong.

European Interim Agreements on Social Security and the European Convention on Social and Medical Assistance.[197]

These agreements were declared applicable to the two agreements on social security and social and medical assistance which the 'Brussels Treaty states' concluded on 7 November 1949. Because of this they have been classified as +A although they only lay down that disputes on interpretation and application should be submitted to an arbitral tribunal, the constitution and procedure of which will be regulated by agreement between the parties.[198]

The other two agreements came about in the context of the European Economic Commission (ECE), viz. the +A Agreement concerning the adoption of uniform conditions of approval and reciprocal recognition of approval for motor vehicle equipment and parts of 20 March 1958 and the Customs Convention on the Temporary Importation of Commercial Road Vehicles of 18 May 1956. Both permit states to make the reservation when signing, ratifying or acceding thereto that they are not bound by the provision on the settlement of disputes.[199]

Ad c. The 5 other agreements classified as +(C)A make unilateral use of arbitration possible by providing for an arbitral tribunal that is formed for a specific period or permanently, or by creating guarantees for the constitution of an ad hoc tribunal.

The *Benelux Protocol concerning the coordination of economic and social policies* of 24 July 1953 lays down that, within 2 weeks after the Protocol becomes effective, each partner must draw up a list of three arbitrators, from which it can nominate one if the need arises. If one of the partners proposes arbitration, it nominates an arbitrator. The other partner appoints its arbitrator within one week. If it fails to do so, the first name on its list is automatically designated. Both arbitrators designate the third one. If they cannot agree on a name, appointment is made by the President of the ICJ at the request of both parties or one of them.[200] Although no provision

[197] *Survey II*, Chap. X, Nos. *26*, Art. 11, p. 683; *27*, Art. 11, p. 692 and *28*, Art. 20, p. 701. Cf. *International Organisation and Integration* : Table showing the deposit of Ratifications of Council of Europe Conventions and Agreements.

[198] *Survey II*, Chap. X, Nos. *18a*, Art. 10, p. 671 and *19*, Art. 12, p. 672 and Annex II of the European Interim Agreements, *Survey II*, p. 685-688 and 696. The Brussels Treaty states are the Benelux countries, France and the UK.

[199] *Survey II*, Chap. IV, No. *8*, Arts. 10 and 11, p. 361 and Chap. V, No. *6*, Arts. 38 and 39, p. 451. The Soviet bloc countries that have ratified or acceded to these agreements have excluded application of the provision on the settlement of disputes. Hungary's position is special — owing probably to political events there at the time — because it made no reservation in the 1956 agreement, but did do so in the 1958 one.

[200] *Survey II*, Chap. III, No. 6, Art. 8, p. 217.

has been made for neither partner drawing up a list, the Protocol has been classified as +A because the period in which a list has to be submitted has been kept so short and it is thus made easier to check fulfilment of the obligation at a time when there is no dispute.

The *Universal Postal Convention* (+A) of 10 July 1964 lays down that in the event of a dispute on its interpretation and application each postal administration involved shall select another administration that is not involved. If one of the parties fails to do so :

> "the International Bureau, if requested, calls on the defaulting Administrations to appoint an arbitrator or itself appoints one *ex officio*."

The arbitrators decide by absolute majority :

> "If the voting is equal the arbitrators select another postal Administration also disinterested in the question at issue to settle the difference. Should they fail to agree on the choice, this Administration is appointed by the International Bureau from among the members of the Union not proposed by the arbitrators."[201]

The parties may only submit a dispute to one arbitrator by mutual agreement. The same procedure is used in the *Postal Union of the Americas and Spain* of 9 November 1955.[202]

The Statutes of the *Bank for International Settlements* (BIS), classified as +A, of 20 June 1930 and the Agreement regarding the complete and final Settlement of the Question of Reparations entrust the settlement of disputes on their interpretation and application to the arbitral tribunal provided for in the latter agreement. This tribunal has 5 members, appointed for 5 years at a time.

The tribunal is not formed ad hoc, if a dispute arises. Although the appointment procedure cannot be completed without the cooperation of the member-states concerned, the Agreement has therefore been classified as +A. An important factor in this is that the treaty provides for the possibility of an interlocutory judgment by the Chairman or member appointed by him to that end, and for a default procedure.[203]

Finally, the *Convention of Association between the EEC and the (18) African and Malagasy States*, classified as +CA, entrusts arbitration to a permanent 5-member tribunal consisting of a Chairman who is appointed

[201] Art. 30. Cf. MENON in *International Conciliation*, No. 552, pp. 46-47.

[202] Art. 26 of this agreement lays down that arbitration shall take place in the manner established in the Postal Convention that is in force when the dispute arises (PEASLEE, p. 1731).

[203] BIS, Art. 56, PEASLEE, p. 82, and Art. XV of the reparations agreement, L.N.T.S., 1930, part CIV, pp. 252-254 .

by the Association Council and four members, two of whom are appointed by the EEC Council and two by the associated states. The respective appointments should be made within 3 months of the treaty's coming into force. As the Court of Arbitration is mentioned in the treaty as one of the permanent treaty organs, and each member-state which is a party to a dispute can submit it to the tribunal, the treaty has been classified as +, although the Chairman can only be appointed by the Asssociation Council by mutual agreement between the EEC and its member-states on the one hand, and the associated states on the other.[204]

5.2.1.2. *Judicial settlement*

The multilateral treaties which contain a special provision classified as +(C)J can be subdivided as follows, according to how judicial settlement can be used :

a. Agreements which do not mention the possibility of making a reservation thereon when the agreement is being ratified or acceded to.

b. Agreements which expressly mention the possibility of making a reservation thereon on ratification of or accession to the agreement.

c. Agreements which exclude, explicitly or otherwise, the possibility of making a reservation thereon on ratification of or accession to the agreement.

d. Agreements in which the special provision classified as +(C)J is contained in a separate protocol, signature of which is optional.

Ad a. The *Convention on the Prevention and Punishment of the Crime of Genocide* (+J) of 9 December 1948, Art. IX of which lays down that disputes on its interpretation and application should be submitted to the ICJ at the request of one of the parties, does not allow for the making of reservations.[205] Nevertheless, 15 states made a reservation in respect of Art. IX, in which the Soviet states in particular maintained their position that 'in each particular case the agreement of all parties to the dispute is essential for the submission of any particular dispute to the International Court for decision.'[206]

On 16 November 1950 the General Assembly accepted a resolution that the ICJ be asked for advice on the question. On the 28 May 1951 the Court advised as follows, by 7 votes to 5 :

"A State which has made and maintained a reservation which has been objected

[204] Arts. 39, 43 and 51, *International Organisation and Integration*, pp. 884-885.

[205] P.N. Drost, *The Crime of State*, part II : *Genocide*, 1959, pp. 118-119.

[206] *Survey II*, pp. 522-527.

to by one or more of the parties to the Convention but not by others, can be regarded as being a party to the Convention if the reservation is compatible with the object and purpose of the Convention; otherwise that State cannot be regarded as being a party to the Convention. If a party to the Convention objects to a reservation which it considers incompatible with the object and purpose of the Convention, it can in fact consider that the reserving State is not a Party to the Convention; if, on the other hand, a party accepts the reservation as being compatible with the object and purpose of the Convention, it can in fact consider that the reserving State is a party to the Convention ..."[207]

The special multilateral treaty should therefore be regarded as a network of bilateral inter-state relations, as is also the case with general multilateral treaties.

The *UN Convention for the Suppression of the Traffic in Persons* of 21 March 1950 (Art. 22) also provides for the unilateral submission of a dispute to the ICJ, without mentioning the possibility of making reservations.[208]
Ad b. The possibility of making reservations is expressly mentioned in the +J convention concluded under UN auspices on the political rights of women and the maintenance convention, as well as the convention on the contract for the international carriage of goods by road concluded through the agency of the ECE (CMR).[209]

In the *Convention on the political rights of women* of 31 March 1953 a reservation was made with regard to the compulsory jurisdiction of the ICJ, by the Soviet countries in particular, maintaining the standpoint mentioned above.[210]

Art. 16 of the *Convention on the recovery abroad of maintenance* of 20 June 1956 (maintenance convention) lays down that a dispute shall be submitted to the Court either by means of a special agreement or by means of a unilateral application by one of the parties to the dispute. It is not clear whether the states are free to choose how this is done, or whether a state

[207] I.C.J. Reports, 1951, pp. 15-69 and *Survey II*, p. 527, which also mentions the states that have not accepted the exclusion by some states of the compulsory jurisdiction of the ICJ; JENKS, *The Prospects of International Adjudication*, pp. 231, 232, 245 and 246; Convention on the Law of Treaties, Arts. 19-23; Doc. A/Conf. 39/27, pp. 686-689 and *A.J.I.L.*, 1967, pp. 317-332. The Convention made the ICJ's advisory opinion (much-contested in the 1950s) the basis of the arrangement in the above Articles and opted for the *flexible* system instead of the *collegial* system advocated at the time (i.e. if a treaty contains no provisions on reservations, they can only be made by unanimous agreement or with the agreement of a large majority, e.g. two-thirds of the number of treaty partners). This illustrates the influence of the new nations on international law.

[208] *Survey II*, Chap. VII, No. 3, p. 544.

[209] *Survey II*, Chap. IV, No. 7, Arts. 47 and 48, p. 360 and Chap. VII, Nos. *4*, Arts, VII and IX, p. 545 and *8*, Arts. 16 and 17, p. 566. Cf. Annex II.

[210] *Survey II*, p. 549.

may submit a dispute unilaterally if the other state is not prepared to conclude a special agreement. The latter was assumed for the purposes of classification, although a number of Soviet countries made *no* reservation on the subject. This can be explained by the fact that it is a treaty which is not sensitive politically and which is wholly administrative in scope: the regulation of cooperation between a number of state bodies which are responsible for the recovery of maintenance abroad at the request of the citizens concerned.

In the *CMR* of 19 May 1956 the only Soviet states that ratified it, Hungary and Poland, ruled out application of the provision on the compulsory jurisdiction of the ICJ.

Ad c. The possibility of making reservations on the unilateral submission of a dispute to judicial settlement is excluded, explicitly or otherwise, in the conventions concluded under UN auspices on the status of stateless persons and the abolition of slavery and institutions and practices similar thereto, and in the International Convention for the Prevention of Pollution of the Sea by Oil and furthermore in the European Convention on Establishment concluded in the Council of Europe — all classified as +J — as well as in the treaties setting up the ECSC (+J), the EEC (+CJ) and EURATOM (+CJ).[211]

The *Convention on the status of stateless persons* of 28 September 1954 came into force between 25 states, none of which belong to the Soviet bloc.

The *Supplementary Convention on the Abolition of Slavery, the Slave Trade and Institutions and Practices similar to Slavery* of 7 September 1956 is in force between most UN members — about 75 — including the Soviet bloc countries.[212] It is after all a treaty protecting one of man's most fundamental rights and freedoms — those relating to his own body. This right is so accepted in the present-day international community that the acceptance of the compulsory jurisdiction of the ICJ over disputes on the interpretation and application of the treaty protecting that right obviously never met any resistance. The wording of Art. 10 of the Convention goes

[211] *Survey II*, Chap. III, Nos. *3* and *4*, Arts. 89 with 87, p. 202; *8* and *9*, Arts. 170 and 219, pp. 236 and 241; *10* and *11*, Arts. 142 and 193; Chap. VII, Nos. *6*, Arts. 9 and 10, p. 556, *7*, Arts. 34 and 38, p. 565; Chap. X, No. *11*, Art. 31, para. 2, p. 664; Chap. XII, No. *4*, Arts. XIII and XIV, p. 894. The Convention relating to certain institutions common to the European Communities applies to the ECSC, the EEC and EURATOM. *Survey II*, Chap. III, No. *12*, Arts. 3 and 4. Cf. Annex II.

[212] *Survey II*, Chap. VII, No. 6, p. 552.

so far to meet Soviet views on compulsory jurisdiction that it leaves open the possibility of parties' choosing another method of settling disputes.

"Any dispute between States Parties to this Convention relating to its interpretation or application. which is not settled by negotiation, shall be referred to the International Court of Justice at the request of any one of the parties to the dispute, unless the parties concerned agree on another mode of settlement."

The *International Convention for the Prevention of Pollution of the Sea by Oil* of 12 May 1954 was signed by 40 countries, including two members of the Soviet bloc : Poland and the USSR. In this Convention too the wording of Art. XIII goes so far towards meeting Soviet wishes on compulsory jurisdiction that it leaves open the possibility of settling disputes by another method, although this is limited to arbitration. Nevertheless, when ratifying the Convention on 3 September 1969, the Soviet Union made the reservation that it is not bound by the Article, with the usual note that when a dispute is submitted to the ICJ 'it is necessary in each case to have agreement of all the Parties to the dispute.'[213]

Finally, the *European Convention on Establishment* of 13 December 1955 is already in force between 7 of the 18 members of the Council of Europe.[214]

Ad d. In the *Conventions on the Law of the Sea* of 29 April 1958 and the *Convention on Diplomatic Relations* of 18 April 1961 the contracting parties, in order to involve as many states as possible in the Conventions, got round the problem of the acceptance of the compulsory jurisdiction of the ICJ over disputes on their interpretation and application by establishing this jurisdiction in an optional Protocol.[215]

The Protocol to the Conventions on the Law of the Sea has come into force between 30 states, among which no Soviet countries are involved.

The Protocol of the Convention on Diplomatic Relations has come into force for 40 states, also without any Soviet countries being involved.[216]

5.2.2. Bilateral treaties

Most bilateral treaties which provide for a form of arbitration or judicial settlement of disputes on interpretation or application which are classified

[213] *Survey II*, Chap. XII, No. 4, p. 893.

[214] Table showing the deposit of ratifications of Council of Europe Conventions and Agreements, *International Organisation and Integration*.

[215] *Survey II*, Chap. XII, No. 5, Art. I, p. 895; No. 7, Art. I, p. 900.

[216] P. CAHIER and L.T. LEE, "Vienna Conventions on Diplomatic and Consular Relations", *International Conciliation*, 1969, No. 571.

as + have been concluded, like the bilateral general treaties, between European countries themselves or between them and countries from other regions. A breakdown by region of the special provisions in bilateral treaties in Table V gives the following :

TABLE XII

Regional grouping of special provisions in bilateral treaties depending on whether they make arbitration (A) or judicial settlement (J) possible for disputes on the interpretation and application of the treaties concerned at the request of one of the parties, with guarantees for the use of arbitration (+).[217]

Region/country \ Class special provision	+A	+CA	+J	+AJ	+CAJ	Total
Africa						
Cameroun	1	–	–	–	–	1
Ethiopia	1	–	1	–	–	2
Madagascar	1	–	–	–	–	1
Sudan	2	–	–	–	–	2
4 countries	5	–	1	–	–	6
Asia						
China (Taiwan)	–	–	–	1	–	1
India	–	1	–	1	–	2
Japan	3	–	–	–	–	3
Korea	1	–	–	–	–	1
Pakistan	2	1	–	2	–	5
Philippines	1	–	–	–	–	1
Thailand	–	–	–	1	–	1
Vietnam	1	–	–	–	–	1
8 countries	8	2	–	5	–	15
Europe (incl. USA)						
Austria	1	1	–	1	–	3
Belgium	2	4	–	1	–	7
Denmark	4	1	–	1	–	6
France	4	4	1	2	2	13
Germany (Fed. Republic)	–	2	–	2	–	4
Greece	–	–	1	1	–	2
Hungary	–	1	–	–	–	1
Iceland	–	–	–	1	–	1
Ireland	–	–	–	1	–	1

[217] The figures given as grand totals of course contain some counted double, as each treaty has been counted for both its parties.

(TABLE XII continued)

Region/country \ Class special provision	+A	+CA	+J	+AJ	+CAJ	Total
Italy	3	2	–	1	–	6
Luxembourg	1	2	–	1	–	4
Netherlands	2	3	1	2	–	8
Norway	1	–	2	1	–	4
Portugal	–	–	–	1	–	1
Spain	1	–	–	–	–	1
Sweden	–	–	1	1	2	4
Switzerland	1	–	–	–	–	1
UK	6	5	6	2	–	19
USA	11	–	1	18	–	30
Yugoslavia	1	2	–	–	–	3
20 countries	38	27	13	37	4	119
Latin America						
Dominican Republic	1	–	–	–	–	1
El Salvador	1	–	–	–	–	1
Guatemala	1	–	–	–	–	1
Mexico	–	–	2	–	–	2
Paraguay	1	–	–	–	–	1
Peru	2	–	–	–	–	2
6 countries	6	–	2	–	–	8
Middle East						
Israel	2	–	–	1	–	3
Jordan	1	–	–	1	–	2
Syria	1	–	–	–	–	1
Turkey	–	1	–	1	–	2
UAR	3	–	–	1	–	4
5 countries	7	1	–	4	–	12
Grand total : 43 countries	64	30	16	46	4	160

In Table XIII the numbers of special provisions in the respective classes have been split according to whether they were concluded between countries in the same region (intra-regional) or from different regions (inter-regional).

TABLE XIII

Intra-regional and inter-regional grouping of special provisions in bilateral treaties depending on whether they make arbitration (A) and judicial settlement (J) possible for disputes on the interpretation and application of the treaties concerned on the initiative of one of the parties, with guarantees being created for the use of arbitration (+).

Region \ Class special provision	+A	+CA	+J	+AJ	+CAJ	Total
Africa						
Intra-regional	–	–	–	–	–	–
Inter-regional :						
Europe	5	–	1	–	–	6
	5	–	1	–	–	6
Asia						
Intra-regional	1	1	–	1	–	3
Inter-regional :						
Europe	6	–	–	3	–	9
	7	1	–	4	–	12
Europe						
Intra-regional	8	13	5	15	2	43
Inter-regional :						
Africa	5	–	1	–	–	6
Asia	6	–	–	3	–	9
Latin America	6	–	2	–	–	8
Middle East	5	1	–	4	–	10
	30	14	8	22	2	76
Latin America						
Intra-regional	–	–	–	–	–	–
Inter-regional ;						
Europe	6	–	2	–	–	8
	6	–	2	–	–	8
Middle East						
Intra-regional	1	–	–	–	–	1
Inter-regional ;						
Europe	5	1	–	4	–	10
	6	1	–	4	–	11

5.2.2.1. *Arbitration*

The same sub-division applies to the organisation of arbitration procedure in the special provisions of bilateral treaties as to special provisions in multilateral treaties.

Ad a. Arbitration by non-judicial bodies is encountered in bilateral air transport agreements. Ten +A special provisions in such agreements enable one of the parties to submit the dispute to the ICAO Council if parties do not manage to form an arbitral tribunal themselves or the ICAO has not formed one.[218] These agreements were all concluded between ICAO member states. As the ICAO, by virtue of the settlement procedure laid down in its constitution, can be regarded as a legal community in the field of civil aviation, the Council's role in these agreements can be described as a form of administrative arbitration.

Ad b. Arbitration by an arbitrator to be appointed by a third party — usually the President of the ICJ — at the request of one of the parties is made possible in particular in special provisions classed as +(C)A in bilateral agreements on social security and economic cooperation if parties do not succeed in reaching agreement on the constitution of an arbitral tribunal or the sole arbitrator to be chosen. There are 12 such agreements between member-states of the Council of Europe on social security to which — insofar as they do not themselves make arbitration possible by an arbitrator to be nominated by the President of the ICJ — the above European Interim Agreements on Social Security apply, and 8 agreements on economic cooperation concluded by the USA with 8 countries, mainly in the 1950s.[219] States which are parties to the latter agreements have not accepted the compulsory jurisdiction of the ICJ. Unlike the +AJ economic cooperation agreements between the USA and countries which have accepted compulsory ICJ jurisdiction which will be discussed below, these agreements, which are designed mainly to create investment guarantees, limit arbitration to disputes over US claims against the party concerned. There is therefore no question of reciprocity.[220]

[218] These agreements have been included in Annex II under III 'Communications and Transport', column +A : *Survey II*, Chap. IV Nos. *14, 15, 17, 24, 25, 28, 31, 33, 40* and *52*.

[219] Annex II under I 'Alliance, etc.', column +A, *Survey II*, Chap. II, No. *11*; VIIId 'Social security', column +CA : *Survey II*, Chap. X, Nos. *13, 14, 15, 16, 20, 21, 23, 29, 33* and *34* — and also in column +A : Nos. *24* and *30*; VIIIe 'Property and Investment', column +A : Chap. X, Nos. *54, 56, 57, 58, 59, 62, 64* and *66*.

[220] The statements in question say : "Any claim thus acquired by the Government of the United States of America against the Government of ... shall be the subject of direct negotiations between the two governments. If, within a reasonable period, they are unable to settle the claim by agreement, it shall be referred for final and binding determination to a sole arbitrator ... etc." (*Survey II*, Chap. X, No. 54), and "That any claim against the Government of ... to which the Government of the United States of America may be subrogated as the result of any payment under such a guaranty ... etc." (*Survey II*, Chap. X, No. 56), or similar formulae are employed (*Survey II*, Chap. X, Nos. 58, 59 62, 64 and 66).

Ad c. Guarantees for the constitution of an ad hoc arbitral tribunal to which a dispute on the interpretation and application of the agreement in question can be submitted on the initiative of one of the parties are encountered in particular in agreements on air transport, social security and economic cooperation. If one of the parties fails to nominate its arbitrator and/or the parties cannot agree on the choice of the third arbitrator, who acts as chairman, either party may ask the ICJ President to make the appointment.[221] There are occasional exceptions to this procedure in other categories of agreement.

A *trade agreement* between *Hungary and Yugoslavia* of 24 July 1947 entrusts arbitration to a 3-man ad hoc tribunal chaired by the USSR trade representative in one of the two countries. He also appoints a party's arbitrator if it fails to nominate one itself.[222]

Finally, the *Indus Waters Treaty* between *India and Pakistan* of 19 September 1960 provides for the formation of a 7-man ad hoc tribunal of whom each country nominates two. The other arbitrators — 'umpires' — are nominated by the parties from a Standing Panel of Umpires by agreement or by lot. If no panel is available when a dispute arises the umpires can be nominated by the parties themselves or by third parties whom they invite to do so after mutual consultation. If the parties fail to agree on the appointment of these 'electors', they each nominate by lot

"for each umpire remaining to be appointed, a person from the appropriate list set out in the Appendix to this annexure, who shall then be requested to make the necessary selection."

If one of the parties refuses to take part in the lottery, the other party may request the President of the World Bank to nominate a person to draw the lots. Although no measures have been taken for the contingency of one of the parties failing to nominate its arbitrators, this special procedure has been classified as +, as the arbitral tribunal is authorised to deal with a case if the three umpires and at least two arbitrators are present. Further-

[221] Annex II under III 'Communications and transport' column +A : *Survey II*, Chap. IV, Nos. *27, 29, 35, 42, 50, 54* and *55*; VII 'Economic matters' (bilateral) column +A : Chap. VIII, No. *21*; VIIIb 'Consular relations' column + AJ, Chap. X, No. *7*; VIIId 'Social security' column +CA : Chap. X, Nos. *25* and *35*; VIIIe 'Property and investment' column +A : Chap. X, Nos. *61, 63* and *65*, that limit the settlement of disputes to claims of the USA against the other party, so that there is no reciprocity; column +AJ, Chap. X, No. *60*; IX, 'Regime in frontier areas' column +CA, Chap. XI, No. *6*, that entrusts appointment to the Executive Secretary of the ECE.

[222] *Survey II*, Chap. VIII, No. 6 (+CA), Art. 11, p. 595.

more, a party is authorised to pay all legal costs if the other party fails to pay its share (50%). Finally, the tribunal may take interim measures at the request of one of the parties by a majority of four members.[223]

5.2.2.2. *Judicial settlement*

The special provisions in bilateral treaties classified as +(A)J can be divided into three groups as regards the acceptance of the compulsory jurisdiction of the ICJ under Art. 36, para. 2 of the ICJ Statute.

a. Provisions which do not themselves make possible unilateral submission of a dispute on the interpretation and application of the agreement in question to the ICJ, with the parties to the agreement already having accepted the Court's compulsory jurisdiction.

b. Provisions which make possible unilateral submission to the ICJ of a dispute on the interpretation and application of the agreement in question, with the parties to the agreement also having accepted the Court's compulsory jurisdiction.

c. Provisions which make possible unilateral submission to the ICJ of a dispute on the interpretation and application of the agreement in question, although the parties to the agreement have not accepted the Court's compulsory jurisdiction.

Ad a. In the period under review only 1 case occurs in which an agreement does not explicitly mention the possibility of submitting a dispute unilaterally to the ICJ, although the parties to it — Mexico and the Netherlands — had previously declared their acceptance of the Court's compulsory jurisdiction. In 1 agreement — between the USA and Japan — one of the parties had previously accepted the compulsory jurisdiction of the ICJ and the other party subsequently did so.[224] The agreements leave open the possibility of parties agreeing on another method of settlement.

Ad b. Most agreements in the period under review which have been classified as +(A)J or +CAJ — 21 out of 33 — which make possible the unilateral submission of a dispute on their interpretation and application were concluded between parties which also, previously or subsequently, made the declaration on the compulsory jurisdiction of the International Court.

[223] *Survey II*, Chap. XI, No. 15, Art. IX and Annex G, paras. 4, 7, 9, 11, 15(b), 23 and 28, pp. 869, 874-877.

[224] *Survey II*, Chap. IX, No. *8* of 27 January 1950, Art. VII, p. 629. The relevant declarations were made by Mexico on 23 October 1947 and by the Netherlands on 5 August 1946 (renewed on 1 August 1956); No. *17* of 2 April 1953, Art. XXIV, p. 639. The relevant declarations were made by the USA on 26 August 1946 and by Japan on 15 September 1958. The treaty has therefore still been classified as —J.

They are mainly agreements to which the UK and the USA are parties.[225] The latter agreements deal with economic cooperation between the USA and the party concerned, and in them, unlike the +A agreements in this sector, the provision on the settlement of disputes is formulated on a basis of reciprocity.[226] Parties to these agreements can also agree to submit the dispute to arbitration. This method has not been elaborated, however. The agreements to which the UK is a party, all classified as +J, also leave open the possibility of parties choosing another method of settlement.

In all these agreements, however, judicial settlement must be regarded as a binding alternative.

Ad c. Of the 9 agreements in the period under review classified as +(A)J which provide for unilateral submission of a dispute on interpretation and application, even though one of the parties has not made the declaration on the compulsory jurisdiction of the International Court, most were also concluded by the USA in the fields of property and investment. The only one to which a non-European country is a party — Jordan — limits the provision on the settlement of disputes to claims of the USA against the country concerned.[227]

The +J agreements lay down that parties may agree on another method of settlement. The +AJ agreements lay down that parties can also settle the dispute by arbitration. In all cases, however, the calling in of the ICJ is a binding alternative.

[225] Annex II under III 'Communications and transport' column +AJ : *Survey II*, Chap. IV, Nos. *19* and *30*; VIIIa 'Trade and navigation' column +J : Chap. IX, No. *9*; VIIIb 'Consular relations' column +J : Chap. X, Nos. *1*, *2*, *3*, *5*; column +CAJ : Chap. X, No. *6*; VIIIc 'Establishment and emigration' column +CAJ : Chap. X, No. *10*; VIIIe, 'Property and investment' column +AJ : Chap. X, Nos. *38*, *40*, *41*, *42*, *45*, *47*, *48*, *49*, *50*, *51*, *52* and *55*.

[226] The statement says "The Governments of the United States of America and ... agree to submit to the decision of the International Court of Justice any claim espoused by either Government on behalf of one of its nationals against the other Government for compensation for damage ... etc." In settling claims by its nationals against the other Government, the USA has applied the methods of lump sum payment or en bloc arrangement. Cf. E.D. Re, "The Presettlement Adjudication of International Claims" , and R.B. Lillich, "International Claims : their Settlement by Lump Sum Agreements", *Liber Amicorum Martin Domke*, pp. 214-225 and 143-156 respectively.

[227] Annex II under III 'Communications and transport' column +AJ : *Survey II*, Chap. IV. No. *43*; VIIIa 'Trade and navigation' column +J : Chap. IX, No. *13*; VIIIb 'Consular relations' column +J : Chap. X, No. *4*; VIIIe 'Property and investment' column +AJ : Chap. X, Nos. *37*, *39*, *43*, *44*, *46* and *53*.

CHAPTER III

PACIFIC SETTLEMENT OF DISPUTES BETWEEN STATES — IMPLEMENTATION OF LAW

Part 1.

Survey of cases

In practice, methods of pacific settlement of disputes between states are applied under general bilateral and multilateral treaties and special provisions in bilateral or multilateral treaties. It also happens that states, although they may not be parties to a general treaty or a treaty with a special provision, take an ad hoc measure on the application of one of the methods of pacific settlement whenever a dispute arises. The number of applications of general treaties, special provisions and ad hoc provisions since 1918 is shown in the table below.

TABLE XIV

Application of general treaties (GT), special provisions (SP) and ad hoc provisions which provide for conciliation (C), arbitration (A) or judicial settlement (J), dependent (—) or not (+) on the cooperation of all parties.[1]

Class / Provision	1918-1945						1945-1965						Grand Total		
	C	J		A		Total	C	J		A		Total			
		—	+	—	+			—	+	—	+		—/+	—	+
Bilateral GT	5	–	2	5	1	13	7	–	2	3	–	12	25	20	5
Multilateral GT	7	–	6	–	–	13	18	–	12	–	–	30	43	25	18
Bilateral SP	–	2	–	5	–	7	2	–	3	1	1	7	14	10	4
Multilateral SP	1	1	7	3	1	13	6	1	3	6	3	19	32	18	14
Ad hoc	2	10	–	36	–	48	3	5	–	3	–	11	59	59	–
Total	15	13	15	49	2	94	36	6	20	13	4	79	173	132	41

[1] In compiling the tables the following publications were used in particular: the Yearbooks of the PCIJ and ICJ; Stuyt, *Survey of International Arbitrations 1794-1970*, 1972; the UN publications Reports of International Arbitral Awards parts I-XVI, 1948-1969, in particular parts XII and XVI, and Docs. A/5694 of 1 May 1964 'Report of the Secretary-General on the methods of fact-finding' and A/AC.119/L. 2 of 10 June 1964 'Summary of the practice of the United Nations and of views expressed in the United Nations by Member States in respect of four of the principles of international law concerning friendly relations and cooperation among states in accordance with the Charter of

A breakdown by region of the countries which have been parties in the 173 cases of settlement of inter-state disputes shown in Table XIV gives the following.

TABLE XV

Breakdown by region of the use of conciliation (C), arbitration (A) and judicial settlement (J), dependent (—) or not (+) on the cooperation of all parties.

Class / Region	1918-1945						1945-1965						Grand Total		
	C	J		A		Total	C	J		A		Total			
		—	+	—	+			—	+	—	+		—/+	—	+
Intra-regional															
Africa	–	–	–	–	–	–	1	–	1	–	–	2	2	1	1
Asia	1	–	–	–	–	1	3	–	1	–	–	4	5	4	1
Europe	11	10	14	25	2	62	14	4	9	10	2	39	101	74	27
Latin America	2	–	–	3	–	5	6	2	1	1	–	10	15	14	1
Middle East	–	–	–	2	–	2	3	–	–	–	–	3	5	5	–
Total	14	10	14	30	2	70	27	6	12	11	2	58	128	98	30
Inter-regional															
Europe with :															
Africa	–	–	–	2	–	2	3	–	1	1	–	5	7	6	1
Asia	–	–	1	–	–	1	3	–	1	–	2	6	7	3	4
Latin America	–	1	–	15	–	16	1	–	1	–	–	2	18	17	1
Middle East	1	2	–	2	–	5	2	–	5	1	–	8	13	8	5
Total	1	3	1	19	–	24	9	–	8	2	2	21	45	34	11
Grand Total	15	13	15	49	2	94	36	6	20	13	4	79	173	132	41

The following countries, by region, were involved in these 173 cases :

the United Nations', and the *Synopses of United Nations Cases in the Field of Peace and Security 1964-1965*, 1966, a publication of the Carnegie Endowment for International Peace, 1966. In the (few) disputes in which different methods were used in succession, *each* method has been counted as a case. Thus, for example, the action of the Security Council in the Corfu Channel dispute has been classed as C and that of the ICJ in the same question under J. The ad hoc provisions on arbitration and judicial settlement have of course been put into classes —A and —J. The tables do not claim to be exhaustive.

TABLE XVI

Countries which have used conciliation (C), arbitration (A) or judicial settlement (J), dependent (—) or not (+) on the cooperation of all parties.

Class / Region/country	C	J —	J +	A —	A +	Total —/+	Total —	Total +
Africa								
Cameroun	–	–	1	–	–	1	–	1
Congo (Kinshasa) *	1	–	–	–	–	1	1	–
Congo (Katanga) *	1	–	–	–	–	1	1	–
Ethiopia	–	–	1	2	–	3	2	1
Ghana	1	–	–	–	–	1	1	–
Liberia	1	–	1	–	–	2	1	1
Morocco	1	–	–	–	–	1	1	–
South Africa	–	–	1	–	–	1	–	1
Tunisia	–	–	–	1	–	1	1	–
9 countries	5	–	4	3	–	12	8	4
* both now in Zaire								
Asia								
Cambodia	1	–	1	–	–	2	1	1
China (Taiwan)	1	–	1	–	–	2	1	1
India	2	–	1	–	–	3	2	1
Indonesia	2	–	–	–	–	2	2	–
Japan	1	1	1	–	2	5	2	3
Pakistan	2	–	–	–	–	2	2	–
Thailand	2	–	1	–	–	3	2	1
7 countries	11	1	5	–	2	19	12	7
Europe (incl. Canada and USA)								
Albania	3	1	–	–	–	4	4	–
Austria	1	–	–	1	–	2	2	–
Belgium	3	3	5	3	–	14	9	5
Bulgaria	2	1	4	1	–	8	4	4
Canada	–	–	–	3	–	3	3	–
Cyprus	1	–	–	–	–	1	1	–
Czechoslovakia	–	1	1	1	–	3	2	1
Denmark	4	1	1	–	–	6	5	1
Estonia	–	–	1	–	–	1	–	1
Finland	1	–	–	1	–	2	2	–
France	6	9	7	12	–	34	27	7
Germany (Fed. Republic)	4	4	3	9	2	22	17	5
Greece	7	2	3	3	1	16	12	4
Hungary	–	–	2	3	–	5	3	2
Italy	4	3	2	9	–	18	16	2
Latvia	–	–	1	–	–	1	–	1
Liechtenstein	–	–	1	–	–	1	–	1
Lithuania	3	–	1	1	–	5	4	1
Luxembourg	1	–	–	–	–	1	1	–
Netherlands	4	1	2	4	1	12	9	3

(TABLE XVI continued)

Region/country \ Class	C	J −	J +	A −	A +	Total −/+	Total −	Total +
Norway	1	–	3	1	–	5	2	3
Poland	2	3	3	3	–	11	8	3
Portugal	3	–	1	1	2	7	4	3
Romania	1	–	–	1	–	2	2	–
Spain	–	1	1	5	–	7	6	1
Sweden	2	1	1	1	–	5	4	1
Switzerland	4	1	2	1	1	9	6	3
UK	5	6	7	14	1	33	25	8
USA	3	1	3	17	1	25	21	4
USSR	2	–	–	–	–	2	2	–
Yugoslavia	2	1	2	1	1	7	4	3
31 countries	69	40	57	96	10	272	205	67
Latin America								
Argentina	–	–	–	1	–	1	1	–
Bolivia	2	–	–	1	–	3	3	–
Brazil	–	1	–	–	–	1	1	–
Chile	1	–	–	2	–	3	3	–
Colombia	–	1	1	–	–	2	1	1
Costa Rica	1	–	–	1	–	2	2	–
Cuba	1	–	–	1	–	2	2	–
Dominican Republic	3	–	–	–	–	3	3	–
Ecuador	1	–	–	–	–	1	1	–
Guatemala	1	–	1	2	–	4	3	1
Haiti	3	–	–	–	–	3	3	–
Honduras	1	1	–	1	–	3	3	–
Mexico	–	–	–	7	–	7	7	–
Nicaragua	2	1	–	–	–	3	3	–
Panama	1	–	–	2	–	3	3	–
Paraguay	1	–	–	1	–	2	2	–
Peru	1	1	1	3	–	6	5	1
Venezuela	–	–	–	1	–	1	1	–
18 countries	19	5	3	23	–	50	47	3
Middle East								
Iran	1	–	1	–	–	2	1	1
Iraq	1	–	–	–	–	1	1	–
Israel	1	–	1	1	–	3	2	1
Jordan	1	–	–	–	–	1	1	–
Lebanon	2	–	2	1	–	5	3	2
Saudi Arabia	1	–	–	1	–	2	2	–
Syria	1	–	–	1	–	2	2	–
Turkey	2	2	–	1	–	5	5	–
UAR	3	–	1	2	–	6	5	1
Yemen	1	–	–	1	–	2	2	–
10 countries	14	2	5	8	–	29	24	5
75 countries	118	48	74	130	12	382	296	86

The tables show that since the end of the First World War 75 countries from all regions have been parties on 382 occasions in the 173 instances of settling disputes, in most of which (132) a method was used based on a '—' class provision.[2] Most instances, then, illustrate the great importance of the element of negotiation in the pacific settlement of disputes between states, for they indicate that states prefer methods which enable them to keep to themselves the decision which can end the dispute or at least, in cases in which this decision is entrusted to third parties, to make their use dependent on their agreement and cooperation.

The tables also reflect the fact that the use of methods of pacific settlement of disputes is mainly a European affair. Apart from the fact that 101 of the 128 intra-regional disputes were European, European countries were parties to all 45 inter-regional disputes.

It can also be inferred from the tables that if states are prepared to apply a method of pacific settlement, they prefer arbitration and judicial settlement. This fits in with the picture given in Chapter II, i.e. that according to the contents of general bilateral and multilateral treaties conciliation is relatively unimportant as an independent method, andt hat in them conciliation is mainly organised on the lines of arbitration and judicial settlement.

The relatively small incidence of the use of conciliation under special provisions in bilateral and multilateral treaties — 9 in all compared with 37 under general treaties — can be considered illustrative of the conclusion drawn in Chapter II that, unlike general treaties, the method of direct negotiation has served as a point of departure for conciliation under special provisions.

In the following sections we shall examine the use of general treaties, special provisions and ad hoc provisions in inter-state relations. In line with the pattern of Chapter II, the cases of conciliation, arbitration and judicial settlement are considered in particular as regards their position in the overall pattern of treaties between parties. Unlike arbitration, conciliation and judicial settlement, as Table XIV shows, were usually used under general treaties or special provisions. Even when an ad hoc provision was the basis, a general bilateral or multilateral treaty was already in force between the states concerned — even with arbitration — or such a treaty subsequently came into force. The main exception is conciliation under the League of Nations Covenant or the UN Charter, which in the relationship concerned offered the only basis at the time of the dispute — and usually continued to do so — for the application of a method of pacific settlement.

The subject of the disputes in settling which conciliation, arbitration and

[2] In some of the 173 disputes several states were parties.

judicial settlement were used usually belongs to the groups of disputes defined in Art. 36, para. 2 of the ICJ Statute. This goes for all instances of judicial settlement and most of those of conciliation under bilateral agreements and of arbitration. The main exception to this is conciliation under multilateral agreements. If the treaty pattern between the states which were parties in these instances is considered, it turns out that conciliation under bilateral agreements was usually no more than an alternative to arbitration and/or judicial settlement, which were also provided for between the parties in question. This is not so in the case of conciliation under multilateral agreements.

In view of this, it can be seen that when the 1961 report of the Institut de Droit International 'La Conciliation internationale' emphasised conciliation under bilateral agreements, it wrongly ignored the treaty pattern on pacific settlement between states which have used conciliation. In view of the aim of the report (to indicate methods of pacific settlement of disputes in those very situations in which arbitration and judicial settlement are not provided for), it would indeed have been more obvious to consider conciliation under multilateral agreements as well — if not exclusively.

Part 2.

Application of provisions on pacific settlement of disputes between states retaining the power to make the decision which can end the dispute

2.1. *Application under bilateral agreements*

Usually — 14 times out of 19 — conciliation under *bilateral agreements* formed part of a previously established procedure between parties which, if conciliation failed, made arbitration and/or judicial settlement possible for all disputes (11 times) or legal disputes (3 times), in most cases on the initiative of only one of the parties. In 2 cases conciliation under an ad hoc provision was used between states whose relationship was also (or subsequently) governed by general bilateral or multilateral treaties on the above lines. In the other 3 ad hoc cases conciliation was used in disputes between countries between which little or no clear provision had been made for the pacific settlement of disputes.

With 3 exceptions the conciliation commissions which operated under bilateral agreements were successful in that their recommendations were adopted by the parties or at least resulted in the limiting of the conflict despite the tense situation.

2.1.1. General treaties

In 12 of the 173 instances of the settlement of inter-state disputes conciliation was used under a bilateral general treaty. With 1 exception — a border dispute between France and Siam (now Thailand) — European countries only were involved.

The applications of the conciliation treaty between Germany and the USSR, under which conciliation — in line with the method of direct negotiation — was used between 1929 and 1932, are hereby counted as one example. WEHBERG relates that, according to information given verbally, less important questions were successfully dealt with by the Deutsch-Russische Schlichtungskommission.[3] In the other cases a form of conciliation was used that was in line with the methods of arbitration and judicial settlement.

The operation of the commissions was a *normal* application of the legal procedure established in the bilateral general treaties, i.e. conciliation (optional or otherwise) on all disputes prior to arbitration or judicial settlement. In accordance with the content of these treaties, the legal disputes were not directly submitted to arbitration or judicial settlement, but first to a conciliation commission. The operation of conciliation commissions under treaties which lay down conciliation for all disputes or legal disputes prior to arbitration or judicial settlement — this has usually been the case since the Second World War — does not indicate a renewed interest of states in conciliation, for such interest was already evident in the treaties themselves. It can be added that the bilateral general treaties applied regulate inter-state relations between the treaty partners, either alone, or with priority, if the partners have also acceded to general multilateral treaties.

The following points can also be made on the instances themselves — particularly on the respective treaty patterns relating to the settlement of disputes.

1. A trade and navigation treaty that was concluded between *Lithuania and Germany* on 30 October 1928 led to a dispute that was submitted in 1931 to the German-Lithuanian conciliation commission that was set up under the general bilateral treaty of 29 January 1928 (IC +IIAJ).[4] Although Art. 2 of the general treaty stipulates that, inter alia, disputes on the interpretation and application of a treaty have to be submitted to the PCIJ at the request of one of the parties, Art. 6 allows for a conciliation procedure

[3] *Survey I*, Nos. 58 with 158 and 222. WEHBERG, "Die Vergleichskommissionen im modernen Völkerrecht", *Z.f.a.ö.R.V.*, 1958, pp. 551-593.

[4] STUYT, *op. cit.*, p. 496, No. B6 and COT, *op. cit.*, p. 95.

before this.[5] Since the commission's report was accepted by both parties, there was no need to proceed to arbitration or judicial settlement. The commission's proposals were based solely on legal considerations.[6]

2. A dispute between *Belgium and Luxembourg* on the interpretation of the treaty of economic union between them of 25 July 1921 was submitted to conciliation in 1934 under the bilateral general treaty of 17 October 1927 (::ICA +IIJ).[7] As the commission's efforts at reconciliation succeeded, there was no need for arbitration or judicial settlement. On 18 May 1929 and 15 September 1930 respectively Belgium and Luxembourg had acceded to the General Act as a framework treaty and had already accepted the compulsory jurisdiction of the PCIJ on legal disputes. The relevant declarations rule out application to disputes for the settlement of which provisions are or will be made in other treaties, so that the bilateral treaty took precedence in the relationship between Belgium and Luxembourg.

3. Under the bilateral general treaty of 6 July 1928 (—ICA +IIJ) between *France and Portugal* both countries wished to use conciliation in 1935 on a dispute on the interpretation of their trade and navigation treaty of 13 March 1934.[8] Unlike the two previous cases, this general treaty expressly lays down that all disputes will be submitted to a permanent conciliation commission, but that

"the High Contracting Parties may always agree that a specific dispute shall be settled direct by the Permanent Court of International Justice or by arbitration without previous resort to the conciliation procedure provided for above."[9]

France wanted to submit the dispute direct to the PCIJ, thus making an exception to the normal procedure of the bilateral general treaty, but in accordance with the fact that both countries had accepted the compulsory jurisdiction of the International Court.[10] Portugal resisted this because it

[5] *Survey I*, No. 2, p. 336.

[6] P. GUGGENHEIM, *Traité de droit international public*, part II, 1954, p. 212.

[7] *Post-War Treaties*, No. 89. Cf. STUYT, *op. cit.*, p. 495 No. B5 and COT, *op. cit.*, p. 96.

[8] *Survey I*, No. 22. Cf. STUYT, *op. cit.*, p. 497, No. B7; COT, *op. cit.*, p. 96.

[9] *Survey I*, p. 409.

[10] France on 25 April 1931 and Portugal on 8 October 1921. Art. 19 of the bilateral general treaty lays down : "Disputes for the settlement of which a special procedure is provided in other agreements in force between the Contracting Parties shall be settled in conformity with the terms of such agreements". (*Survey I*, p. 412). The French declaration on the compulsory jurisdiction of the PCIJ contained a similar provision (*Post-War Treaties*, p. 880), but Portugal's declaration remained silent on the subject (*ibid.*, p. 874). On the basis of the principle of reciprocity Portugal was able to assume that the bilateral general treaty took precedence in the relationship between the countries.

felt the dispute was more economic than legal, which was wholly in accordance with the normal procedure of the bilateral general treaty, but an exception to the above declarations on the compulsory jurisdiction of the PCIJ. Before the commission began its activities the parties succeeded in settling the dispute by direct negotiation.

4. The use of conciliation under a bilateral general treaty between *Denmark and Lithuania* concerned the interpretation of a contract between a Danish company and the Lithuanian Government for the construction of a railway.[11] The agents based themselves on legal considerations. In the end the parties reached a solution on the basis of the commission's recommendation. The bilateral treaty (Art. 3) rules that conciliation shall be used in all cases before a dispute is submitted for arbitration or judicial settlement. Denmark and Lithuania had accepted the compulsory jurisdiction of the PCIJ on 13 June 1925 and 14 January 1930 respectively, so that in their relationship the bilateral general treaty ratified on 11 December 1926 had come into force first and therefore took precedence under its Art. 2.[12]

5. A dispute between *Romania and Switzerland* on the content of diplomatic immunity led in 1949 to a Romanian conciliation intitiative under the bilateral general treaty between the countries of 3 February 1926 (+ICAJ), under which a permanent conciliation commission had been appointed on 1 February 1927.[13] As the commission had not been formed, the President of the ICJ, under Art. 4 of the treaty with Art. 37 of the ICJ Statute, appointed the three members whom the parties had jointly to appoint themselves.[14] Because Romania in vain requested the Swiss court to drop criminal proceedings against a Romanian diplomat, it ceased to cooperate in the conciliation procedure, upon which the commission gave up its task and the case was not subsequently submitted to arbitration or judicial settlement.

6. A classic example of conciliation attuned to arbitration procedure is provided by the operation of the permanent *Belgian-Danish* conciliation commission in 1952 on a dispute on the legality of certain measures taken by Belgium in 1940 in respect of two Danish merchant vessels in the port of Antwerp as the German invaders drew near.[15] This is because the permanent commission had remained intact and both parties, in accordance

[11] Treaty of 11 December 1926 (+ICAJ) *Post-War Treaties*, No. 74. Cf. STUYT, *op. cit.*, p. 493 No. B3 and COT, *op. cit.*, p. 96.

[12] *Post-War Treaties*, p. 514.

[13] *Post-War Treaties*, No. 58, p. 381. This commission had to be reconstituted at the time of the dispute. Cf. HAMZEH, *op. cit.*, p. 49, note 1 and COT, *op. cit.*, p. 97.

[14] *Post-War Treaties*, pp. 375-376.

[15] *Post-War Treaties*, No. 79. Cf. ROLIN (Belgian member of the commission), "Une conciliation belgo-danoise, *R.G.D.I.P.*, 1953, pp. 353-371.

with Art. 5 of the general bilateral treaty of 3 March 1927 (— ICA + IIJ) were able jointly to approach the President of the Commission.[16]

Although both countries had acceded to the General Act as a framework treaty — and to the 1949 Revised General Act — and had made the declaration on the compulsory jurisdiction of the ICJ, the bilateral general treaty took precedence in their relationship under its Art. 2 with Art. 29 of the General Act and on the basis of the content of the Belgian declaration.[17]

Because the parties complied with the commission's recommendation and were able to assess the damages payable by Belgium to Denmark, there was no need for arbitration or judicial settlement.

7/8. The general bilateral treaty concluded by *France and Switzerland* on 6 April 1925 (— ICA + IIJ) was applied in 1954 to two disputes between them on the cost of interning a Polish division in Switzerland during the Second World War and on whether French Customs officials had infringed Swiss territoriality.[18] Both countries had acceded to the General Act as a framework treaty and accepted the compulsory jurisdiction of the ICJ.[19]

The treaty in question rules that conciliation shall be applied to all disputes before arbitration or judicial settlement, although parties can agree to go directly to the international court or an arbitral tribunal.

Under Art. 29 of the General Act and the content of the French declaration the bilateral general treaty took precedence. Although these were legal disputes — as defined by Art. 36, para. 2 of the ICJ Statute — it was wholly in accordance with the legal procedure laid down in the bilateral general treaty for Switzerland to appeal unilaterally (under Art. 5) to the chairman

[16] The permanent commission had been constituted on 30 March 1928. In 1952 two of the original members of the commission still held office, viz. Prof. J.P.A. François, who had been appointed by both countries, and the Belgian member Prof. H. Rolin. The President in 1952 was the Swede Mr. Sändstrom, who was a member of, inter alia, the Permanent Court of Arbitration.

[17] The Danish declaration contains no reservation in respect of inapplicability if other treaties are in force but does make the proviso that it applies towards other countries that have accepted the same obligation.

[18] *Post-War Treaties*, No. 38, p. 226. Cf. VAN ASBECK (chairman of the permanent Franco-Swiss conciliation commission), "La tâche et l'action d'une commission de conciliation", *N.T.I.R.*, 1956, pp. 1-9 and "La procédure suivie par la Commission permanente de la conciliation franco-suisse", *N.T.I.R.*, 1956, pp. 209-219.

[19] The French declaration on compulsory jurisdiction makes a reservation in respect of disputes for the settlement of which provisions are or shall be made elsewhere. The Swiss declaration does not make a reservation of this kind but applies on the basis of reciprocity.

of the permanent conciliation commission.[20] Since the commission's recommendation was accepted by the parties in both cases, there was no need for arbitration or judicial settlement.

9. The issue in the *Italo-Swiss* dispute submitted by Switzerland in 1956 to the permanent Italo-Swiss conciliation commission provided for in the bilateral general treaty of 20 September 1924 (+ ICJ) was the interpretation of the establishment treaty concluded between them on 22 July 1868.[21]

Both countries had acceded to the General Act as a framework treaty. Under Art. 29 of the General Act the bilateral treaty took precedence. Art. 1 of the bilateral general treaty makes conciliation compulsory before recourse is had to the ICJ.[22] Italy was therefore acting in accordance with the treaties between the two countries on pacific settlement when it did not agree to the original Swiss proposal to submit the dispute to arbitration but persevered with conciliation. Under Art. 5, para. 2 of the bilateral treaty Switzerland then unilaterally submitted the dispute to the permanent conciliation commission.

In its unanimously adopted report the commission emphasises that it considers it its duty to examine the juridical aspects of the dispute first.[23] The parties accepted the recommendation given.

10. Also in 1956 a settlement was made by the *Greek-Italian* permanent conciliation commission, to which both countries submitted a dispute in 1955 under their bilateral general treaty of 23 September 1928 (+ ICJ) which concerned the need for Italy to compensate Greece for the fact that an Italian submarine had torpedoed a Greek vessel in August 1940 when Greece was still neutral.[24] Both countries had acceded to the General Act as a framework treaty. The treaty in question has the same pattern as the Italo-Swiss treaty. The Greek-Italian commission too stated its position on juridical problems after which it recommended that Italy should compensate

[20] VAN ASBECK points out (*N.T.I.R.*, 1956, p. 211) : "il faut applaudir à cette possibilité, ouverte par les traités de règlement pacifique de différends, de saisir une commission de conciliation par requête unilatérale". In the context of treaties like this one, in which conciliation is a preliminary stage before arbitration or judicial settlement, unilateral recourse to a conciliation commission cannot however be regarded as anything special.

[21] *Post-War Treaties*, No. 29. Cf. the report, published in 1960 by the Italian Foreign Ministry, of the Commissione Permanente di Conciliazione fra la Republica Italiana e la Confederazione Svizzera : 'Atti relativi alla vertenza per l'applicazione ai cittadini svizzeri dell'imposta straordinaria italiana sul patrimonio'.

[22] *Post-War Treaties*, pp. 164 and 165.

[23] Cf. the publication of the Italian Foreign Ministry mentioned in note 21.

[24] *Survey I*, No. 53. Cf. COT, *op. cit.*, pp. 99-100; HAMZEH, *op. cit.*, pp. 56-57.

Greece, also for reasons of equity.[25] The parties accepted the recommendation.

11. Finally, the *Franco-Siamese* Treaty of Friendship, Commerce and Navigation of 7 December 1937, classified as :: ICA + IIJ, because it declares the General Act applicable as a framework treaty in the relationship between the parties, provides the sole example of a bilateral general treaty between countries from different regions on the basis of which conciliation was used. The case in question was a border dispute between Siam (now Thailand) and what was then French Indo-China.[26] The bilateral general treaty was applied under an agreement of 17 November 1946 between the two countries, signed through the intermediary of the United Kingdom and the United States, Art. III of which states, as far as is relevant here :

"La Commission commencera ses travaux aussitôt que possible après que le transfert des territoires visés au deuxième paragraphe de l'article I aura été effectué. Elle sera chargée d'examiner les arguments ethniques, géographiques et économiques des parties en faveur de la révision ou de la confirmation des clauses du traité du 3 octobre 1893, de la convention du 13 février 1904, et du traité du 23 mars 1907 maintenues en vigueur par l'article 22 du traité du 7 décembre 1937."

The remarkable thing about the agreement is that, according to its Art. I, it cancels the Tokyo Convention of 9 May 1941 — "précédemment répudiée par le Gouvernement français" — and thereby restores the status quo, as a consequence of which the parts of Indo-China handed over to Thailand, as Siam was called in the Second World War, with Japanese support as part of the 'Greater Thai' idea, were returned to France. According to the French agent on the conciliation commission, the result of this cancellation was that the treaty of 7 December 1937 had again come into force.[27]

The conciliation commission's intervention was therefore based both on an ad hoc provision and on a general treaty. The situation becomes even more complicated if it is borne in mind that, after France had again taken over the administration of Laos and Cambodia, Siam presented itself to world opinion as the victim of border incidents and wanted the UN to intervene.[28] The 1937 Treaty completed a series of treaties between France and Siam on the establishment of frontiers between Siam (now Thailand

[25] François, "Le Palais de la Paix en 1956", *N.T.I.R.*, 1957, p. 71.

[26] *Survey I*, No. 217. Cf. S. Bastid, "La Commission de conciliation franco-siamoise", in *La Technique et les Principes du Droit Public, Études en l'honneur de Georges Scelle*, 1950, pp. 1-20 and the commission's report, published in, inter alia, I.C.J. Pleadings, Oral Arguments, Documents 1962, pp. 21-90.

[27] I.C.J. Pleadings 1962, p. 86.

[28] Bastid, *op. cit.*, p. 8.

again) and French Indo-China (now Laos and Cambodia) concluded on 3 October 1893, 13 February 1904 and 23 March 1907. For ethnic, geographical and economic reasons Siam pleaded, in its request of 5 May 1947 to the chairman of the conciliation commission, which had by then been constituted in accordance with the General Act, for revision of the border with Indo-China which was again in force because of the re-introduction of the status quo.[29]

The issue in the dispute was therefore more political than legal. The commission acted more legally than politically, however, by construing narrowly its advisory function in respect of whether a treaty revision was possible and desirable.

In the conclusion of its report the commission emphasised that, within its terms of reference, it had confined itself to examining the ethnic, geographical and economic arguments adduced, to the exclusion of political and historical considerations. It was indeed difficult to determine the scope of these terms of reference because, on the one hand, France adhered relentlessly to the status quo and on the other, Siam created the impression of asking too much. In such a situation there is hardly any agreement between the parties on the subject of the dispute that separates them and a conciliation commission cannot perform its bridging function. Because the report, apart from a few recommendations to facilitate movements in the unchanged border area, rejected the Siamese demands, it was not surprising that France accepted it and Siam did not. It is worthy of note that Siam, after receiving a new government shortly after rejecting the report, implicitly accepted it by declaring that it was dropping its demands on frontier changes.

The report had a striking aftermath in the dispute between Cambodia and Thailand on the ownership of the Preah Vihear temple, that Cambodia submitted to the ICJ in 1961. The Court rejected Thai objections to maps produced in evidence by Cambodia to support its view that the temple was on its territory on grounds of estoppel. This conclusion was supported, among other things, by recourse to the conciliation procedure, which in the Court's opinion constituted "an outstanding opportunity to claim a rectification of the frontier at Preah Vihear on the ground that the delimitation embodied a serious error..."[30] Thailand then passed this opportunity up, however.

Thailand's attitude during the conciliation procedure was thus seized upon by the Court in basing its opinion of estoppel. There was indeed an

[29] I.C.J. Pleadings 1962, p. 37.

[30] I.C.J. Pleadings 1962, p. 28; VERZIJL, "International Court of Justice; Case concerning the Temple of Preah Vihear". *N.T.I.R.*, 1962, p. 245.

opportunity to do so because the General Act, unlike many bilateral general treaties and the Pact of Bogota, contains no provision to the effect that parties will never be bound by considerations of fact and law which have been accepted by the commission.[31]

2.1.2. Special provisions

Two instances can be mentioned of conciliation under special provisions. Both of them concerned the interpretation of Air Transport Services Agreements, viz. those concluded by the USA with France on 27 March 1946 and with Italy on 6 February 1948.[32] Both contain a provision that a dispute on interpretation or application shall be submitted to a tribunal of three arbitrators with a request for a recommendation. The parties promise to do their utmost to abide by the recommendation. These provisions can therefore be classified as C.[33]

There was in fact arbitration in the dispute between the *USA and France*, because both countries had agreed, in an exchange of letters on 8 December 1962/9 January 1963 which had preceded the signing of the 'compromis' on 22 January 1963, to regard the recommendation as binding.[34]

In the dispute between the *USA and Italy* the task of the 'arbitral tribunal' was confined, in accordance with the special provision, to the making of a recommendation.

At the time of the dispute the relationship between America and France as regards the pacific settlement of disputes was governed by the acceptance of the compulsory jurisdiction of the ICJ. However, both countries' declarations make the reservation that they do not apply to disputes for whose settlement other procedures are or shall be provided for.[35] There was also a bilateral general treaty of 6 February 1928 (—IC IIA) in force between the countries, which under Art. 1, however, only applies "... when the High

[31] Cf. *Survey I*, pp. 251-253, Nos. XXII-XXVII.

[32] Reports of International Arbitral Awards — to be referred to hereinafter as Arb. A. — part XVI, 1969, pp. 5-108. Both agreements are not included in *Survey II* and have not been included in the tables in Chapter II.

[33] USA-France Art. X (Arb. A., part XVI, p. 7) and USA-Italy Art. 12 (Arb. A., part XVI, p. 82). In both cases the procedure was established in a "compromis' in a way that was wholly in conformity with arbitration (Arb. A., part. XVI, pp. 7-10 and 77-79).

[34] Arb. A., part XVI, pp. 11. The tribunal's decision of 22 December 1963 was unanimous. On 28 June 1964 the tribunal again unanimously interpreted the above decision (*ibid.*, pp. 68 and 73).

[35] *Annuaire* 1967-1968 of the ICJ, pp. 47 and 49.

Contracting Parties do not have recourse to adjudication by a competent tribunal..."[36]

There was therefore scope for special provisions, although the agreement in this case to regard the recommendation as binding was wholly in line with general provisions in force. A general treaty of 19 April 1928, supplemented on 23 September 1931 (— IC IIA), was (and is) in force between the USA and Italy.[37] Under its Art. 1 disputes which are not settled by conciliation are to be submitted to the Permanent Court of Arbitration or another competent tribunal. This special provision, which provides for conciliation for legal disputes, is in line with this.

2.1.3. Ad hoc provisions

Conciliation under an ad hoc provision has been used in disputes between European (2), Latin American (1) and Asian (1) countries themselves and between a European and an African country (1).

The instances of conciliation in European inter-state relations conform to the picture already described of use of conciliation under general bilateral treaties. In the other cases there were few, if any, clear inter-state relations in the field of pacific settlement of disputes, with the exception of membership of the UN. These instances concern long drawn-out disputes arising from and illustrating bad relations between parties. The result of conciliation in these circumstances cannot be considered encouraging. In 1 case the dispute was eventually settled by arbitration.

1. On 30 March 1921 *Germany and the Netherlands* agreed to set up an international commission to investigate the loss of the Dutch ship 'Tubantia' on the night of 16 March 1916, for which the Netherlands held a German submarine reponsible.[38] At the time there was no general bilateral treaty between the countries. They were both parties to the 1907 Hague Convention, in which the formation of commissions of inquiry was recommended. The provisions of the relevant chapter (III) of the Convention were declared applicable to the commission's procedure. As such commissions were formed ad hoc by special agreements, the bilateral provision took precedence and the Hague Convention could be regarded more as a recommendation.[39] The commission in question kept scrupulously to the terms of reference advised in Art. 9 of the Hague Convention, with the consequence, incidentally, that Germany made good the damage caused.

[36] *Survey I*, No. 3, p. 340.

[37] *Survey I*, No. 10 with 160, p. 367.

[38] COT., *op. cit.*, pp. 43 et seq.; Doc. A/5694, paras. 54-61; SCHURMANN, *op. cit.*, pp. 15/16.

[39] *International Organisation and Integration*, p. 2.

2. In a exchange of letters on 15 November 1961 *Denmark and the United Kingdom* set up a three-man commission to inquire into the circumstances surrounding the arrest of the British trawler "Red Crusader" on the night of 29 May 1961.[40]

The relationship between the two countries was governed in 1961 by the 1907 Hague Convention, the General Act and the European Convention as framework treaties and the declarations on the compulsory jurisdiction of the ICJ, which are also confined to disputes for whose settlement the parties have not agreed or will not agree upon any other procedure.[41]

On the grounds that they were parties to the Hague Convention, both countries were acting in accordance with their existing inter-state relationship in respect of the pacific settlement of disputes when they set up a commission of inquiry.

3. At the beginning of 1929 *Bolivia and Paraguay* entered into hostilities over the area known as Grand Chaco. By the intermediary of the Pan-American Conference on Conciliation and Arbitration, which was in session in Washington at the time, and the League of Nations, both countries signed a Protocol on 3 January 1929 in which they agreed to have the cause of the dispute investigated by a special commission.[42]

Bolivia and Paraguay had not ratified the treaty on compulsory arbitration of 29 January 1902, that also provided for the setting up of an international commission of inquiry. Furthermore, only Paraguay had at that time ratified the Treaty of Investigation of 3 May 1923 (the Gondra Convention).[43] The parties had not concluded any bilateral general treaty. No procedures were therefore laid down in their mutual relationship in respect of the pacific settlement of disputes.[44] The fact that the difference of opinion on the Grand Chaco had been dragging on for many years will not have been unconnected with this.

The commission succeeded in having negotiations re-opened, but its

[40] Report of the Commission of Enquiry, Investigation of certain incidents affecting the British trawler "Red Crusader" (the "Red Crusader" incident), 1962.

[41] *Annuaire* 1967-1968 of the ICJ, pp. 47 and 65. The British declaration made a reservation in respect of disputes for the settlement of which other provisions are or shall be made. The Danish declaration does not do this, but makes the reservation in respect of reciprocity.

[42] STUYT, *op. cit.*, p. 499 No. B9. Cf. also J. BROWN SCOTT, "La Conférence panaméricaine et le conflit de la Bolivie et du Paraguay, 1929"; COT., *op. cit.*, p. 93 and the above-mentioned Doc. A/5694, paras. 130-136.

[43] *Post-War Treaties*, p. 77.

[44] The fact that the treaty relationship at the time was not very intensive is clear from tables A and B in The *Inter-American System*, pp. 506 et seq.

mandate expired before a settlement was made. In 1938 the dispute was finally submitted to an arbitral tribunal under the Treaty of Peace, Friendship and Boundaries of 21 July 1938 (class — ICA) and it made its award on 10 October 1938.[45]

4. A *Franco-Moroccan* conciliation commission was convened under an agreement of 5 January 1957 over a dispute which arose when an aircraft carrying Algerian nationalist leaders was forced by French planes to land in Algiers.[46] Apart from their UN membership, the two countries were not parties to any general bilateral or multilateral treaties.

The commission, consisting of five members, including a Frenchman and a Moroccan, followed a procedure in line with that of arbitration and judicial settlement. It did not manage to prevent a deadlock, or final failure, when the Moroccan agent persisted in his demand that all those on the captured plane should be heard, while the majority of the commission (the three Western members) felt that in the first instance the testimony of the captain and stewardess would suffice. This view was not shared by the non-Western members. The Moroccan delegation then decided to boycott the commission, the result being that this bilateral conciliation between countries from different regions failed.

5. Border difficulties led *Cambodia and Thailand* to ask the UN Secretary-General in October 1962 to appoint a personal envoy in the area for a period of one year, beginning 1 January 1963. His terms of reference would, in general, require him to place himself at the disposal of the parties to assist them in solving all problems that have arisen or may arise between them.[47] Both countries agreed to pay jointly all costs of the mission.

The frontier problems between the countries were long-standing. They gave rise to the involvement of the Franco-Siamese conciliation commission in 1946 and to the submission of the case of the Preah Vihear temple to the ICJ. The appeal by both countries to the UN Secretary-General illustrates his opportunities for diplomatic action outside the framework of the other UN organs.[48]

At the time of the request the treaty position of Cambodia and Thailand regarding the settlement of mutual disputes was no longer clear. When unilaterally submitting the Preah Vihear temple dispute to the ICJ in 1959

[45] *Survey I*, No. 218, p. 1118 and STUYT, *op. cit.*, No. 407.

[46] HAMZEH, *op, cit.*, pp. 60-67.

[47] Doc. A/5694, paras. 313 and 314.

[48] J. SIOTIS, *Essai sur le Secrétariat International*, 1963, in particular pp. 185 et seq., and S. SUCHARITKUL, "Good Offices as a Peaceful Means of Settling Regional Differences," *Liber Amicorum Martin Domke*, pp. 341-343.

Cambodia had invoked the mutual declaration on compulsory jurisdiction and the Franco-Siamese treaty of 7 December 1937 mentioned above. Thailand contested the ICJ's jurisdiction because its declaration was not supposed to be legally valid and because, even if the other treaty provisions cited by Cambodia had empowered the Court to deal with a dispute of such a nature between Thailand and France, Cambodia could not yet independently invoke them in a dispute with Thailand. The Court, after unanimously rejecting Thailand's first counter-argument, did not pronounce on the second.[49]

In 1962 the Thai declaration on the compulsory jurisdiction of the ICJ (PCIJ) no longer applied and it had not made any further declaration.

2.2. *Application under multilateral agreements*

Conciliation was used under *multilateral agreements* within the League of Nations (6 times), the UN Charter (11), inter-American general treaties (8), the European Convention for the Protection of Human Rights and Fundamental Freedoms — the Rome Convention — (3) and the ILO Constitution (2).

The feature common to the cases under the League of Nations Covenant and the UN Charter is that these two general multilateral treaties provided the only available basis in the relationship between the parties to the disputes concerned for the use of a method of pacific settlement.

The cases from the Latin-American region constitute application of inter-American general treaties, in combination with general bilateral treaties or otherwise, that make conciliation a normal part of a previously established pacific settlement procedure that also provides for arbitration and/or judicial settlement for legal disputes (classes —IC IIA or —IICA (5 times), combined in 3 cases with the compulsory jurisdiction of the ICJ) and/or arbitration and judicial settlement for all disputes. With one exception the procedure provided for in the European Human Rights Convention and the ILO Constitution was used in inter-state relationships which were also governed by general bilateral and/or multilateral treaties.

All cases relate to disputes connected with or arising from the threat or

[49] It would have been interesting to know the position of the ICJ on this question of succession of states, all the more so as the treaty provisions on the pacific settlement of disputes are part of treaties settling frontiers whose effects also bind Thailand, as is shown in the pronouncement of the Court on the merits dated 15 June 1962. In my opinion Cambodia could rather have opposed it if the opposite had happened and Thailand had unilaterally filed an application against Cambodia to the Court under the relevant general bilateral treaties.

use of force between neighbouring states or between colonial powers and colonies striving for independence, usually in politically tense relationships. These cases were therefore usually brought to the attention of the OAS, the League of Nations or the UN with an appeal to these organisations' peace-keeping function, after which, however, the emphasis was usually shifted to the mediating function.

In spite of this, attempts at conciliation usually resulted in a solution of the conflict, the normalisation of relations or at least a containment of the conflict situation. The number of complete failures has remained low. The result of mediation, which was not automatically and wholeheartedly accepted by the parties, illustrates regional and international organisations' responsibility for the pacific settlement of disputes between states.

2.2.1. General treaties

The use of conciliation under general multilateral treaties can be illustrated by 25 cases, including 7 from the period of the League of Nations. A breakdown by region gives the following :

TABLE XVII

Breakdown by region of cases of conciliation under general multilateral treaties.[50]

	1918-1945	1945-1965	Total
Intra-regional			
Africa	–	1	1
Asia	1	1	2
Europe	5	2	7
Latin America	1	6	7
Middle East	–	3	3
Total	7	13	20
Inter-regional			
Europe with :			
Asia	–	2	2
Latin America	–	1	1
Middle East	–	2	2
Total	–	5	5
Grand total	7	18	25

[50] More examples can be mentioned of the action of the League of Nations, UN and the OAS, but the emphasis in these cases is not so much on the conciliatory as on the peace-keeping function. Peace-keeping does include both pacific settlement of disputes and military measures to preserve or keep order and peace. Cf. R.B. RUSSELL, *Develop-*

2.2.1.1. *Conciliation under inter-American general multilateral treaties*

The multilateral treaties invoked were the Convention of Inter-American Conciliation of 5 January 1929 (once) and the Inter-American Treaty of Reciprocal Assistance (Treaty of Rio) of 2 September 1947 (7 times).[51] The *Dominican Republic and Haiti* invoked the former treaty (class IC) in 1937, when they submitted to the permanent Commission of Inquiry provided for in Art. 2 and 3 a dispute that arose when Haitian nationals were molested in the Dominican Republic and ordered to leave the country.[52] The parties were able to reach agreement. The Dominican Republic undertook to compensate Haiti.

The Rio Treaty was invoked in disputes between the Dominican Republic and Haiti — in 1949 and 1963; Costa Rica and Nicaragua (in 1948); Ecuador and Peru (1955); Honduras and Nicaragua (1957); Bolivia and Chile (1962) and Panama and the USA (1964).

The OAS Charter grants powers to OAS organs in the field of collective security, elaborated in the Rio Treaty, but not in that of pacific settlement of disputes.[53] In this the organs remain dependent on the consent of both

ment by the United Nations of Rules Relating to Peacekeeping, Proc. ASIL, 1965, pp. 53-60. In this study the term is used to indicate the policing (executive) function of IGO's to distinguish it from the peaceful settlement function (judicial function in the widest sense). The criterion taken is whether the terms of reference confine themselves to instructing the relevant organ of the international organisation to investigate and report, or whether it is also instructed to try to bring parties to settle the dispute peacefully.

[51] Cf. Annex III. The mutual treaty positions of the parties in the dispute are as follows (or have become so) — see also Chap. II, note 140.

Treaty / Parties	Inter-American conc. and arb.	Pact of Bogota	ICJ	Bil. GT
Dominican Rep. - Haiti	×	×	×	SI' No. 64 —IICA
Costa Rica - Nicaragua	×	×	–	–
Ecuador - Peru	×	–	–	–
Honduras - Nicaragua	×	×	×	–
Bolivia - Chile	×	–	–	–
Panama - USA	×	–	×	–

') SI = *Survey I.*

[52] Stuyt, *op. cit.*, p. 500; Cot, *op. cit.*, p. 94.

[53] Cf. OAS Charter Arts. 63 and 81 with Rio Treaty Arts. 6-8 (initiative and measures), 17 (decisions by two-thirds majority of states that have ratified treaty) and 18 (parties excluded from voting). Examples are the measures against the Dominican Republic in 1960 and Cuba in 1964 in respect of the aggression against Venezuela. Cf. with regard. to the Dominican Republic *The Inter-American System*, p. 139 and Doc. A/5694, para.

parties.[54] The preference of parties for the Rio Treaty above other general treaties is connected with the fact that settlement of disputes in the framework of the treaty is hedged with more sanctions. Apparently this easily tempts OAS member-states, even if they have already regulated their relationship in the field of settlement of disputes in general bilateral and/or multilateral treaties, to present the case to the OAS as a threat to collective security.[55] If a party to the dispute does not comply with the decision of the ICJ or arbitral tribunal, Art. 50 of the Pact of Bogota only obliges the other party to convene a Meeting of Consultation between OAS Foreign Ministers before going to the Security Council "to agree upon appropriate measures to ensure the fulfilment of the judicial decision or arbitral award", while Art. 7 of the Rio Treaty lays down : "The rejection of the pacifying action will be considered in the determination of the aggressor and in the application of the measures which the consultative meeting may agree upon."[56]

In the dispute between the *Dominican Republic and Haiti* the efforts of the Permanent Council of the OAS resulted in agreement between the parties to begin formal negotiations at the headquarters of the Pan-American Union under the auspices of a special commission.[57]

In the dispute between *Costa Rica and Nicaragua* the Permanent Council successfully took steps both in the field of collective security — it condemned Nicaragua and set up a commission of military experts — and in that of the pacific settlement of disputes.[58]

345 and with regard to Cuba *The Inter-American System*, pp. 166 et seq and 181 et seq. and Doc. S/5586 of 9 March 1964 'Report of the Investigating Committee appointed by the Council of the Organization of American States, acting provisionally as Organ of Consultation'. Also FENWICK, "The Dominican Republic : Intervention or Collective Self-Defence", *A.J.I.L.*, 1965, pp. 987-988 (resolution) and 1966, pp. 64-67.

[54] OAS Charter, Arts. 82 et seq., in particular Art. 87, *International Organisation and Integration*, p. 1055.

[55] Cf. *The Inter-American System*, p. 203 : "Nevertheless, if the inter-American system of pacific settlement were not deficient, as has been mentioned, surely the parties would have refrained from requesting the application of the Rio Treaty and the recourse to the machinery for collective security would have been avoided".

[56] *The Inter-American System*, pp. 387 and 394.

[57] Since the OAS Charter came into force in 1951 the Permanent Council of the OAS has served provisionally as Organ of Consultation (Arts. 12 and 26 Rio Treaty with Arts. 63 (formerly 43) and 81 (formerly 52) of the OAS Charter amended in 1967). Cf. CH.O. LERCHE, Jr., *Development of Rules Relating to Peacekeeping by the Organization of American States*, Proc. ASIL, 1965, pp. 60-64.

[58] Doc. A/5694, paras. 331, 332, 335-337; *The Inter-American System*, pp. 122 and 132.

Ecuador, in its dispute with *Peru*, withdrew its complaint without their longdrawn-out border conflict thereby coming to an end.

In the dispute between Bolivia and Chile the OAS accepted on 24 May 1962 a very carefully-worded resolution in which a 'friendly plea' was addressed to both governments to use one of the methods of pacific settlement provided for in the inter-American system. Bolivia desired mediation, Chile preferred judicial settlement. The dispute, which was over the drainage by Chile of the Lauca River, was not solved, and led Bolivia to withdraw from OAS activities.[59]

In the dispute between *Panama and the USA* the OAS Council appointed a general commission consisting of all members, with the exception of the disputants, to investigate the situation.[60] Its efforts led to a joint declaration by the disputants that they would appoint special ambassadors with full powers "to seek the prompt elimination of the causes of conflict between the two countries, without limitations or pre-conditions of any kind."

Finally, the long drawn-out conflict between *Honduras and Nicaragua* on the establishment of their common frontier forms the clearest illustration of the function of conciliation in the inter-American region as the prelude to and extension of arbitration. The conflict led in 1894 to have the settlement of the frontier entrusted by treaty to a mixed commission. Disputes which arose would be submitted to an arbitral tribunal. If it could not be constituted, one possibility was to appoint the King of Spain as an arbitrator. This happened in 1902. In 1906 the King pronounced, but Nicaragua refused to accept his award.[61] In 1937 the conflict came into the limelight again — the USA had tried in 1918 to break the deadlock by offering its good offices — when Nicaragua issued a postage stamp on which the disputed area was shown as being part of Nicaragua. Both states had ratified the Gondra Convention of 1923 and the inter-American conciliation and arbitration treaties of 1929.[62] The 1937 offer by Costa Rica, Venezuela

[59] *The Inter-American System*, pp. 150-153; *Synopses of UN Cases*, pp. 71 and 72; Doc. A/5694, paras. 338 and 339. Cf. on the conflict between Ecuador and Peru G. Maier, "The Boundary Dispute between Ecuador and Peru, *A.J.I.L.*, 1969, pp. 28-46. Of interest in relation to the dispute between Bolivia and Chile is the study by P.B. Potter, *Article XIX of the Covenant of the League of Nations*, 1941, Geneva Studies, part XII, No. 2, pp. 27-33.

[60] *The Inter-American System*, pp. 146-150.

[61] L. Cavaré, "L'arrêt de la C.I.J. du 18 novembre 1960 et les moyens d'assurer l'exécution des sentences arbitrales, " *Mélanges Rolin*, pp. 39-54.

[62] With regard to the 1929 General Treaty of Inter-American Arbitration Honduras however made the reservation that it did not apply to pending international disputes (*Survey I*, p. 503). The surveys of treaties in *The Inter-American System*, p. 143 et seq.

and the USA to conciliate can be seen against the background of these treaties, which provide for permanent three-member commissions who can also offer their good offices of their own accord.[63] In this case both states accepted the offer, but the commission was unable to achieve much more than an end to hostilities. Since 1 September 1955 the Pact of Bogota has been in force between the two countries, with the reservation by Nicaragua that "the signature of the Nicaraguan Delegation to the Treaty in question cannot be alleged as an acceptance of any arbitral decisions that Nicaragua has attacked and the validity of which is not certain."[64]

Despite this the two countries submitted the border dispute after one other to the OAS Council in May 1957 under the Rio Treaty, after hostilities had broken out again.

The commission of inquiry set up by the Council recommended that an ad hoc commission be charged to investigate whether a final peaceful settlement was possible. The commission's work led to a resolution in which both parties agreed to the application of the Pact of Bogota.[65] This resulted in the submission to the ICJ in 1958 of the dispute over whether Nicaragua was obliged to implement the King of Spain's arbitral award. In its Judgment of 18 November 1960 the Court, after investigating whether the irregularities put forward by Nicaragua did in fact exist, decided that the King's award was valid and had to be implemented by Nicaragua.[66]

In this case the OAS Council, although approached under the Treaty of Rio, therefore put its mediating role in the forefront. The matter did not end with the ICJ's judgment. On 16 February 1961 Nicaragua requested the Inter-American Peace Committee to propose methods and steps which could contribute to a solution of "the questions that have arisen about the execution of the judgment of the International Court of Justice..." After obtaining the agreement of Honduras to its operations, the Committee prepared a

show also that Honduras and Nicaragua have ratified a considerable number of inter-American treaties from that period, including the Inter-American Anti-War Treaty of Non-Aggression and Conciliation of 10 October 1933 (Saavedra Lamas Pact).

[63] Art. III of Gondra Convention with Art. 3 of 1929 Inter-American Conciliation Convention.

[64] *Survey I*, p. 1175.

[65] *The Inter-American System*, p. 135.

[66] *The Inter-American System*, p. 136. The Court did not investigate the soundness of the arbitral award as an appeal court, because under the Gámez-Bonilla treaty of 7 October 1894 the award could not be the subject of an appeal. It did no more than investigate whether the irregularities alleged by Nicaragua constituted grounds for annulling the award. The Court felt that this was not the case (I.C.J. Reports 1960, p. 217; CAVARÉ, *op. cit.*,p. 49).

[67] *Ibid.*, pp. 100-102.

'Basis of Agreement' and set up a mixed commission representing both countries. On 16 July 1963 the Inter-American Peace Committee was able to report to the OAS Council that the dispute on the 1906 arbitral award of the King of Spain had finally been settled.[67]

2.2.1.2. *Conciliation in the League of Nations*

Six cases can be mentioned of the role of the League of Nations in the pacific settlement of disputes between states. They all relate to the extent of the territories of the parties concerned. Four of them arose in the early 1920s, between Finland and Sweden; Poland and Lithuania and Germany respectively; and Albania and Greece/Yugoslavia. The other two related to the Bulgarian-Greek border incident at Demir-Kapu in 1925 and the Sino-Japanese dispute over Manchuria in 1931.

Except for the 1907 Hague Convention and membership of the League of Nations in some relationships the parties had not at the time concluded any general bilateral or multilateral treaties.[68]

Although the parties usually contented themselves with invoking the peacekeeping function of the League of Nations, enshrined in Arts. 10 and 11 of the Covenant, the League nevertheless laid emphasis on its function in respect of the pacific settlement of disputes, which was entrusted to its Council in Art. 15.[69]

1. In the dispute between *Sweden and Finland* in 1920 on sovereignty over the Aaland islands the Council did this by forming a three-member commission of jurists — the plan to set up an International Court had not by then been realised — whose task was to issue a recommendation on whether the Finnish recourse to domestic jurisdiction against the Council's interference, provided for in Art. 15, para. 8 of the Covenant, was justified.

When its powers had been confirmed by the commission, the Council finally unanimously laid down that Finland had sovereignty over the archi-

[68] After this the mutual treaty position became as follows

Parties \ Treaty	PCIJ	Gen. Act.	Bil. GT
Finland - Sweden	×	×	PT'' No. 26 with No. 56
Lithuania - Poland	–	–	–
Germany - Poland	–	–	PT'' No. 48
Albania - Greece/Yugoslavia	–	–	–
Bulgaria - Greece	×	–	–
China - Japan	–	–	–

'' PT = *Post-War Treaties.*

[69] *International Organisation and Integration*, pp. 15 and 16.

pelago, but that it had to give special guarantees to protect the Swedish section of the population.[70]

2. In the conflict between *Poland and Lithuania* over sovereignty over Wilna and its environs, the Council made mediation proposals, although Poland had raised the matter under Art. 11 of the Covenant. The proposals were refused by both parties. Lithuania appealed to the Assembly of the League of Nations, which did not feel competent to deal with the matter further.[71]

3. Although *Albania*, in its dispute with the adjoining countries of *Greece* and *Yugoslavia* on their common frontiers, explicitly based its appeal to the Council on, among others, Art. 15, the Council refrained from intervening but left determination of the frontiers to the organs designated therefor in the respective peace treaties, although Albania was not a party to them.[72]

4. The dispute between *Germany and Poland* on the status of Upper Silesia was submitted to the League of Nations Council under Art. 11 in August 1921 by the Supreme Council, which under the Versailles Peace Treaty was responsible for establishing the frontier between the two countries. On that occasion too the Council did not resolve the problem itself, but entrusted the making of an arrangement to 4 countries. The work of this 'quartet' resulted in a German-Polish Convention concerning Upper Silesia of 15 May 1922, which provides for the submission of disputes on interpretation and application to the PCIJ. Under the relevant special provision the Court was approached on 8 occasions.[73] This procedure is significant because of the background against which the arising of such conflicts must be seen : the re-drawing by the Allies and associated powers of the frontiers of Europe after the First World War, contained in the respective peace treaties.

Bearing in mind later developments between Germany and Poland, culminating in the German invasion of Poland which started the Second

[70] W. SCHÜCKING, *Das Völkerrechtliche Institut der Vermittlung*, 1923, Publications de l'Institut Nobel Norvégien, part. V, pp. 228-254; H.A. COLIJN, *La Décision de la Société des Nations concernant les Iles d'Aland*, 1923.

[71] SCHÜCKING, *loc. cit.*, and G.P. PINK, *The Conference of Ambassadors (Paris 1920-1931)*, 1942, Geneva Studies, part XII, Nos. 4-5, pp. 27-28, 36, 104-106 and 182-183.

[72] The (main) allied and associated powers who were parties to the peace treaties drawn up during the Paris Peace Conference in 1919 — except for the USA, which did not ratify them — formed a 'Supreme Council'. This Council set up a 'Conference of Ambassadors' which was responsible for detailing the peace treaties and supervising their implementation. Cf. PINK, *op. cit.*, p. 27-28, 36, 106-116 and 203- 206, and SCHÜCKING, *op. cit.*, pp. 254-260.

[73] Arts. 23 and 72, para. 3. Cf. VERZIJL, *op. cit.*, part I, pp. 146, 254 and 318 and SCHÜCKING, *op. cit.*, pp. 263-272.

World War, we can see in the frequent use of judicial settlement not so much a manifestation of respect for judicial settlement as a political manoeuvre : to win back the lost territory via the PCIJ and through legal channels to lighten the burden of peace treaties.[74]

5. The border incident between *Greece and Bulgaria* at Demir-Kapu on 19 October 1925 was completely unexpected and was therefore the first case of a "normal" application of the procedure of peace-keeping in the League of Nations Covenant other than the above conflicts which arose after the re-drawing of the map of Europe by peace treaties after the First World War and after the collapse of the Czarist Empire.[75]

After Bulgaria had invoked Art. 11 of the Covenant, the Council constituted a commission to investigate the incident and gather evidence which would enable the Council to establish responsibility, determine compensation if any and make proposals to the governments involved to avoid similar incidents in future.[76] The commission, on which the parties themselves were not represented, carried out an on-the-spot inquiry and concluded, after hearing both sides, that "the operations carried out by the Greek troops were not technically justified", the result being that "the Greek Government is responsible for the expenses, losses and suffering caused to the Bulgarian people and Government..."[77] The report was accepted by the Council, after which both parties complied with it.

6. Finally, the League was less successful in the conflict between *China and Japan* over Manchuria, submitted to the League of Nations Council by China on 21 September 1931 under Art. 11.[78] At Japan's suggestion, and with the consent of both parties, the Chairman of the Council constituted a commission under the chairmanship of Lord Lytton. The commission's task was to investigate any circumstance which threatened to disturb the peace between China and Japan.

The commission's proposals included that the parties should conclude a bilateral general treaty with provisions on conciliation and arbitration, non-aggression and mutual assistance.

[74] Poland and Germany, on the other hand, brought the record number of disputes between them before the PCIJ. This record has not been broken since the ICJ was set up.

[75] LoN Doc. C. 727.M.270. 1925. VII. Report of the Commission of Enquiry into the Incidents on the Frontier between Bulgaria and Greece, published in Official Journal LoN, 1926, pp. 196-209 and Doc. A/5694, paras. 91-97.

[76] Doc. A/5694, paras. 92 and 93.

[77] LoN Report, pp. 203 and 204. A similar argument and conclusion can be found — nearly 40 years later — in the "Red Crusader" report, p. 22 (cf. this Chapter, part 2.1.3).

[78] Doc. A/5694, paras. 98-103; LoN Doc. C.663.M.320. 1932. VII. Appeal by the Chinese Government, Report of the Commission of Enquiry.

The Council — again at China's request, this time under Arts. 10, 11 and 15 of the Pact — referred the dispute to the Assembly on 26 November 1932 under Art. 15, para. 9 of the Covenant. The Assembly charged a special commission with studying the report of the Lytton commission. This did not lead to acceptance of the report by the parties either or to the conclusion of the treaties. This was despite the fact that the Assembly, when a solution proved impossible, accepted the report on 24 February 1933 with only one country dissenting, although it was Japan. The only result was that Japan left the League of Nations.

2.2.1.3. *Conciliation in the United Nations*

The eleven cases of attempts at conciliation in the context of the UN Charter relate to disputes in which force was used or threatened in inter-state relationships which were *not* governed by general bilateral treaties or other general multilateral treaties than the Charter, with a few exceptions in which, however, the use of these other general treaties in the conflicts concerned was explicitly or implicitly excluded.[79]

In all disputes UN intervention was preceded directly or indirectly by an appeal by at least one of the parties to the dispute. In all cases but 2 the UN bodies involved — the Security Council, General Assembly, Secretary-General, acting together or otherwise — entrusted mediation to commissions and/or a mediator.

In 3 cases the mediating role was performed exclusively by the Security Council — under Art. 35 of the Charter — with relative success.

1. In the dispute between *Iran and the USSR* which arose after armed intervention by the Soviet Union in Iran in 1946, the Council did no more

[79] The treaty position of the parties whose mutual relationship was governed by other general treaties is as follows :

Parties \ Treaty	ICJ	Mult. GT	Bil. GT
Netherlands-Indonesia	–	–	S II* Chap. I No. 14')
India - Pakistan	×'')	–	–
Lebanon - UAR	–	SI* No. 130''')	–
Jordan - UAR	–	SI No. 130''')	–

*) SI = *Survey I*; S II = *Survey II*.

') Round Table Conference Agreement of 2 November 1949, in force until 18 August 1954; under Art. 2 of the accompanying Charter of Transfer of Sovereignty not applicable to West Irian.

'') For disputes arising after 26 January 1950.

''') Pact of the League of Arab States for disputes not involving the independence of a State, its sovereignty or its territorial integrity.

than accept unanimously a resolution in which, taking into consideration the willingness of the parties to negotiate directly, the Council called upon parties to keep it informed of the results and also reserved the right to make enquiries itself.[80] On 5 April 1946 the Iranian Premier and the Soviet Ambassador in Teheran reported in a joint communiqué that agreement had been reached between parties. This led to a discussion of whether, in these circumstances, the Council could keep a question on its agenda. The majority of the Council emphasised the Council's own responsibility. The minority, consisting of France, Poland, and the USSR, contested this with regard to *disputes*, because a dispute "exists only by virtue of the opposition between the interested parties."

With regard to *situations* being considered by the Council under Arts. 34 or 35 of the Charter, the minority also recognised the Council's own responsibility. The Secretary-General supported the minority view.

The majority view was confirmed in other cases by the Council's attitude, the consequence being that the Council is in an ambivalent position on the pacific settlement of disputes. On the one hand it can only mediate if the parties want it to, and on the other it has a supervisory role, independent of the approval of the parties. In the latter role too, however, the Council is unable to force through a pacific settlement as long as it operates under Chapter VI — pacific settlement of disputes — of the Charter.

2. In the *UK's* dispute with *Albania* on the Corfu Channel the Council decided not to pronounce on whether the minefield had been laid by Albania or with its knowledge, but to advise the parties to submit the case to the ICJ. The UK did so on 22 May 1947. On 25 March 1948 the parties concluded a special agreement on the jurisdiction of the Court over this case.[81]

3. The first '*Indonesian question*' was submitted to the Security Council on 31 July 1947 by India (at Indonesia's request) and Australia. This meant the end of Dutch attempts to settle the case without involving third parties.

Australia tabled a draft resolution appealing to the parties to end hostilities and, with reference to Art. 17 of the Agreement of Linggadjati of 25 March 1947, to submit the disputes to arbitration.[82] The Netherlands

[80] Doc. A/AC.119/L.2, paras 241-244; Repertoire of the Practice of the Security Council 1946-1951, pp. 300-301 and 303-306.

[81] Doc. A/5694, paras. 260-265 and A/AC.119/L.2, paras. 149-153; T.J. KAHNG, *Law, Politics and the Security Council*, 1964, pp. 150-161.

[82] Doc. A/5694, paras. 266-278; KAHNG, *op. cit.*, pp. 36-42; Organization and Procedure of United Nations Commissions, 1949-1950 (hereinafter called UN Series) No. IV 'The Security Council Consular Commission at Batavia', and V 'The Security Council Committee of Good Offices on the Indonesian Question'. The provision, which can be classed as —CA, has not been mentioned in the tables in Chapter II or in the Annex of special

resisted involvement of the Security Council in vain, invoking Art. 2, para. 7 of the Charter because under the Agreement Indonesia was not yet a sovereign state, and subsequently it successfully resisted the arbitration proposal.[83] The Security Council did, however, accept a resolution on 25 August 1947, at the USA's suggestion, in which the Council offered its good offices. Both parties accepted it.

On 2 November 1949 the question of the transfer of sovereignty from the Netherlands to Indonesia was settled in a 'transfer charter' with an accompanying agreement on the establishment of a Netherlands-Indonesian Union.[84]

4. When dealing with the long drawn-out dispute on Kashmir the Security Council also called in the UN Secretary-General after the second armed conflict between *India and Pakistan.*

On 1 January 1948, some months after India and Pakistan became independent (August 1947), India, under Art. 35 of the Charter, asked the Security Council to consider the question. The UN then formed a commission, originally of three and later of five members, one of whom was chosen each by India and Pakistan.[85] The commission's work resulted on 13 August 1948 in a resolution recommending both parties to cease fire (part I), to conclude a truce agreement (part II) and establishing the desire of both parties to have the future of the disputed area decided by the people themselves in a plebiscite (part III).[86]

The dispute has not yet been settled. It even led in 1965 to a second armed conflict, although the UN, and the Security Council in particular, had not ceased their efforts at mediation. On 20 September 1965 the Council adopted a resolution requesting a cease-fire from 22 September and requesting the Secretary-General "to exert every possible effort to give effect to this resolution, to seek a peaceful solution, and to report to the Security Council thereon."[87]

provisions, because the Linggadjati Agreement has lapsed since the agreement of 2 November 1949. Cf. *Survey II*, Chap. I No. 14, pp. 28-34 (classed as —IIA).

[83] The arbitration provision had been included in the Agreement at Indonesia's request. The Dutch refusal of arbitration can partly be explained in the light of the general Dutch position that it would not be a suitable method for the settlement of political disputes. Incidentally, the Australian and Indian representatives on the Council had declared that the dispute was not a 'purely legal question' (KAHNG, *op. cit.*, pp. 41 and 42).

[84] *Survey II*, Chap. I, No. 14, pp. 28 et seq.

[85] Doc. A/5694, paras. 279-285; A/AC.119/L.2, paras. 159-182; LALL, *op. cit.*, pp. 84-86, 130, 131; UN Series No. XI 'The United Nations Commission for India and Pakistan'.

[86] Doc. A/5694, Paras. 286 and 287; UN Series No. XI, pp. 50-52.

[87] In respect of the conflict the Secretary-General set up, in addition to the 1948

An offer of good offices from the Soviet Premier led the heads of government of both countries to attend a conference at Tashkent in January 1966.

5. The Security Council and the General Assembly were involved when the UN dealt with the *Greek border incidents* in 1946. On 19 December 1946 the Security Council unanimously adopted a resolution setting up a commission of inquiry into the Greek border incidents under Art. 34 of the Charter.[88] While the report was being discussed in the Security Council, discussion on continuing the investigation — a proposal to that effect had been made by the USA and opposed by Albania, Bulgaria and Yugoslavia — concentrated on the question whether the investigation required the consent of both parties. Some representatives emphasized that, unlike conciliation, an investigation could take place irrespective of the parties' attitude. On the other side, particularly by the USSR, this was seen as a breach of sovereignty.[89] This discussion was repeated in the General Assembly, and it resulted in the adoption of a resolution by 40 votes to 6 (all Soviet countries), setting up a special commission, the work of which however was clearly made dependent on the cooperation of parties.[90] Another solution, in view of the inability of the General Assembly to impose sanctions (only the Security Council can do so, under Chapter VII of the Charter), would indeed have been impossible. The special commission was unable to achieve much. After the end of the guerilla war in late 1949 relations between the 4 countries gradually improved, however.

6. The General Assembly was occupied for years with the '*Second Indonesian Question*', which the UN Secretary-General finally helped to solve. In 1949 the question of sovereignty over West Irian had not been solved.[91]

In 1961 this situation led to armed Indonesian intervention in West Irian, whereupon the USA took the initiative in 1962 of instructing Ambas-

United Nations Military Observer Group (UNMOGIP), another group of observers, the United Nations India-Pakistan Observation Mission (UNIPOM). UNMOGIP's sole task was to check the peace line in Kashmir. UNIPOM had to supervise the frontier between the two countries themselves.

[88] Doc. A/5694, paras. 249-259; Doc. A/AC.119/L.2, paras. 260-275; GOODRICH, *The United Nations*, p. 201; UN Series Nos. I and II 'UN Commission of Investigation Concerning Greek Frontier Incidents', and the Subsidiary Group of this Commission set up by the Security Council; and VI 'UN Special Committee on The Balkans' set up by the General Assembly.

[89] Doc. A/AC.119/L.2, para. 263.

[90] Res. 109 (II), UN Series No. VI, p. 27.

[91] Cf. Art. 2 of the agreement of 2 November 1949, Survey II, Chap. I, No. 14, p. 30. Cf. also Report of a Study Group on the Peaceful Settlement of International Disputes, Annexe III; D.W. BOWETT, "The United Nations and Peaceful Settlement", p. 176.

sador Ellsworth Bunker to bring the parties to the negotiating table. When he succeeded in doing so, he was appointed by the Acting Secretary-General of the UN as his personal representative and placed at the parties' disposal as a mediator in this capacity. The negotiations resulted in an agreement, signed on 13 August 1962, under which Indonesia, after an interim period of UN administration lasting 6 to 7 months, would be granted administrative control on condition that the people themselves could determine their own future.

In treatment of the other disputes the Security Council, the General Assembly and the Secretary-General were all involved, supported in one case by a recommendation of the ICJ.

7. In 1954 Greece brought to the General Assembly's attention the position of Cyprus as a British Crown colony as enshrined in the Treaty of Lausanne of 24 July 1923 with Turkey, invoking the principle of equal rights and self-determination for all peoples.[92] During its eleventh session the Assembly adopted a resolution appealing to the parties — *Greece, Turkey and the UK* — to resume negotiations with a view to reaching a pacific settlement. In 1959 agreement was reached between the parties on the status of Cyprus as an independent nation.[93] In 1963 fighting broke out between Greek and Turkish Cypriots, which led to the stationing on the island of a UN force, on the recommendation of the Security Council and with the consent of Cyprus. In addition the Secretary-General appointed a mediator in consultation with the parties. The question is still occupying the UN.[94]

8/9. In 1953 *Jordan and the Lebanon* applied to the Security Council with a complaint against the *UAR* about intervention in their internal affairs.[95] The Lebanese complaint of 22 May 1958 led the Security Council, after originally postponing consideration so that the Arab League could consider the question, to send a group of observers (UNOGIL) to the Lebanon. In the middle of July, at the request of the respective governments, American troops landed in the Lebanon and British troops in Jordan to protect these states' sovereignty. Shortly afterwards Jordan too submitted a complaint against the UAR to the Security Council.

This foreign intervention in the Middle East led the UN Secretary-General to summon the third extraordinary session of the General Assembly

[92] Repertory of Practice of United Nations Organs, Suppl. No. 1, part. I, 1958, pp. 42 and 43 and Suppl. No. 2, part II, 1964, pp. 350-353; LALL, *op. cit.*, p. 42-44, 158, 292-294.

[93] Zürich and London agreements, signed on 19 February 1959 in London by Greece, Turkey, the UK and the Greek and Turkish communities in Cyprus.

[94] *International Conciliation*, latterly 1971, No. 584, pp. 31 and 32.

[95] Doc. A/5694, paras. 203 and 295-300.

at which a resolution drafted by 10 Arab countries was unanimously adopted in which "noting that the Arab states have agreed, in the *pact of the League of Arab States*, to strengthen the close relations and numerous ties which bind the Arab states and to support and stabilize those ties", the Secretary-General was invited to make such arrangements, in consultation with the respective governments, as would serve the objectives and principles of the UN and facilitate the withdrawal of foreign troops.[96] The Secretary-General's efforts resulted for Jordan in the nomination of his special representative for that country. On 17 November 1958 the Lebanese Foreign Minister reported to the Security Council that the dispute with the UAR had been settled and requested it to be removed from the list. This was done and UNOGIL withdrew. Relations between the UAR and Jordan were also normalised.

The special character of conciliation in the framework of the Charter, i.e. that the general interest — the maintenance of peace and security — imposes a responsibility on the UN for the nature of the solution and thus sets limits to freedom of parties in this, is clear in the treatment of the Palestine problem and in particular that of the question of the former Congo.

10. Since it was founded in 1948, *Israel* has been in a state of conflict with the Arab countries, particularly *Iraq*, *Lebanon*, *Saudi Arabia*, *Syria*, the *UAR and Yemen* and the UN has been involved in these from the beginning.[97] As early as 1948 the Security Council appointed the Security Council Truce Commission for Palestine and the General Assembly appointed a UN Mediator on Palestine to "promote a peaceful adjustment of the future situation of Palestine" in cooperation with the Commission.

The duties of this mediator were then taken over by the United Nations Conciliation Commission for Palestine, also constituted by the General Assembly, its terms of reference being to help the governments and authorities to achieve a final settlement of all disputes, to propose measures to promote economic development in the area, including arrangements on access to ports and airports and transport and communications and furthermore "to facilitate the repatriation, resettlement and economic and social rehabilitation of refugees and the payment of compensation."

[96] LALL, *op. cit.*, p. 78 (author's italics).

[97] HAMZEH, *op. cit.*,; Doc. A/5694, paras. 288-294; UN Series No. III 'The United Nations Special Committee on Palestine', No. VII 'The United Nations Palestine Commission', No. IX 'The Security Council Truce Commission for Palestine" and No. X 'The United Nations Mediator (and Acting Mediator) for Palestine'; E.V. ROSTOW, *Legal Aspects of the Search for Peace in the Middle East*, and Q. WRIGHT, *The Middle Eastern Crisis*, Proc. ASIL, 1970, pp. 64-77.

If the duty to report regularly to the Security Council, General Assembly and Secretary-General are taken into consideration, the conciliation commission appears more as an organ to assist the UN, which acts not only as a mediator but also carries out operational duties.[98]

11. Finally, in the *Congolese question*, the General Assembly, convened in emergency session by the Secretary-General, adopted a resolution on 20 September 1960 supporting the Security Council resolutions and the Secretary-General's actions and appealing to all Congolese in the Congolese Republic "to seek a speedy solution by peaceful means of all their internal conflicts for the unity and integrity of the Congo, with the assistance, as appropriate, of Asian and African representatives appointed by the Advisory Committee on the Congo, in consultation with the Secretary-General, for the purpose of conciliation."[99]

This conciliation differs from other cases in that a world organisation composed a wider ranging commission than ever before consisting entirely of Afro-Asian countries — members of the 'Third World' — to mediate in an internal conflict with one central assumption : the unity of the state, without the parts of that state having been known in the constitution and formulation of the mandate.[100]

Although, in a resolution of 20/21 February 1961, the Security Council expressed its conviction that "the solution of the problem of the Congo lies in the hands of the Congolese People themselves without any interference from outside and that there can be no solution without conciliation", armed intervention by the UN peace-keeping force and economic sanctions against Katanga put an end to the secession.[101]

The Congolese question thus illustrates that the UN does not always need to make its mediation efforts neutral, in particular when it considers that there is a threat to the achievement of its main objective : the maintenance of international peace.[102] By this an international organisation was able for

[98] UN Series No. IX, p. 21 and No. X, pp. 65-70. HAMZEH directs his criticism towards this in his book mentioned above (pp. 137-148).

[99] *Kongo en de Verenigde Naties* (The Congo and the UN), Ministry of Foreign Affairs, The Hague, No 68, p. 208. The advisory commission consisted of representatives of countries which had provided troops for the UN police force in the Congo. On 24 November 1960 the advisory commission constituted a conciliation commission of 15 national representatives.

[100] Letter of 22 November 1960 from President Kasavubu to the UN Security Council; cf. *ibid.*, p. 290.

[101] VAN LANGENHOVE, *op. cit.*, pp. 156 et seq.

[102] This objective led the ICJ in its advisory opinion on the 'certain expenses' to justify them and therefore answer in the affirmative the question whether Art. 19 of the Charter

the first time to demonstrate that an appeal to a general interest is also possible in international relations and that there is therefore a limit to the contracting freedom of states and to their freedom to settle disputes as they choose.

2.2.2. Special provisions

The 7 cases concern disputes on the interpretation and application of the 1923 Treaty of Lausanne with Turkey (1), GATT (1), the European Convention for the Protection of Human Rights and Fundamental Freedoms — the Rome Convention (3) — and the ILO Forced Labour Conventions (2). Four of these arose from the latter two treaties between states whose mutual relations were also governed by general bilateral and/or multilateral treaties.[103] Under the special provision — in this case Art. 62 of the Rome Convention — or the general treaty, however, the special procedure took precedence.

1) The settlement of the border between Iraq and Turkey after the First World War led to a dispute between *Turkey and the United Kingdom* which was submitted by the UK in 1924 to the League of Nations Council under Art. 3, para. 2 of the Treaty of Lausanne.[104]

When Turkey, unlike the UK, refused to accept the Council's decision as binding, the Council decided to ask the PCIJ for advice on whether Art. 3,

—the removal of voting rights from countries that are behind with their contributions—applied to them (I.C.J. Reports 1962, pp. 166-170).

[103] The treaty position between the parties in the disputes concerned is (or became) the following :

Parties \ Treaty	PCIJ/ICJ	Gen. Act	European Convention	Bil. GT
Turkey - UK	×	×	–	–
India - Pakistan	×')	–	–	–
Greece - UK	–	×	–	–
Austria - Italy	–	–	×	SI* No. 33
Greece-Denmark	–	×	–	SI No. 184
-Netherlands	–	×	–	–
-Norway	–	×	–	–
-Sweden	–	×	–	SII* Chap. I No. 36
Ghana - Portugal	–	–	–	–
Liberia - Portugal	×	–	–	–

') with a reservation for special procedures agreed or to be agreed between Commonwealth countries.

*) SI = *Survey I*; SII = *Survey II*

[104] Doc. A/5694, paras. 85-90; Report of commission of enquiry Doc. C.400.M.147. 1925. VII.

para. 2 of the Lausanne Treaty allocated to the Council the role of mediator, recommender or arbitrator. The Court advised that the Council's decision was binding, that the decision had to be unanimous, and that parties to the dispute could vote, but that their votes did not count towards unanimity.

The Council accepted the Court's view, only Turkey dissenting. Turkey rightly argued — it had also been against asking the Court's advice — that arbitration could not just be assumed, but had to be explicitly provided for.[105]

The Council then tried to make the parties agree, at first in vain, although the mediation helped prevent a solution by force. In the end the parties, in direct negotiations, accepted the border proposed by the commission of inquiry. Thus the Council's decision to attribute an arbitral character to its standpoint on the dispute, in accordance with the PCIJ's advice, was overtaken by subsequent events.

2) The method of settling disputes in the General Agreement on Tariffs and Trade (GATT), designed to encourage direct negotiations between parties, has been used on several occasions in practice. Since 1953 a small Panel of Complaints can be formed from states not directly involved in the complaints that either settles the disputes while dealing with them or whose recommendations can be included in the resolutions of the Contracting Parties.[106] In addition the GATT organisation can offer its good offices. This happened, for example, in the dispute between *India and Pakistan* in 1952 on the discriminatory charging of duty on jute exports to India. The chairman of the Contracting Parties succeeded, via his good offices, in making the parties agree on a basis for negotiation, with the result that in 1953 they signed a long-term agreement on jute exports to India.[107]

3) The procedure for the pacific settlement of inter-state disputes arising from the interpretation and application of the Rome Convention has been used 4 times, twice between the same states on the same question. These cases clearly illustrate a conciliation procedure by analogy with the procedure of arbitration and judicial settlement by virtue of the contesting of the Com-

[105] Official Journal LoN, 1926, p. 120; certainly, now that the commission itself had argued that Iraq could not lay any claim to the disputed territory, there was even less reason to assume in the case concerned an obligation to arbitrate on *all* disputes against the background of the usual treaty pattern in respect of arbitration, with nothing explicit having been laid down.

[106] McMahon, *op. cit.*, pp. 254-256; and Jackson, *op. cit.*, pp. 144-155, who mentions that 58 complaints have been submitted in the context of GATT, 15 of them in 1962 by Uruguay against the same number of countries. A settlement of one kind or another was reached in about three-quarters of the complaints.

[107] McMahon, *op. cit.*, p. 256.

mission's competence by the defendant state, the Commission's decision thereon and the content of the Commission's report to the Committee of Ministers (of the Council of Europe). They also reflect the Commission's own responsibility as a treaty organ for the peaceful settlement of the dispute and the possibility of political pressure which is built into the Convention in combination with the Statute of the Council of Europe, in which context the Convention was concluded. Under Arts. 28 and 29 the Commission's function in the process of settling disputes and guarantees for its observance, however, insofar as the Commission itself can bring about a solution, is a conciliatory one. That the term "règlement amiable" (amicable settlement) is used in this article instead of 'conciliation' is due to a recommendation from the Committee of Experts that 'conciliation' should be replaced by 'règlement amiable' "étant donné que ce premier terme est surtout employé en cas de conflits entre États, alors que la Commission s'occupe également des conflits entre États et particuliers."[108]

In none of the cases did the Commission's conciliation succeed, which, in view of the contesting of the Commission's competence by the state against which the complaint was directed, is not surprising, as the fact of contesting presupposes a formal approach by the defendant state and indicates that it is not willing to call in the Commission. The Commission's operation, as the procedure also shows, is from the beginning drawn into the legal sphere.

The complaints of *Greece* against the *UK* lapsed when the Cyprus problem was settled politically, when the two countries let it be known that in their opinion no further measures were necessary. In the first case the Committee of Ministers adopted these remarks, and in the second the Commission asserted that "when an Application alleging a breach of the Convention had been referred to the Commission, the withdrawal of the Application was a matter which concerned the Commission as well as the Parties and the Commission must satisfy itself that the termination of the proceedings was calculated to serve, and not to defeat, the purposes of the Convention."

The Committee of Ministers, on 14 December 1959, agreed to the Commission's subsequent decision to close the case.[109]

Regarding *Austria*'s complaint against *Italy* in 1960 over infringement of

[108] SCHERMERS, *Het Europese Verdrag tot bescherming van de rechten van de mens en de fundamentele vrijheden*, (the European Convention for the Protection of Human Rights and Fundamental Freedoms) on Art. 28, column 75; COT, *op. cit.*, para. 117, pp. 274-278; MCMAHON, *op. cit.*, pp. 227-229. It should be noted that the Convention on the settlement of investment disputes between States and nationals of other States of 18 March 1965 does use the term conciliation (cf. in particular Arts. 28 et seq.).

[109] *Yearbook* II, pp. 175-199.

the Rome Convention in criminal proceedings against South Tyroleans, Italy at first in vain contested the Commission's competence. However the Commission decided to reject Austria's complaint, a decision with which the Committee of Ministers agreed.[110]

Finally, the complaints of the *Scandinavian countries and the Netherlands* against *Greece* because of infringement of the Rome Convention by the Greek Government were made in a climate that no longer afforded the Commission much latitude to conciliate. After all, the Council of Europe's Consultative Assembly had more or less put the regime in default by expressing the wish, before the complaint was made, that the governments of treaty partners "refer the Greek case, either separately or jointly, to the European Commission of Human Rights" and it certainly did so after the complaint by condemning, while the Commission was considering the matter, the violation of normal constitutional procedures in Greece since April 1967 and deciding "to recommend to the Committee of Ministers, at the latest in the spring of 1969, the suspension or expulsion of Greece from the Council of Europe if by then an acceptable parliamentary democracy has not been restored in that country or to do so even before that time if it appears that the undertakings given by the Greek regime have not been respected".[111]

The Assembly had also appointed its own observer in this case. On 30 January 1969 it decided not to recognise the Greek representative's credentials "until such time as the Assembly is satisfied that freedom of expression is restored and a free and representative parliament is elected in Greece" and to recommend the Committee of Ministers to bring these and other conclusions to the attention of the Greek Government and take suitable measures in the interests of the Greek people. On the basis of this recommendation the Committee, on 6 May 1969, also expressed its concern at the situation in Greece, anticipating the report of the Commission on Human Rights.

Not until its resolution of 15 September 1970 did the Committee of Ministers deal in its deliberations with the result of the report issued to the Committee by the European Human Rights Commission on 18 November 1969. Endorsing the conclusions of the report regarding the violation noted

[110] *Yearbook* IV, pp. 116-183 and VI, pp. 740-801. The part of the Commission's report devoted to the attempt at pacific settlement has not been published.

[111] *Yearbook* X, pp. 94-98 and 586-593 and *Jaarboek van het Ministerie van Buitenlandse Zaken*, The Hague (Yearbook Neth. Ministry Foreign Affairs). 1967-1968, Annexes 3 and 4, pp. 248-354, 1968-1969, Annexes 6-8, pp. 199-208 and 1969-1970, pp. 20-31; cf. BÜRGERTHAL, "Proceedings against Greece under the European Convention of Human Rights", *A.J.I.L.*, 1968, pp. 441-450.

of the Rome Convention, the Committee of Ministers concluded that now that the Greek Government had repudiated the Convention (on 12 December 1969) and it was clear that it was not prepared to comply with the treaty obligations by which it was still bound, the question could not be dealt with in the circumstances provided for in the treaty, and that there were thus no grounds for intervening under Art. 32 of the Convention, except to publish the Commission's Report.

Irrespective of whether the complaints against Greece were justified, we must conclude that the procedure for the pacific settlement of disputes arising from the interpretation and application of the Rome Convention failed in this case. While the complaint was still being dealt with by the European Human Rights Commission, Greece had already been condemned in the political forum of the Consultative Assembly and the Committee of Ministers and had thereby been induced to leave the Council of Europe.

4) The ILO Constitution (Art. 26) allows a member-state to submit to the ILO a complaint against another member-state on the ground of violation of a treaty that has been accepted by the General Conference of the ILO and that both have ratified.[112] This was invoked in 1961 — for the first time in the ILO's 40 years' existence — by *Ghana* against *Portugal.* The complaint, made on 25 February 1961, concerned Portugal's alleged failure to apply the 1957 Abolition of Forced Labour Convention (No. 105) satisfactorily in its African territories. On 19 June 1961 the Governing Body appointed a three-man commission with wide international experience and made it issue a declaration analogous to the one made by the judges of the ICJ when they accept their appointment. The Commission followed a conciliation procedure analogous to that of arbitration and judicial settlement. In its report it points out that the Governing Body "en instituant la Commission, a mis spécialement l'accent sur le caractère judiciaire de la mission confiée à celle-ci."

Conscious of the fact that the claimant and the defendant states "ont tous deux le droit, en vertu de la Constitution, s'ils n'acceptent pas les conclusions ou les recommandations contenues dans le rapport, de soumettre le différend à la Cour internationale de Justice", it refrained from making a political judgment.[113] Both states, and the Board of Administration, accepted the report.

[112] VAN ASBECK, "Nieuwe proeven in de beslechting van statengeschillen" (New experiments in the settlement of disputes between states), *N.T.I.R.*, 1964, pp. 119-128; MCMAHON, *op. cit.*, pp. 193-199; D.G. PARTAN, *The Development of International Law by the International Labor Organization*, Proc. ASIL, 1965, pp. 139-146.

[113] Bulletin Officiel, Bureau International du Travail, part. XLV, No. 2, Supplement

TABLE XVIII

Breakdown by region of cases of arbitration under general treaties (GT), special provisions (SP) or ad hoc provisions (ah), depending (—) or not (+) on the cooperation of all parties.

Provision / Region	1918-1945									1945-1965											
	Bilateral						Multilateral			Bilateral						Multilateral			Grand Total		
	GT		SP		ah	total	SP		total	GT		SP		ah	total	SP		total			
	—	+	—	+	—	—/+	—	+	—/+	—	+	—	+	—	—/+	—	+	—/+	—/+	—	+
Africa	–	–	–	–	–	–	–	–	–	–	–	–	–	–	–	–	–	–	–	–	–
Asia	–	–	–	–	–	–	–	–	–	–	–	–	–	–	–	–	–	–	–	–	–
Europe	3	1	5	–	15	24	2	1	3	1	–	–	1	3	5	6	1	7	39	35	4
Latin America	1	–	–	–	2	3	–	–	–	1	–	–	–	–	1	–	–	–	4	4	–
Middle East	–	–	–	–	1	1	1	–	1	–	–	–	–	–	–	–	–	–	2	2	–
Total	4	1	5	–	18	28	3	1	4	2	–	–	1	3	6	6	1	7	45	41	4
Europe with :																					
Africa	1	–	–	–	1	2	–	–	–	1	–	–	–	–	1	–	–	–	3	3	–
Asia	–	–	–	–	–	–	–	–	–	–	–	–	–	–	–	–	2	2	2	–	2
Latin America	–	–	–	–	15	15	–	–	–	–	–	–	–	–	–	–	–	–	15	15	–
Middle East	–	–	–	–	2	2	–	–	–	–	–	1	–	–	1	–	–	–	3	3	–
Total	1	–	–	–	18	19	–	–	–	1	–	1	–	–	2	–	2	2	23	21	2
Grand Total	5	1	5	–	36	47	3	1	4	3	–	1	1	3	8	6	3	9	68	62	6

On 30 August 1961 Portugal took its revenge with a complaint against Liberia regarding the failure of that country to comply with the 1930 Forced Labour Convention (No. 29). The complaint was dealt with in the same way as the one above, with the same result.[114]

Part 3.

THE ELEMENT OF NEGOTIATION IN THE APPLICATION OF ARBITRATION AND JUDICIAL SETTLEMENT

3.1. *Arbitration*

The results of the cases of arbitration broken down in Table XVIII (p. 165) can be summarised as follows as far as their effect for the claimant is concerned :

TABLE XIX

Survey of results of arbitration for claimant state. [115]

Result / Provision	Mutual agreement	Successful	Neither successful	Both successful	Miscellaneous	Total
Bilateral GT	1	3	1	2	2	9
Bilateral SP	1	3	1	2	–	7
Ad hoc	2	14	7	16	–	39
Multilateral SP	–	4	2	6	1	13
Total	4	24	11	26	3	68

Apart (perhaps) from the use of arbitration to settle borders in 5 cases — 2 under a IA class treaty and 3 under an ad hoc povision — the cases related to legal disputes within the meaning of Art. 36, para. 2 of the ICJ Statute. In half the instances of arbitration under an ad hoc provision this method was used to settle claims of nationals of one state against another state.

II, paras. 701-703, pp. 243 and 244. Whether the Commission is interpreting Arts. 29 and 32 correctly by speaking of a right, thereby implying that it is the other party's duty to consent to the application to the Court, is debatable — if both parties have not recognised the compulsory jurisdiction of the ICJ.

[114] Bulletin Officiel, Bureau International du Travail, part. XLVI No. 2, Supplement II, 1963.

[115] A claimant is considered to be the side which as the most interested party took the initiative in arriving at the compromise on the application of a method for the peaceful settlement, or — in case of a general or special treaty of the + class — on the unilateral application.

The great significance of the element of negotiation in the pacific settlement of inter-state disputes is illustrated by the fact that most instances of arbitration are based on an ad hoc provision (39). This high figure, compared with conciliation under ad hoc provisions, confirms the phenomenon noted in the analysis of treaties in Chapter II that once parties are willing to settle a dispute peacefully, they are usually also prepared to entrust settlement to a third party. The fact that in most party relationships general bilateral and/or multilateral treaties have come into force after the use of arbitration under an ad hoc provision is in line with this.

In addition, the important role of negotiation as a basis for the use of arbitration is shown by the fact that most of the general bilateral treaties and special provisions in bilateral or multilateral treaties which have led to arbitration have to be classified as —.

The few instances (6 in all) of the use of arbitration on the basis of a provision classified as + also illustrate the importance of cooperation between the parties, because after all a special 'compromis' preceded the use of arbitration or the use of arbitration rested partly on supplementary agreements in which this method was elaborated.

In the only case of arbitration without the cooperation of the parties — under Art. 31, para. 3 of the Universal Postal Convention in a dispute between Portugal and Yugoslavia — the claim (by Portugal) was turned down, so the problem that a judgment delivered in this way can produce did not arise.

3.1.1. Bilateral agreements

3.1.1.1. *General treaties*

With one exception the 9 general treaties under which arbitration was used date from before 1945. Two of them led to arbitration after 1945. The treaties can be classified as IC +IIAJ (once), —ICA +IIJ (once), —ICA (twice), —IC IIA (three times) and — IIA (twice).[116] In the only case in which a general treaty with a class + IIA arbitration provision was invoked — in a dispute between Germany and Switzerland in 1935 over the abduc-

[116] Cf. Annexes II and III. In this and following notes in which cases of arbitration and judicial settlement are mentioned the party which as the most interested party took the initiative in arriving at the compromise as a basis for the procedure is mentioned first. Although in these procedures, which can only be instituted by virtue of mutual agreement, there is no claimant and defendant in the normal sense (this is also clear from arbitral judgments which are not uncommonly formulated diplomatically), the state mentioned first is subsequently indicated as claimant or claimant party.

tion of a German political refugee from Switzerland — arbitration was preceded by a special agreement on the application of the general treaty to the dispute (the Berlin Convention of 26 July 1935) and the parties settled the dispute by mutual agreement before the procedure ended.

Experience with the treaty on the setting up of a Franco-Tunisian arbitration board illustrates the fact that cooperation by parties in the application of treaties is essential. When France applied to the board on 3 June 1955, but the Tunisian arbitrators refused to cooperate in the procedure, the Chairman of the board, who at the time was French, could do no more than note, after thorough deliberation in which it was emphasised that the treaty was in force because it had not been denounced, that the Tunisian arbitrators, including the Vice-President, had withdrawn, that there were therefore vacancies and that consideration of the case was suspended, pending the filling of these vacancies.[117]

With 2 exceptions the general treaties under which arbitration was used only provide for arbitration for all disputes or legal disputes, whether or not in combination with conciliation. With regard to the two treaties that also allow for judicial settlement for legal disputes, it should be noted that when the bilateral general treaty was concluded the parties had accepted the compulsory jurisdiction of the International Court but this was no longer the case when the dispute arose. In the other cases the general treaties formed the only provisions on the settlement of disputes between the parties concerned, apart from the League of Nations Covenant or the UN Charter.

An analysis of the cases according to the result of the settlement shows that the claimant was successful on 3 occasions and unsuccessful once, that in 2 cases both claimant and defendant were vindicated on a number of points and that in one case the tribunal dismissed the complaint because the international responsibility of one of the States in the dispute was not at stake.[118]

[117] Arb. A. part XII, pp. 277-280 and STUYT, *op. cit.*, No. 423. The fact that the mixed commission was given an arbitral function is clear from Arts. 21 with 22 of the Franco-Tunisian (general) Convention of 3 June 1955.

[118] *Agreement*: Germany-Switzerland, STUYT, *op. cit.*, No. 404 with *Survey I* No. 32; *Claimant successful*: France-Spain, STUYT, *op. cit.*, No. 425 and Arb. A. part XII p. 281 with *Survey I*, No. 87; Norway-USA, STUYT, *op. cit.*, No. 339 and Arb. A. part I p. 309 with general treaty of 4 April 1908 (cf. *Survey I* No. 65); Netherlands-USA, STUYT, *op. cit.*, No. 366 and Arb. A. part II No. 331 with general treaty of 2 May 1908 (cf. *Survey I*, No. 113); *Claimant unsuccessful*: Sweden-USA, STUYT, *op. cit.*, No. 395 and Arb. A. part II p. 1241 with *Survey I* No. 40; *Both successful*: Bolivia-Paraguay, STUYT, *op. cit.*, No. 407 and Arb. A. part III p. 1819 with *Survey I* No. 218; Argentina-Chile, STUYT, *op. cit.*, No. 432 and Arb. A. part XVI p. 111 with general treaty of 28 May 1902; *Miscellaneous*: Italy-Ethiopia, STUYT, *op. cit.*, No. 384 and Arb. A. part

With regard to the 3 instances of arbitration under a general treaty classified as IA, it can be noted that the reasons for the disputes were the interpretation of a treaty (France-Spain), a military incident (Italy-Ethiopia) and the settlement of a border between neighbouring states (Bolivia-Paraguay) after conciliation, also as a consequence of an armed encounter. Except for the last two cases, the instances of arbitration under bilateral general treaties related to legal disputes within the meaning of Art. 36, para. 2 of the ICJ Statute.

3.1.1.2. *Special provisions*

With one exception, the special provisions under which arbitration was used belong to treaties concluded before 1945. One of them led to arbitration after 1945. The provisions can be classified as —A (3), —CA (3) and +A (1).[119] In the only case in which a special provision classified as +A was invoked — the dispute between *Greece and the UK* on the Ambatielos claim — Greece had, before arbitration, (the UK being unwilling to cooperate therein) to appeal to the ICJ for a ruling on whether the UK was obliged to submit the dispute to arbitration and then, when the Court answered in the affirmative, an agreement was concluded between the parties on 24 February 1955 on the composition of the tribunal and the substance of the disputes the tribunal was to deal with. The UK's initial refusal to go to arbitration was based, it is true, on a difference of opinion as to whether the special provision applied to the dispute and not on any objection to arbitration as such — incidentally the UK is not a party to any other agreement with a +A provision — but that does not alter the fact that it did not want to lay this question before an arbitral tribunal. It is illustrative of the importance of negotiation, even when arbitration is being used, that the ICJ decided that it was not competent as such to intervene because the parties had omitted clearly to indicate the conditions on which it could do so. This was despite the fact that, according to the treaty, the PCIJ had to act as an arbitration court unless otherwise agreed.[120]

An analysis of the cases according to the outcome of the procedure

III p. 1659 with *Survey I* No. 24; France-Tunisia, STUYT, *op. cit.*, No. 423 and Arb. A. part XII p. 273 with general treaty of 3 June 1955.

[119] No case has been found in the Reports of International Arbitral Awards of the application of the arbitral provisions included in Table II and Table V. Cf. note 121 and Annex II Category I, column —A(1) and —CA(1); Category VI column —CA(1); Category VIIIa, column —A(1) and +A(1); Category VIIIc column —CA(1) and Category VIIIe column —A(1).

[120] ICJ Reports 1952, pp. 28-88; VERZIJL, *op. cit.*, part II, pp. 148-168.

shows that in 1 case the parties settled the dispute between themselves before the end of the procedure, in 3 cases the claimant was successful and in 1 case not, and that in the application of 2 arbitration provisions each of the parties in some cases saw their standpoint confirmed, and in others not.[121]

3.1.1.3. *Ad hoc provisions*

With 3 exceptions the 39 cases of use under ad hoc provisions date from before 1945, most from the 1920s. The countries most frequently involved were the USA (11 times), the UK (11 times) and France (7 times). If membership of the League of Nations or UN is not counted, in most cases there were no general bilateral and/or multilateral treaties in force between the parties when the dispute was sent for arbitration. The few cases in which this was so involved disputes that arose from an incident which occurred before the general provision was made and/or from war conditions.

An analysis of the cases according to the outcome of the procedure shows that in 2 cases the parties settled the dispute between themselves before the procedure ended, in 14 cases the claimant was successful and 7 not, in 3 cases both parties were vindicated on a number of points, and that on the basis of 13 ad hoc provisions more claims were dealt with by the arbitral tribunal then set up, some of which were sustained, some dismissed.[122] The subject of arbitration under an ad hoc provision was usually

[121] *Agreement* : Israel-Germany, STUYT, *op. cit.*, No D1 and Arb. A. part XVI p. 3; *Claimant successful* : France-Poland, STUYT, *op. cit.*, No. 343 and Arb. A. part III p. 1671; UK-USA, STUYT, *op. cit.*, No. 357 and Arb. A. part III p. 1611; Germany-Lithuania, STUYT, *op. cit.*, No. 359 and Arb. A. part III p. 1721; *Claimant unsuccessful* : *Greece-UK*, STUYT, *op. cit.*, No. 422 and Arb. A. part XII p. 83; *Both successful* : Germany-Romania, STUYT, *op. cit.*, No. 387 and Arb. A. part II p. 901 and part III p. 1639, 1845 and 1883; *Poland-Germany*, STUYT, *op. cit.*, No. 345 (these are arbitral provisions under which a number of claims have been dealt with). General bilateral or multilateral treaties were applicable at the time of the dispute between the states printed in italics.

[122] *Agreement* : *USA-Canada*, STUYT, *op. cit.*, No. 431 and *N.T.I.R.*, 1969, p. 161; UK-Peru, STUYT, *op. cit.*, No. 340; *Claimant successful* : STUYT, *op. cit.*, Nos. 338 USA-Peru (Arb. A. part I, p. 347); 349 Peru-Chile (Arb. A. part II, p. 923); 356 USA-Turkey; 364 Netherlands-Germany; 378 *UK-Ethiopia* (*id.* p. 823); 389 USA-Cuba (*id.* p. 915); 390 USA-Guatemala (*id.* p. 1081); 392 France-UK (*id.* p. 1115); 394 UK-Portugal (*id.* p. 1147); 397 *Finland-UK* (Arb. A. part III p. 1481); 400 *France-Switzerland* (*id.* p. 1457); 403 *USA-Canada* (*id.* p. 1907); 405 *Belgium-France* (*id.* p. 1703); *408 Hungary-Czechoslovakia; *Claimant unsuccessful* : STUYT, *op. cit.*, Nos. 337 Italy-Venezuela (Arb. A. part II p. 977); 347 France-Spain (Arb. A. part I p. 302); 374 Germany-France (Arb. A. part II p. 799); 396 USA-Egypt (*id.* p. 1163); 396a Saudi Arabia-Yemen; 398 *UK-Panama* (Arb. A. part III p. 1441); 420 *Greece-UK* (Arb. A. part XII p. 53); *Both successful* : STUYT, *op. cit.*, Nos. 342 UK-Costa Rica (Arb. A. part I p. 371); 350 Germany-USA;

the settlement of claims by nationals of one state against another state (20 times) or the interpretation of agreements or rules of international law, whether or not with establishment of compensation in cases of breach thereof (16 times).[123] In the other 3 cases the dispute involved the settlement of borders between neighbouring countries. Except perhaps for these cases, arbitration under an ad hoc provision was thus applied to legal disputes within the meaning of Art. 36, para. 2 of the ICJ Statute.

3.1.2. Multilateral agreements

The 9 special provisions in multilateral treaties under which arbitration was used on one or more occasions come into classes —A (4), —CA (2), +A (2) and +AJ (1).[124] With 3 exceptions, they are part of peace treaties concluded after the First World War between the central and allied powers and after the Second World War between Italy and Japan respectively and the Allies. Arbitration in the first group of treaties was entrusted to one or more arbitrators appointed by the League of Nations or to a mixed commission which was joined by a third impartial member if the 2 party members could not agree. Art. 83 of the Peace Treaty with Italy (—CA) is in line with this provision.

Two of the 3 +A special provisions belong to peace treaties and/or agreements arising therefrom.

The arbitration between *Germany and Portugal* in 1930 under the Agreement regarding the complete and final Settlement of the Question of Reparations of 20 January 1930 between the Allied powers and Germany (+A) was preceded by an exchange of Notes in which both parties established that,

352 Spain-UK (Arb. A. part II p. 615); 355 USA-Mexico (Arb. A. part IV); 358 Germany-Poland (Arb. A. part I p. 403); 363 France-Mexico (Arb. A. part V p. 309); 365 Austria/Hungary-USA; *367 Germany-Mexico (*id.* p. 563); *371 Spain-Mexico; 375 Panama-USA (Arb. A. part VI p. 297); 376 UK-Mexico (Arb. A. part V p. 3); *379 Italy-Mexico; 386 Belgium-Mexico; 393 Guatemala-Honduras (Arb. A. part II p. 1309); 396b *France-Greece* (*id.* p. 155); 410 Italy/UK/USA-Spain, (Arb. A. part XII p. 1).

At the time of the dispute general bilateral and/or multilateral treaties were in force between the states printed in italics. In the cases marked * no general bilateral and/or multilateral treaty was subsequently signed outside the League of Nations Covenant and the UN Charter.

[123] Most ad hoc provisions formed the basis of arbitral tribunals to which more claims were submitted (particularly the Mexican claims commissions). These cases have been counted as one case in each instance per party relationship.

[124] Cf. note 128 and Annex II Categories I, column —A(4), —CA(1) and +AJ(1); II column —CA(1) and III column +A(1); IV column +A(1) and Annex III.

No cases have been found in STUYT's survey or the Reports of International Arbitral Awards of the application of arbitration on the basis of general multilateral treaties.

as soon as Portugal ratified the Agreement, which it did on 11 July 1931, they would submit a dispute on the implementation of a specific arbitral pronouncement to the arbitral tribunal provided for in the treaty.[125]

Art. 22 of the Treaty of Peace with *Japan* provides for a special 'claims tribunal'. If no solution is found by this or any other way, the dispute will be submitted to the ICJ at the request of one of the parties.

On 12 June 1952 an Agreement for the Settlement of Disputes arising under Art. 15(a) of the Treaty of Peace which Japan was produced for signature. Settlement of disputes on the restitution of property by Japan is thus entrusted to 'property commissions', which, unlike the Italian conciliation commissions, can be constituted if necessary without the cooperation of both parties.[126] Under Arts. II and IV of the agreement, the commissions consist of three members, one nominated by each party and the third by the parties together. If one of the parties fails to nominate its member, or no agreement is reached on the nomination of the third member, the government which has already nominated its member, or in the latter case the party which is most ready to do so, may request the President of the ICJ to appoint the member or members concerned. This provision can therefore be classified as +A. On this basis Japanese-Dutch and Japanese-American property commissions have already operated. Their composition was agreed by the parties concerned.

The only instance of arbitration without the cooperation of one of the parties is the dispute between the postal authorities of *Portugal and Yugoslavia.* When Yugoslavia resisted arbitration, the International Bureau of the Universal Postal Union, for the first time in the history of postal arbitration, used its power under Art. 31, para. 3 of the Universal Postal Convention of 11 July 1952 to appoint ex officio an arbitrator for the party which failed to do so.[127] The commission so constituted, however, did not sustain the Portuguese claim against the Yugoslav postal authorities, so that the problem of implementing a judgment against a country that had refused to cooperate in the procedure was avoided.

Apart from this last example, that relates more to the settlement of disputes between members of an international organisation — internal settlement — than to a normal inter-state relationship, the above cases can be

[125] STUYT, *op. cit.*, No. 391.

[126] STUYT, *op. cit.*, No. 416 and Arb. A. part XIV, pp. 465 and 501.

[127] Art. 31, para. 3; Arb. A. part XII pp. 341 and 346/347. Of the 26 cases of postal arbitration, 20 have been settled by 2 arbitrators and 6 by 3 arbitrators. In 5 cases the third arbitrator was chosen in mutual consultation and in 1 case — this particular one — he was chosen ex officio by the Bureau. Cf. MCMAHON, *op. cit.*, p. 211.

summed up as showing that the cooperation of parties has also been the starting point in the application of + class arbitral provisions. In the 7 cases in which arbitration was used under a special multilateral provision, while a general bilateral and/or multilateral treaty was in force between the parties, the latter treaties enable special procedures to be followed.

An analysis of cases according to the result of the judgment shows that the claimant's case was accepted on 4 occasions and rejected on two. Under the peace treaties with Italy and Japan 4 and 2 arbitral tribunals, to which various matters were submitted, operated respectively. In one case — that concerning ownership of Albanian gold — the arbitrator's sole task was to establish ownership of the gold in connection with possible further action by the UK and Italy, which both had claims against Albania.[128]

3.2. *Judicial settlement*

Table XX on page 174 gives the breakdown by region of cases of judicial settlement under general treaties (GT), special provisions (SP) or ad hoc provisions (ah) depending (—) or not (+) on the cooperation of all parties.

[128] *Claimant successful*: *Greece-Bulgaria* under Art. 181 of the Neuilly Peace Treaty (STUYT, *op. cit.*, No. 330 and Arb. A. part III p. 1391); Hungary-Yugoslavia under Art. 304 of the Trianon Peace Treaty of 4 June 1920 with Art. 320 of the St. Germain-en-Laye Peace Treaty (STUYT, *op. cit.*, No. 332); Germany-Portugal under the German reparations agreement (STUYT *op. cit.*, No. 391); Syria/Lebanon-Egypt under telecommunications treaty of 9 December 1932, Art. 15, para. 1 (STUYT, *op. cit.*, No.399); *Claimant unsuccessful*: *Netherlands-Belgium* under Art. 4 of Benelux Protocol (STUYT, *op. cit.*, No. 414 and Arb. A. part XII pp. 321-322); Portugal-Yugoslavia under Art. 31 of Universal Postal Convention of 12 July 1952, applied in 1956 (Arb. A. part XII, p. 339); *Both successful*: *Italy-France* (STUYT, *op. cit.*, No. B12, Arb. A. parts XIII, XIV and XV and Recueil des Décisions de la Commission de Conciliation Franco-Italienne); *Italy-Netherlands* (STUYT, *op. cit.*, No. B14 and Arb. A. part XIV); *Italy-UK* (STUYT, *op. cit.*, No. B13 and Arb. A. part XIV) and *Italy-USA* (STUYT, *op. cit.*, No. B15 and Arb. A. part XIV) under Art. 83 of the Italian Peace Treaty; *Netherlands-Japan* (STUYT, *op. cit.*, No. 416 and part XIV p. 501) and *USA-Japan* (STUYT, *op. cit.*, No. 416 and Arb. A. part XIV p. 465) under Art. 22 of the Japanese Peace Treaty with the Agreement for the Settlement of Disputes arising under Art. 15(a) of the Treaty of Peace with Japan.

With the states printed in italics the provisions have been used more than once — the Franco-Italian conciliation commission, for example has already issued about 200 judgments, but they have only been counted as one case in the tables.

TABLE XX

Provision / Region	1918-1945											1945-1965											Grand Total		
	Bilateral						Multilateral					Bilateral						Multilateral							
	GT		SP		ah	total	GT		SP		total	GT		SP		ah	total	GT		SP		total			
Region	—	+	—	+	—	—/+	—	+	—	+	—/+	—	+	—	+	—	—/+	—	+	—	+	—/+	—/+	—	+
Africa	–	–	–	–	–	–	–	–	–	–	–	–	–	–	–	–	–	–	–	–	1	1	1	–	1
Asia	–	–	–	–	–	–	–	–	–	–	–	–	–	–	–	–	–	–	1	–	–	1	1	–	1
Europe	–	2	2	–	7	11	–	5	1	7	13	–	1	–	1	3	5	–	7	1	–	8	37	14	23
Latin America	–	–	–	–	–	–	–	–	–	–	–	–	1	–	–	2	3	–	–	–	–	–	3	2	1
Middle East	–	–	–	–	–	–	–	–	–	–	–	–	–	–	–	–	–	–	–	–	–	–	–	–	–
Total	–	2	2	–	7	11	–	5	1	7	13	–	2	–	1	5	8	–	8	1	1	10	42	16	26
Europe with :																									
Africa	–	–	–	–	–	–	–	–	–	–	–	–	–	–	–	–	–	–	–	–	1	1	1	–	1
Asia	–	–	–	–	–	–	–	1	–	–	1	–	–	–	–	–	–	–	1	–	–	1	2	–	2
Latin America	–	–	–	–	1	1	–	–	–	–	–	–	–	–	–	–	–	–	1	–	–	1	2	1	1
Middle East	–	–	–	–	2	2	–	–	–	–	–	–	–	–	2	–	2	–	2	–	1	3	7	2	5
Total	–	–	–	–	3	3	–	1	–	–	1	–	–	–	2	–	2	–	4	–	2	6	12	3	9
Grand Total	–	2	2	–	10	14	–	6	1	7	14	–	2	–	3	5	10	–	12	1	3	16	54	19	35

The results of the cases of judicial settlement according to their effect for the claimant can be summarised as follows.

TABLE XXI

Survey of results for the claimant of judicial settlement used with (—) or without (+) the consent of all parties.[129]

Result / Provision	Successful		Unsuccessful (incl. court not competent)		Both successful		Claim withdrawn		Total	
	—	+	—	+	—	+	—	+	—	+
Bilateral GT	–	1	1	1	–	1	–	1	–	4
Bilateral SP	1	1	–	–	–	–	1	2	2	3
Ad hoc	8	–	5	–	–	–	2	–	15	–
Multilateral GT	–	2	–	13(8)	–	1	–	2	–	18
Multilateral SP	1	–	1(1)	7(2)	–	–	–	3	2	10
Total	10	4	6(1)	21(10)	–	2	3	8	19	35

With 2 exceptions the ad hoc provisions on judicial settlement were made in inter-state relations in which general bilateral and/or multilateral treaties that enabled a dispute to be submitted unilaterally to the International Court were already in force during the dispute or came into force afterwards. This points to a link between the willingness of states to decide, at least in consultation, to apply to the International Court and the general treaty pattern on the pacific settlement of their inter-state disputes which was already in existence or developing. This conclusion is confirmed by the fact that in cases in which the one party does not comply with a unilateral offer of judicial settlement by the other party no general bilateral or multilateral treaty was ever in force between those states that made judicial settlement possible by mutual consent or at the request of one of the parties.

That mutual agreement between states also remained the basic assumption behind the willingness of parties to submit their dispute to the International Court in inter-state relations containing a + class provision on judicial settlement is clear from the fact that in most cases the defendant state contested the Court's jurisdiction in the concrete case with the Court declaring that it was not competent in quite a few of the cases — 10 out of 21.

129 The figures in brackets indicate the number of cases in which the International Court declared that it was not competent.

In line with this is the fact that in cases submitted under a — class provision the Court's judgment was more often in favour of the claimant than in those submitted under a + class provision. Apart from the merits of the individual cases, this could after all be seen as an indication that the International Court is more inclined to find for the claimant if it was clear that *both* parties agreed to the submission of the case to it. In any event this situation is not surprising in the overall picture of pacific settlement of interstate disputes, in which negotiation still plays a predominant part.

Finally, another feature illustrating the significance of the element of negotiation is that only in half the cases in which the claimant was successful did the Court's judgment in fact involve the legal ending of the conflict. In the other cases the claimant took further action in the form of arbitration or conciliation.

3.2.1. Bilateral agreements

3.2.1.1. *General treaties*

The use of judicial settlement under bilateral general treaties can be illustrated by 4 cases, 2 from the period since 1945.

1. In the dispute between *Belgium and Bulgaria* on the Electricity Company of Sofia and Bulgaria, Belgium unilaterally submitted the case to the PCIJ on the grounds of the acceptance of the Optional Clause by both parties in 1921 (Bulgaria) and 1926 (Belgium) and under the bilateral general treaty of 23 June 1931 (—ICA +IIJ).

Bulgaria opposed the jurisdiction of the PCIJ, partly because the declaration on compulsory jurisdiction contained a reservation in respect of disputes arising from incidents previous thereto — in this case a concession contract dating from 1898 that had been transferred to a Belgian company in 1909 — and because the general treaty that did not contain such a reservation was no longer applicable. This was because it had expired on 4 February 1938, having been terminated by Bulgaria (in view of this same dispute). It was admittedly after Belgium submitted the dispute to the Court on 26 January, but it was before the condition laid down in the general treaty relating to exhaustion of local remedies had been fulfilled. After considering the differing contents of the declarations and the bilateral general treaty, the Court concluded by 9 votes to 5 that both were applicable at the same time and independently of each other and therefore had to be investigated. Only if both were invalid was the Court not competent.[130]

[130] *Survey I*, No. 157; PCIJ Series A/B, No. 77, p. 76.

The Court in the end maintained its competence on the basis of the declarations, but owing to the outbreak of the Second World War it did not pronounce on the merits.

2. When, in an arbitration procedure between Greece and the Société Commerciale de Belgique (Socobel), Greece had been ordered to pay damages for non-fulfilment and refused to pay, *Belgium* unilaterally submitted the case to the PCIJ under its general treaty with Greece of 25 June 1929 (+ICA IIJ). It had previously tried in vain to do so in consultation with *Greece*. The PCIJ thus had to consider the first case in which its compulsory jurisdiction was based solely on a general bilateral treaty, although both states had made the declaration on the compulsory jurisdiction of the PCIJ and had acceded to the General Act.[131]

Although Greece was not prepared to cooperate in Belgian efforts to conclude a 'compromis' as a basis for the Court's jurisdiction (illustrating the conviction of both states that negotiations were the basis of pacific settlement and compulsory jurisdiction was something special), it did not contest the competence of the Court. On the other hand, the process was more one of 'continuation of diplomatic discussions and negotiations carried on under the supervisory eye of the Court, than a true legal battle'.[132]

3. In 1948 *Belgium*, acting as in previous cases for the rights of a private company (the Barcelona Traction, Light and Power Company), submitted to the ICJ a dispute with *Spain* under the bilateral general treaty of 19 July 1927 (—ICA +IIJ). After withdrawing the case in 1961 and trying to reach a settlement by further negotiation, Belgium filed a new application before the Court on 7 August 1962. This time Spain contested the Court's competence, arguing among other things that the bilateral general treaty was no longer in force. This failed, for the Court declared itself competent against the will of Spain.[133] In this case too, however, it is difficult to indicate the significance of this as in its judgment of 5 February 1970 on the merits the Court found against Belgium by 15 votes to one, as with regard to Belgium 'no jus standi before the Court (had) been established'.[134]

[131] *Survey I*, No. 85; PCIJ Series A/B, No. 78.

[132] VERZIJL, *op. cit.*, p. 597. This did not affect the fact that Socobel's claim against the Greek State, although awarded, was not met. This led Socobel in 1950 to seek redress in the Belgian courts via recovery of Greek assets in Belgium. (Cf. SH. ROSENNE, *The Law and Practice of the International Court*, 1965, pp. 129-133.).

[133] *Post-War Treaties*, No. 85; I.C.J. Reports 1961 p. 9, 1964 p. 6 and 1970 p. 3; cf. *A.J.I.L.*, 1965, pp. 131-160.

[134] I.C.J. Reports 1970, pp. 3 et seq., paras. 101-103; cf. *A.J.I.L.*, 1970, pp. 653-693 and H.W. BRIGGS, "Barcelona Traction : The Jus Standi of Belgium", *A.J.I.L.*, 1971, pp. 327-345. It is not within the scope of this study to go into the merits of this and other judgments.

4. Finally, the granting of asylum by the Colombian Embassy in Lima to the Peruvian insurgent Victor Raül Haya de la Torre in 1949 led to 3 cases between *Peru and Colombia* being brought before the ICJ.

Although both countries had ratified in 1935 a bilateral Protocol on friendship and cooperation that can be classified as +IIJ, an ad hoc provision was needed — the 'Act of Lima' of 31 August 1949 — to submit the first 'Asylum case' to the ICJ. In this Act the parties agreed that now it was not possible to call upon the ICJ by mutual agreement, each party could approach the Court.[135]

In the Haya de la Torre case Colombia based its application to the Court on the bilateral Protocol of 1934, among others. The Court was unable to settle the dispute. It indeed laid down that the asylum should end but that Columbia was in no way obliged to do this by surrendering the refugee. The Court assumed that as good neighbours the parties should seek a practical and satisfactory solution.[136] In other words, the only remedy was direct negotiation.

In November 1953 Colombia approached the Inter-American Peace Committee for help in finding a solution. Peru refused the offer of good offices and maintained that unless the request was made by both parties the Committee was not competent to deal with the matter. The Committee nevertheless recommended the parties in January 1954 — over 2 ½ years after the ICJ's last pronouncement — to settle the dispute by direct negotiation in the American capital agreed on by them.[137]

The results of the 4 cases can be summed up as follows. In the first case the ICJ did not pronounce on the merits; in the third and fourth cases the defendant party did not see judgment go against it, and the second process had more of the character of negotiation between the parties under the watchful eye of the Court.

3.2.1.2. *Special provisions*

Five cases were submitted to the International Court under 3 special provisions in bilateral treaties. One of them can be classed as —J, although there was no clear agreement between the parties that the Court should consider the cases in question. This case involved Art. 23 of the *German-Polish* Convention concerning Upper Silesia of 15 May 1922, under which two cases were brought unilaterally before the PCIJ, viz. those concerning

[135] *Survey I*, No. 200, p. 1073; I.C.J. Reports 1950, pp. 266 and 395 and 1951, p. 71.

[136] I.C.J. Reports 1951, p. 81.

[137] *The Inter-American System*, pp. 88 and 89.

German interests in Upper Silesia and — arising therefrom — those of the nitrogen factory at Chorzow.[138] Although this Article did not explicitly lay down that either party could submit unilaterally, the Polish objections to the competence of the Court were not directed against that. When the Court upheld its jurisdiction in the first case — German interests in Upper Silesia — it pronounced, in accordance with the German request, on the significance of the Articles involved in the case, establishing that Poland had taken a number of expropriation measures in violation of the treaty. Within the framework thus created, both countries then tried in vain to reach agreement by negotiation, which led Germany to submit the matter to the Court again, but this time in respect of the Chorzow nitrogen factory. It invoked the general bilateral treaty which had by then been concluded with Poland at Locarno as the basis for the jurisdiction of the Court, but the Court did not act on this. In the face of Polish objections the Court nevertheless upheld its jurisdiction under Art. 23 of the German-Polish Convention concerning Upper Silesia. Again, the objections did not concern unilateral submission. The Court did underline the need for cooperation between parties.

> "It has been argued repeatedly in the course of the present proceedings that in case of doubt the Court should decline jurisdiction. It is true that the Court's jurisdiction is always a limited one, *existing only insofar States have accepted it.*" [139]

In its judgment on the merits the Court decided to constitute a commission of experts to establish the compensation payable by Poland to Germany for the nitrogen factory. In the end the Court did not have to revert to the case because both countries managed to settle it by mutual agreement.[140]

The third example is the Ambatielos claim by *Greece* against the *UK* mentioned earlier. This was brought under Art. 29 of the Treaty of Commerce and Navigation between the countries signed on 16 July 1926 (+A).

[138] The relevant judgments of the PCIJ are Series A, No. 6 (jurisdiction) and No. 7 (merits) on German interests in Upper Silesia; No. 9 (jurisdiction), No. 17 (merits) and No. 13 (interpretation of No. 7) on the Chorzow nitrogen factory (VERZIJL, *op. cit.*, part I, pp. 145-176). It should be noted that the Convention on Upper Silesia was (partly) due to conciliation in the context of the League of Nations.

[139] PCIJ Series A, No. 9, p. 32, author's italics. The Court is not demanding a formal acceptance of its jurisdiction, but it is prepared to infer the consent of parties thereto from certain behaviour. This is called 'forum prorogatum', Cf. JENKS, *op. cit.*, pp. 134 and 135; E.K. NANTWI, *The Enforcement of International Judicial Decisions and Arbitral Awards in Public International Law*, dissertation, 1966, pp. 50-58.

[140] VERZIJL, *op. cit.*, part I, p. 176. The fact that parties maintain their freedom to have the case settled by mutual agreement even during the procedure before the Court is in itself indicative of the extent of freedom states have to settle disputes in the manner they choose.

Although arbitration was desired, it is worth mentioning this example in the context of judicial settlement by the ICJ, which pronounced not as an arbitral tribunal — as provided for in the above Article — but as a court of justice.[141]

The last two cases involved *France and the Lebanon* in 1950 and 1960. They were brought before the ICJ by France under Art. 23 of an agreement with the Lebanon of 24 January 1948 which can be classified as +J.[142] France withdrew the case in both instances because agreement had been reached with the other party.

It can therefore be concluded that, insofar as the provisions can be classified as +J, the disputes concerned were finally either settled by agreement or the Court's judgment was only a stage in the pacific settlement of the dispute between the states in question.

In the other cases the Court's competence, after unilateral application by one party, was not contested by the other party on those very grounds. These cases too were finally settled by agreement. In other words, no problems arose which could arise from the implementation of a judgment delivered in a process carried on against the will of one of the parties.

3.2.1.3. *Ad hoc provisions*

Fifteen cases were submitted to the International Court under ad hoc provisions — 10 to the PCIJ and 5 to the ICJ — all except 2 of them involving European countries only or at least one European country. With 2 exceptions, including the Corfu case already discussed, general bilateral and/or multilateral treaties governed the relationship between the countries concerned, viz. in 11 cases the 1928 General Act and/or the declaration on the compulsory jurisdiction of the PCIJ (ICJ), and in the two inter-American cases inter-American treaties, which provided for unilateral submission of at least legal disputes to the International Court, in 7 cases when the dispute was already in progress. In 2 cases the special 'compromis' was the result of a recommendation of the Security Council (Corfu Channel) or of conciliation in the context of the OAS (arbitral award of the King of Spain).[143]

That a connection can be inferred from this between the existing or developing treaty pattern of states and their willingness to resort at least jointly to the International Court is confirmed by the fact that in eight disputes between the USA and Hungary, Czechoslovakia and the USSR

[141] I.C.J. Reports 1952, pp. 28 et seq. and 1953, pp. 10 et seq.

[142] I.C.J. Reports 1954, pp. 107 et seq. and 1960, pp. 186 et seq.

[143] Cf. pp. 148-150 and 154.

respectively and the UK and Argentina and Chile, the USA and the UK tried in vain to get the other side to accept the jurisdiction of the ICJ. No general bilateral of multilateral treaties had ever been in force between these states which provided for judicial settlement by mutual agreement or at the request of one of the parties.[144]

Although the negotiation element played an important part in starting the procedure in all these cases, the seven cases in which parties had already provided in their relationship for unilateral application to the PCIJ (ICJ) are particularly illustrative of the contracting freedom of states, even where the pacific settlement of disputes is concerned. In 4 of these cases the cause of the dispute was the interpretation and application of treaties and agreements dating from before the general bilateral and multilateral treaties, viz. the disputes between France and Yugoslavia (the Serbian Loans), Greece (concessions on lighthouse maintenance) and the UK (territorial ownership) respectively and between the Netherlands and Belgium (sovereignty over certain frontier areas). In the first 2 cases there had been a succession of states since the agreements were made. The 3 other cases originated in colonial situations (Oscar Chinn case) and in sensitive subjects such as the murder of a diplomat (Borchgrave case) and the granting of asylum (Haya de la Torre case). Although the last case but one was cleared after Belgium and Spain had reached agreement, it is worth mentioning because it is the only example of a dispute in which the Court's jurisdiction, although based on a special agreement between the parties, was subsequently contested by one of them (Spain).[145]

Because these cases were submitted to the International Court by means of a 'compromis' there was no claimant or defendant in the real sense. If the Court's judgments are analysed according to their effect for the party which can be regarded as taking the initiative on the 'compromis' — thus as 'claimant' — it proves that this party was successful on 8 occasions and unsuccessful on 5. In 2 cases parties reached agreement before the judgment.[146]

[144] Concerned here are the disputes on the treatment of USA air crews in Hungary and the USSR, an air incident with Czechoslovakia, Bulgaria and the USSR and the Antarctica cases (I.C.J. Reports 1954 pp. 99 et seq., 1956 pp. 6-17, 1958 pp. 158 et seq., 1959 pp.264 et seq. and 276 et seq., 1960, pp. 146 et seq.).

[145] VERZIJL, *op. cit.*, part I, p. 538, points out that although this case had been submitted on the basis of a 'compromis', the procedure developed in such a way that Belgium acted as claimant and Spain as defendant. This can perhaps be explained by the fact that at the time it was possible in the relationship between the states to submit disputes unilaterally to the PCIJ.

[146] *Agreement*: PCIJ Series A/B Nos. *51, Italy-Turkey (cf. Survey I No. 14); 72, Belgium-Spain (cf. PT No. 85); *Claimant successful*: PCIJ Series A/B Nos. *20, France-Yugoslavia (cf. PT No. 91); *21, France-Brazil; 23, Denmark/Germany/France/Czecho-

In the cases of the Serbian loans and the Baarle-Nassau and Baarle-Duc enclaves the Court's judgment also ended the dispute. In the case of the Brazilian loans difficulties arose regarding payment by Brazil in accordance with the judgment. In the 4 other cases the claimant had to take further action in the form of arbitration — on the basis of an ad hoc provision — or conciliation.[147]

3.2.2. Multilateral agreements

3.2.2.1. *General treaties*

Since the International Court sat for the first time in January 1922 18 cases have been brought before it by unilateral application by virtue of the acceptance of the Optional Clause in the party relationship concerned.[148] With one exception these involved European countries alone, or at least one European country. A breakdown by treaty pattern shows that in 11 cases the reciprocal acceptance of compulsory jurisdiction over legal disputes was the only basis for calling on the Court.[149] In 6 cases the states in question had acceded to the 1928 General Act, and in 2 cases a bilateral general treaty was also in force.[150] In 1 case — between Cambodia and Thailand — a bilateral general treaty between France and Siam was invoked, therefore raising the question of succession of states, though the Court did not pronounce on that point.[151] The considerable extent to which mutual agreement remained the starting point in these cases for the Court's determination of its jurisdiction is clear from the fact that in 11 cases the defen-

slovakia/UK and Sweden-Poland; *22, 24, 46, Switzerland-France (cf. PT No. 38); 71, *France-Greece*; I.C.J. Reports 1948 p. 15 and 1949 p. 4, UK-Albania; idem 1959, p. 209, *Belgium-Netherlands*; *idem 1960 p. 192, Honduras-Nicaragua; *Claimant unsuccessful*: PCIJ Series A(/B) Nos. *3 and 4, Greece-Bulgaria; *10, France-Turkey; 63, *UK-Belgium*; I.C.J. Reports 1950 p. 266, Peru-Colombia (cf. *Survey I* No. 200); *idem* 1953 p. 111, *France-UK.*

The party relationship at the time of the dispute between the states printed in italics was governed by mutual acceptance of the compulsory jurisdiction of the International Court and/or the General Act. Bilateral general treaties which were in force are indicated in brackets. In the cases marked * general bilateral and/or multilateral treaties later came into force.

[147] Cf. p. 149 and part 3.1.1.3.

[148] Cf. Annex III, p. 223.

[149] Cf. Annex III, p. 223, Nos. 1, 3, 6, 8-10. 12, 13 and 15-17.

[150] *Ibid.*, Nos. 2, 4, 5, 7, 11 and 14.

[151] Cf. note 49.

dant state objected to the Court's jurisdiction, in 8 cases successfully.[152]

The ICJ's judgment in the case between *France and Norway* on the Norwegian loans illustrates the need for mutual agreement between parties. Unlike the Norwegian declaration on the compulsory jurisdiction of the ICJ, the French declaration contained the reservation that it only applied in respect of disputes

"qui s'élèveraient au sujet de faits ou situations postérieurs à la ratification de la présente déclaration".

and did not apply to disputes on matters

"qui relèvent essentiellement de la compétence nationale telle qu'elle est entendue par le Gouvernement de la République française".[153]

The Norwegian declaration stated that it applied vis-à-vis parties which had given the same undertaking. On these grounds the ICJ acknowledged Norway's right to determine itself — as it had done — that the matter belonged to its domestic jurisdiction. The Court remarked that it found itself

"en présence d'une disposition que les deux Parties au différend considèrent comme exprimant *leur volonté commune quant à sa compétence*. La Cour ne se tient donc pas pour appelée à entrer dans un examen de cette réserve à la lumière de considérations *qui ne sont pas liées aux données du procès*. Sans préjuger la question, elle applique la réserve telle qu'elle est, et *telle que les Parties la reconnaissent*."[154]

Of the 8 cases in which the case proper was considered the claimant was wholly or partly successful in three.[155] In one of them — the dispute between Thailand and Cambodia — further action by the claimant proved necessary in the form of conciliation.[156]

[152] Cf. Annex III, p. 223. In the cases contained under Nos. 10 (Liechtenstein-Guatemala), 12 (Portugal-India) and 18 (Cambodia-Thailand) the Court declared itself competent. In the other cases its non-competence was based on :

a) non-exhaustion of local remedies : Annex III, Nos. 6 and 13;
b) date of dispute previous to acceptance of optional clause : *ibid.*, Nos. 5 and 9;
c) 'domestic jurisdiction' : *ibid.*, No. 11;
d) loss of validity of optional clause : *ibid.*, No. 15, after which the cases under Nos. 16 and 17 were withdrawn.

[153] I.C.J. Reports 1957, p. 21. In the declaration renewed in 1966 the last reservation was objectivised (*Yearbook* 1967-68 of the ICJ, p. 49).

[154] *Ibid.*, p. 27, author's italics.

[155] *Agreement* : Annex III, p. 223, Nos. 1 (Belgium-China) and 3 (Switzerland-Yugoslavia); *Claimant successful* : *ibid.*, Nos. 2 (Denmark-Norway), 8 (France-USA) and 18 (Cambodia-Thailand); *Claimant unsuccessful* : *ibid.*, Nos. 4 (Netherlands-Belgium), 7 (UK-Norway), 10 (Liechtenstein-Guatemala), 12 (Portugal-India) and 14 (Netherlands-Sweden).

[156] Cf. para 2.1.3. Sub 5.

3.2.2.2. *Special provisions*

The 9 special provisions - 7 in class +J and 2 in class —J - on the basis of which 12 cases in all were entrusted to the International Court belong to treaties connected with the ending of the First and Second World Wars, or with the former colonial status of certain countries.[157]

In ten cases, including one on the basis of a —J class provision, the competence of the Court was contested, in 3 cases successfully, viz. the Mavrommatis case between Greece and the UK as mandatee of what was then Palestine, the case of the Albanian gold between Italy and France, the UK and the USA, and the case of the Northern Cameroons between Cameroun and the UK.[158]

The case between *Italy* on the one hand and *France, the UK* and *the USA* on the other is a noteworthy example of the need for cooperation between parties, even in the event of judicial settlement. When, on 19 May 1953, Italy accepted the jurisdiction of the ICJ over disputes mentioned in the Washington Statement of 25 April 1951 (—J), it brought forward on the same day the case concerning the ownership of the gold removed from Rome by the Germans in 1943 — and then itself contested the competence of the Court, with success. France, the UK and the USA had agreed, under the Agreement on Reparation from Germany, on the Establishment of an Interallied Reparation Agency and on the Restitution of Monetary Gold of 14 January 1946 to have the question whether Albania was the owner of the gold of the Albanian national bank that had been removed from Rome answered by an arbitrator, and if he answered in the affirmative, to allow the UK to clear Albania's outstanding debt in respect of the Corfu Channel question, unless this was contested by either Albania or Italy. The arbitrator laid down that Albania was the owner. Albania did not contest the compensation scheme, but Italy did on the grounds of a previous claim on Albania. After its approach to the ICJ Italy claimed that the Court was not competent because the dispute really involved Albania — i.e. the question whether Albania had a debt towards Italy — while Italy was not involved. The Court shared this view, the result being that the UK did not receive compensation, as the condition thereof — that Albania and/or Italy should not contest the scheme — had not been fulfilled.

In the 7 cases in which the Court, against the objections of the defendant state, confirmed its jurisdiction after unilateral submission by the claimant,

[157] Cf. Annex II categories I column —J(2) and +J(2); VI column +J(4) and X column +J(1) and Annex III.

[158] PCIJ Series A, Nos. 2 with 5 and 11; I.C.J. Reports 1954, p. 19; idem 1963, p. 15.

the judgment went in favour of the defendant or the claimant (in 2 cases) withdrew the case for political reasons. In the 2 other instances in which jurisdiction was not contested the case was settled by agreement or the claimant was vindicated.[159]

In the dispute between *Germany and Poland* on the German minority schools in Upper Silesia, the PCIJ declared itself competent, despite Polish objections, arguing that the *consent* of the parties, if not clear from an explicit declaration, may be apparent from the attitude of the opposing party. It stated

"Il paraît difficile de nier que le fait de plaider le fond (as Poland had done - author), sans faire des réserves sur la compétence, ne doive être regardé, comme une manifestation non équivoque de la volonté de l'État d'obtenir une décision sur le fond de l'affaire".[160]

The Court's judgment vindicated Poland in theory but Germany in practice.[161]

Another illustration of the element of negotiation in pacific settlement is the case of the mandated territory of South-West Africa brought in 1960 against the mandatee *South Africa* by *Ethiopia and Liberia* under Art. 7 of the Mandate for German South-West Africa of 17 December 1920.

In its judgment on the merits on 18 July 1966 the Court noted, among other things, that

"In the international field, the existence of obligations that cannot in the last resort be enforced by any legal process, has always been the rule rather than the exception, — and this was even more the case in 1920 than today".[162]

The Court finally decided, although it had confirmed its jurisdiction in 1962 in spite of South African objections, to reject the Ethiopian and Liberian complaint after noting that the

"Applicants did not, in their individual capacity as States, possess any separate self-contained right which they could assert, independently of, or additionally to, the right of the League, in pursuit of its collective institutional activity, to require

[159] *Agreement* : I.C.J. Reports 1952 p. 176 (France-UAR); *Claimant successful* : PCIJ Series A No. 1 (France-Germany); *Claimant unsuccessful* : PCIJ Series A(/B) Nos. 47 with 49 (France/Italy/Japan/UK-Lithuania); 15 with 40 (Germany-Poland); 61 (Czechoslovakia-Hungary); 66 with 68 (Hungary-Yugoslavia); I.C.J. Reports 1962 p. 319 with 1966 p. 6 and 1971 p. 16 (Ethiopia/Liberia-South-Africa); *Withdrawn* ; PCIJ Series A(/B) Nos. 52 with 54 and 59 (Germany-Poland); 58 (Germany-Poland).

[160] PCIJ Series A, No. 15, p. 24.

[161] An advisory opinion of the PCIJ was (consequently) necessary to clarify the situation in 1931, after Germany had asked the Court accordingly.

[162] I.C.J. Reports 1966, p. 46.

the performance of the Mandate in discharge of the sacred trust" (and that they) "cannot be considered to have established any legal right or interest appertaining to them in the subject-matter of the present claims."[163]

This is in line with previous conduct — as far as the result for the claimant is concerned, not the reasoning. This conduct implies that the Court acts with the utmost caution in cases brought unilaterally against the will of the defendant.

Finally, the only case in which the defendant state did not dispute unilateral submission by the claimant and lost the case was also the first contentious case which the International Court had to deal with after it was founded half a century ago : the Wimbledon case laid before the PCIJ by *France*, supported by Italy, Japan and the UK, against *Germany* under Art. 386, para. 1 of the Peace Treaty of Versailles. Although this Article contains no provision on the duty of a state to appear before the Court after another state has gone to it (the provision is therefore classed as — J), Germany left the Court to decide whether it was competent.[164] The PCIJ had no difficulty in answering this in the affirmative, dealt with the case and ordered Germany to pay compensation.[165]

This account of use of judicial settlement under +J class special provisions can be completed by noting that, under the relevant provisions in the European Communities treaties, in all the cases submitted to the European Court, only once has a state (Belgium) instituted judicial proceedings against another state (France), but it was settled in good time.[166]

3.3. *Cooperation between parties as a basic assumption in the jurisprudence of the International Court*

The International Court's basic assumption in determining its jurisdiction is that its competence is based on voluntary acceptance by states. This all conforms to the general pattern of inter-state relations, in which the

[163] *Ibid.*, pp. 29 and 51. In an article on "The Revocation of the Mandate for South West Africa", *A.J.I.L.*, 1968, pp. 78-97, J. DUGARD notes that the Court announced that the 'political organs of the League had been the appropriate agencies for investigating a mandatory's administration of her 'sacred trust' under the mandates system, not the Court itself'.

[164] PCIJ Series A, No. 1, p. 20.

[165] The Reparation Commission, however, refused Germany permission to pay France the damages, France, as a member of the Commission, not having resisted this decision (ROSENNE, *op. cit.*, p. 119).

[166] L.J. BRINKHORST and H.G. SCHMERMERS, *Judicial Remedies in the European Communities; a Case Book*, 1969, p. 4.

sovereignty of states is crucial. In its judgment on the Free Zones of Upper Savoy and the District of Gex the PCIJ considered

"que *le règlement judiciaire* des conflits internationaux, en vue duquel la Cour est instituée, *n'est qu'un succédané au règlement direct et amiable* de ces conflits entre les Parties; que dès lors, il appartient à la Cour de faciliter, dans toute la mesure compatible avec son Statut, pareil règlement direct et amiable..."[167]

This pronouncement runs like a thread through the jurisprudence of the International Court. In the 50 years of its existence the Court has studiously avoided compromising the freedom of states to decide to approach it, even if they had made the declaration accepting its compulsory jurisdiction over legal disputes, if not in its decision on the preliminary objections to its jurisdiction by the defendant state in cases of unilateral submission, then in that on the merits.

Apart from its treatment of requests for interpretation of the UN Charter and resolutions of UN organs, the Court has carefully avoided states being 'judged' via the advisory procedure without being involved themselves. In its advisory opinion on the Status of Eastern Carelia, over which *Finland* and the *USSR* differed, both basing themselves on the Finno-Russian peace treaty of 14 October 1920, the PCIJ refused to issue the opinion requested by the League of Nations Council because the USSR declined to cooperate in the procedure :

"It is well established in international law that no State can, without its consent, be compelled to submit its disputes with other States either to mediation or arbitration, or to any other kind of pacific settlement".[168]

This view also led the PCIJ, in its advisory opinion on the interpretation of an arbitration clause in the Peace Treaties with Bulgaria, Hungary and Romania issued in 1950 at the request of the UN General Assembly, on the one hand to confirm the duty of states to cooperate in the agreed constitution of an arbitral tribunal by nominating their arbitrators — obvious in the light of the old adage 'pacta servanda sunt'. On the other hand it did not thereby extend the UN Secretary-General's power to nominate the third arbitrator at the request of one of the parties if they fail to agree

[167] PCIJ Series A, No. 22, p. 13, author's italics; E. HAMBRO, *The Case Law of the International Court*, 1952, part III 'The Peaceful Settlement of Disputes'; VERZIJL, *op. cit.*, part I, pp. 243- 250, 'The Task of the Permanent Court of International Justice'; L. GROSS, "The International Court of Justice : Consideration of Requirements for Enhancing its Rôle in the International Legal Order", *A.J.I.L.*, 1971, pp. 253-326, in particular pp. 265-266.

[168] PCIJ Series B, No. 5, p. 27.

thereon so as to cover the nomination of a party's arbitrator in the name of the state which fails to do so itself:

> "Le pouvoir du Secrétaire général de désigner le tiers membre *n'a d'autre source que la volonté des parties* telle qu'elle s'est exprimée dans la clause de règlement des différends. Par sa nature, même une telle clause est de droit strict et l'on ne peut en étendre les effets en dehors du cas expressément prévu ..."[169]

The advisory opinions on South-West Africa differ from the above examples in that they concern the interpretation of the Charter and resolutions of UN organs relating to the attitude of member states which draw their rights and duties at stake from an agreement which was not concluded with another state but with an international organisation — the League of Nations. In this difference we can see, apart from the merits of the case, an explanation of the fact that the advisory opinion issued by the ICJ on 21 June 1971 at the request of the Security Council in respect of 'legal consequences for States of the continued presence of South Africa in Namibia (South-West Africa) notwithstanding Security Council Resolution 276 (1970)' amounts to a condemnation of South Africa, although that country disputed the Court's competence on the matter, referring inter alia to the PCIJ advisory opinion on the Status of Eastern Carelia. Apart from the fact that at the time one of the states parties to the dispute was not a member of the League of Nations and had not appeared before the PCIJ, the Court considered this advisory opinion immaterial because the Security Council's request did not relate to a

> "legal dispute actually pending between two or more States. It is not the purpose of the request to obtain the assistance of the Court in the exercise of the Security Council's functions relating to the pacific settlement of a dispute pending before it between two or more States. The request is put forward by a United Nations organ with reference to its *own* decisions and it seeks legal advice from the Court on the consequences and implications of these decisions". (I.C.J. Reports 1971, p. 24 — author's italics).

It can be argued that South Africa itself even implicitly maintained that this was not a dispute between *states* by asserting that

> "the question relates to a dispute between South Africa and other *Members* of the United Nations ..." (I.C.J. Reports 1971, p. 22 — author's italics).

Nor can it be denied, however, that it was a dispute between a member state and the United Nations. The origin of the dispute, after all, was the very question whether the UN took over all rights and duties of the League

[169] Peace Treaties, advisory opinion 2nd phase, I.C.J. Reports 1950, p. 227.

of Nations and on that basis the UN organs could invoke certain powers against a member state which had concluded an agreement with the League of Nations. Paragraph 87 of the advisory opinion puts this clearly :

"The Government of France in its written statement and the Government of South Africa throughout the present proceedings have raised the objection that the General Assembly, in adopting resolution 2145 (XXI), acted *ultra vires.*" (I.C.J. Reports 1971, p. 45).

The UN Charter has no provision on the settlement of disputes on its interpretation and application. In its advisory opinion the Court refers clearly to this lacuna, and notes that, unless it is explicitly requested

"Undoubtedly, the Court does not possess powers of judicial review or appeal in respect of the decisions taken by the United Nations Organs concerned". (I.C.J. Reports 1971, p. 45).

Although it was not explicitly requested, the Court took into consideration the objections to the resolutions of the General Assembly and the Security Council in the conclusion :

"A binding determination made by a competent organ of the United Nations to the effect that a situation is illegal cannot remain without consequence. Once the Court is faced with such a situation, it would be failing in the discharge of its judicial functions if it did not declare that there is an obligation, especially upon Members of the United Nations, to bring that situation to an end". (I.C.J. Reports 1971, p. 54).

Unlike in the previous advisory opinions on the South-West Africa case and in the action brought in the Court by Ethiopia and Liberia against South Africa, the ICJ could in this case fall back on a clear pronouncement of the UN's 'legislative' body: the General Assembly's resolution of 27 October 1966, in which South Africa's mandate over South-West Africa was withdrawn, in combination with the Security Council resolution of 30 January 1970, stating

"that the continued presence of the South African authorities in Namibia is illegal and that consequently all acts taken by the Government of South Africa on behalf of or concerning Namibia after the termination of the mandate are illegal and invalid."

The treatment of this case by the various UN organs, including the Court, was from the outset considered by the UN member state in question, South Africa, not so much a legal as a political matter. In contesting the Court's competence to issue the advisory opinion, the South African Government argued that "even if the Court had competence to give the opinion requested, it should nevertheless, as a matter of judicial propriety, refuse to exercise its competence ... because of political pressure to which the Court, according to the Government of South Africa, has been or might be subjected". (I.C.J. Reports 1971, p. 23).

From the point of view of juridical organisation one can maintain, along with the Court, however, that the treatment of the South-West Africa question, even during the recent advisory procedure, constitutes no exception to the Court's view that no state can be forced against its will to submit disputes with other *states* to pacific settlement. The course of events indicates, however, that the UN, in order to be able to grow into a real legal community with adequate guarantees of communication between members themselves and with the community organs, even when a dispute arises, has an indispensable need of an administrative legal procedure for disputes between the international organisation and a member state.

The Court has indeed been willing to lay down no formal requirements for the consent of parties to its jurisdiction. The principle of 'forum prorogatum' has also been applied with caution, however. The decrees which could support such a principle have usually been issued in cases submitted under —J class bilateral special provisions or ad hoc provisions. In the only case in which the principle was raised in a case submitted on the grounds of the acceptance of the compulsory jurisdiction of the Court under Art. 36, para. 2 of the Statute — the Anglo-Iranian Oil Co. case — the Court saw no cause for 'extended jurisdiction'.

3.3.1. Competence on the basis of the acceptance of compulsory jurisdiction

If one of the parties contests the competence arising from the mutual acceptance of compulsory jurisdiction over legal disputes, the International Court has always attributed a central position to the freedom of states to contract, even in this field. The declarations on the acceptance of the compulsory jurisdiction of the International Court in inter-state relations form 'the consensual band, which is the basis of the Optional Clause'.[170] The least far-reaching declaration determines the competence of the Court, as was shown in the cases dealt with by the ICJ concerning the Norwegian loans and the Anglo-Iranian Oil Co.[171]

However, the freedom of states to contract, as reflected in declarations

[170] ICJ judgment on dispute between Portugal and India on the Right of Passage over Indian Territory, I.C.J. Reports 1957, pp. 145-146.

[171] Anglo-Iranian Oil, I.C.J. Reports 1952, p. 103.

made unilaterally but admittedly on a basis of reciprocity, is interpreted by the Court in such a way that the Court does not easily allow itself to be attributed the political function of a legislative organ. However widely the declarations on the acceptance of the compulsory jurisdiction of the Court may be formulated, the Court assumes that parties regard its function as formation of law in concrete, as to arrive with reference to a 'legal right or interest' of the claimant state 'in the subject-matter of its claim', at a judgment that merely binds parties.[172] In other words, the Court is not easily inclined to assume such wide powers that it can honour an *actio popularis* :

"But although a right of this kind may be known to certain municipal systems of law, it is not known to international law as it stands at present: nor is the Court able to regard it as imported by the 'general principles of law' referred to in Article 38, paragraph 1 (c) of its Statute." [173]

The fact that the Court (the majority opinion of the judges) acts with as much restraint as possible when a state resists its jurisdiction fits in with the system of inter-state relations in which the reference of a dispute to the Court is always a *choice* by the states that they regard judicial settlement as the most suitable means of settling a problem which arises between them.[174] In addition it is the states that, by the substance of their submission of a case to the Court, define the Court's capacity to decide and in a way also determine the content of that decision.

[172] ICJ judgment on South-West Africa, I.C.J. Reports 1966, p. 42.

[173] *Ibid.*, p. 47. In my opinion, the criticism of this judgment of the Court contained in the dissenting opinion of the American judge JESSUP (I.C.J. Reports 1966, pp. 379 et seq.) does not make a sufficient distinction between the question whether the 'actio popularis' is known in international law and if so to which organ it can be submitted. The following notes can be made on the examples given. The European Commission for Human Rights and the Governing Body of the ILO — to which any member state can make a complaint — Art. 24 of the European Human Rights Convention and Art. 26 of the ILO Constitution — are not judicial bodies. The consequence of the ICJ's advisory opinion on the Genocide Treaty is that that multilateral treaty is to be regarded more as a network of bilateral provisions. The Mavrommatis claim was dealt with partly on the basis of an ad hoc agreement and was not sustained. Nor do the two cases submitted under the German-Polish Minorities Treaty indicate in either their history or outcome that the International Court is prepared to declare an 'actio popularis' receivable. The Wimbledon case was submitted on the basis of a — class provision. The conclusion must be that no case is known in which the International Court declared in favour of an 'actio popularis' against a state.

[174] ROSENNE, *op. cit.*, pp. 90 et seq.

3.3.2. The request of parties as the basis of the judgment

In its advisory opinion of 23 July 1926 on the power of the ILO 'to regulate, incidentally, the personal work of the employer' the PCIJ clearly stated that it

"would exceed its own competency should it essay to consider controversial cases, actual or hypothetical, on which its opinion is *not* asked, and to intimate what, in its judgment, the decision upon them should be."[175]

In its judgment of 20 November 1950 on the right of asylum the ICJ repeated

"le principe que la Cour a le devoir de répondre aux demandes des parties telles qu'elles s'expriment dans leurs conclusions finales, mais aussi celui de s'abstenir de statuer sur des points non compris dans les dites demandes ainsi exprimées."[176]

In the case of the Norwegian loans the Court based its jurisdiction solely on the Norwegian and French declarations accepting compulsory jurisdiction and not on the 1928 General Act, because this was not contained in the French request :

"Dans ces conditions, la Cour ne saurait rechercher, pour établir sa compétence, un fondement autre que celui que le Gouvernement français a lui-même énoncé dans sa Requête, et sur lequel l'affaire a été plaidée devant la Cour par les deux Parties."[177]

In other words, the parties not only determine whether the Court is competent but also the scope which it has within that competence to arrive at a judgment.[178]

"Indeed, the extent to which the attitude of the parties determines the efficacy of the employment of the Court as an instrument for the settlement of international disputes is not sufficiently generally appreciated."[179]

The above-mentioned restraint of the Court if a state opposes its jurisdiction and the influence of parties outlined above not only on the competence itself but also on the court's freedom of movement within that competence means that the significance of the distinction between legal and

[175] PCIJ Series B, No. 13, p. 24, author's italics.

[176] I.C.J. Reports 1950, p. 402.

[177] I.C.J. Reports 1957, p. 25.

[178] ROSENNE, *op. cit.*, para. 31 'The Judicial Role of the Court' : 'This — the *non ultra petita* rule — gives the parties the last word in the efficacy of the Court to settle their dispute' (p. 97).

[179] ROSENNE, *op. cit.*, p. 98.

political disputes in general treaties, that in theory is disputable, is in practice very small, at least from the Court's point of view. In the dispute between Germany and Poland over the Rights of the Minorities in Upper Silesia the PCIJ stated :

"La juridiction de la Cour dépend de la volonté des Parties. La Cour est toujours compétente du moment où celles-ci acceptent sa juridiction, car il n'y a aucun différend que les États admis à ester devant la Cour ne puissent lui soumettre."[180]

In its advisory opinion on the conditions of admittance of new members to the UN, the ICJ declared that it could not

"attribuer un caractère politique à une demande, libellée en termes abstraits, qui, en lui déférant l'interprétation d'un texte conventionnel l'invite à remplir une fonction essentiellement judiciaire."[181]

The distinction between legal and political disputes is important not for the Court, but for the States, firstly in determining their choice of the method of pacific settlement and then in deciding on the implementation of the Court's judgment.

"The Court has demonstrated that the distinction between legal and political disputes, or between justiciable and non-justiciable disputes, which has given rise to so many theoretical difficulties in the history of international arbitration and in the development of an effective system for pacific settlement, has no validity as an abstract pıoposition in law, despite its ıeali mportance as a matter of practical politics".[182]

3.3.3. Implementation of judgments of international legal organs in disputes between States

In 24 of the 68 cases of arbitration in inter-state disputes between 1918 and 1965 the claimant was vindicated. They include only one example of arbitration under a +class provision, a case in which the 'losing' state accepted the judgment. Furthermore, 14 of the cases were based on ad hoc provisions.[183] The claimant's case was accepted in 14 of the 54 instances of judicial settlement. Four of these came about under a + class provision and 8 under an ad hoc provision. In only 7 of these 14 cases did the judgment end the dispute — two of these were based on a + class provision — it

[180] PCIJ Series A, No. 15, p. 22.

[181] I.C.J. Reports 1950, pp. 6-7.

[182] ROSENNE, *op. cit.*, p. 94.

[183] Cf. Table XIX and O. SCHACHTER, "The Enforcement of International Judicial and Arbitral Decisions", *A.J.I.L.*, 1960, pp. 1-24; NANTWI, *op. cit.*,; W.M. REISMAN, *The Enforcement of International Judgments*, Proc. ASIL, 1968, pp. 13-25.

being understood that in 2 cases compliance raised difficulties or further action was needed by the private legal person favoured by the judgment in his (its) own national courts.[184] This illustrates that a judgment of an arbitral or judicial body binding the parties need not end the conflict. The International Court is not involved in the implementation of its judgment. As soon as the Court or an arbitral tribunal has determined the legal relationship between the parties in its judgment the matter ends as far as it is concerned — except for any requests for clarification — and it is up to the parties to take care of compliance.[185] A party has the following means at its disposal apart from the sanctions it may impose itself : appeal to the cooperation of other states — as in the Albanian gold case — of international or regional organisations or of national judicial bodies. Only in the Haya de la Torre case did the International Court explicitly pronounce (or was it able to) that implementation was the responsibility of the parties themselves. The subject of this dispute was, among other things, the way in which the judgment of 20 November 1950 should be complied with. The Court adopted the following position :

"La forme interrogative qu'elles (i.e. the parties) ont donnée à leurs conclusions montre qu'elles entendent que la Cour opère un choix entre les diverses voies par lesquelles l'asile peut prendre fin. Mais ces voies sont conditionnées par des éléments de fait et par des possibilités que, dans une très large mesure, les Parties sont seules en situation d'apprécier. Un choix entre elles ne pourrait être fondé sur des considérations juridiques, mais seulement sur des considérations pratiques ou d'opportunité politique; il ne rentre pas dans la fonction judiciaire de la Cour d'effectuer ce choix." [186]

That the Court was not led in more cases by parties — except for requests for interpretation — to pronounce on the implementation of its judgments and arbitral awards is connected, it may be assumed, with the fact that the

[184] When SCHACHTER (*op. cit.*, p. 1) and NANTWI (*op. cit.*, p. 103) note that there are no cases of judgments of the PCIJ that states have refused to carry out they are right, but they do not tell the whole story, if it is borne in mind that most of the (not very numerous) cases in which the defendant state was found against were submitted under — class provisions and that in the two cases submitted under a + class provision — the Socobel and the Greenland judgments — a willingness was shown, either before or during the procedure, to bring the dispute to a pacific settlement.

[185] ROSENNE, *op. cit.*, pp. 115-162 and JENKS, pp. 663-726. REISMAN, *op. cit.*, p. 14, notes that : 'In developing a socially relevant and useful conception of judgment enforcement, then, we must emphasize the essential integrality of all decision functions. Judgments alone do not make law. The procedures by which policy is clarified, authorized and realized, in short, in which decisions are made, are executed in a number of different functions. *The court phase represents at best one of them*' — author's italics.

[186] I.C.J. Reports 1951, p. 79.

claimant party, relatively and absolutely, has had such little success in cases which it submitted to judicial settlement or arbitration under a + class provision.[187]

Whether and how a party whose claim is allowed wants to compel compliance with the decision concerned is *its* choice and responsibility. It is not for the Court to ensure that its decisions are implemented.[188] In principle this also applies to national legal systems. The great difference between inter-state and national communities is that in the former the executive, like the legislative function, is not yet sufficiently formed.

"The absence, and the inapplicability, of any solution to these problems based upon any element of international force makes for no alternative than to stress the role and the duties of the various States as the principal execution agents of international judgments."[189]

As the sovereignty of states is the cornerstone of the present organisational structure of inter-state society, this means that the cooperation of parties is also needed in the implementation of a decision by a third party, settling a dispute between states, and that this decision is a more or less decisive stage — depending on the relationship between the states concerned — in the negotiating process in the implementation of law. The Study Group on the Peaceful Settlement of International Disputes, set up in 1962 by the David Davies Memorial Institute of International Studies, therefore recognises that

"a greater measure of *common agreement* on the substance of many parts of international law would help to overcome the reluctance to have recourse to judicial procedures'.[190]

The fact that, as the group says,

"the process of judicial settlement itself has, as in the past, an important contribution to make to the clarification and development of international law"

does not contradict this, although the influence of this contribution, like that of writers on subjects in international public law, is weighed by the

[187] Usually, of course, the application of arbitration or judicial settlement will be the only or the last remedy for the claimant party. If it does not produce a result, there will be no option but to resign oneself to the situation. Assessment of the degree of compliance with international arbitral awards and court judgments should partly be seen in this light.

[188] ROSENNE, *op. cit.*, p. 117; JENKS, *op. cit.*, p. 667; SCHACHTER, *op. cit.*, pp. 6 et seq.

[189] ROSENNE, *op. cit.*, p. 162.

[190] Cf. the above-mentioned report para. 49 'Uncertainty of the Law and the Settlement of Legal Disputes', p. 37 (author's italics).

international community itself, the structure of which can still be described as anti-authoritarian.[191] The fact that this description has taken on a new gloss in many Western countries with an already stable balance between the legislature, the judiciary and the executive emphasises the continuing responsibility of states and individual citizens for the forming and also the maintenance of the international community.

[191] *Ibid.* One can also say : Not yet authoritarian, because there has not yet been any question of a supra-national authority.

SUMMARY

The Charter of the United Nations, adopted in 1945, states, with regard to the pacific settlement of international disputes, that the "parties to any dispute, the continuance of which is likely to endanger the maintenance of international peace and security, shall, first of all, seek a solution by negotiation, enquiry, mediation, conciliation, arbitration, judicial settlement, resort to regional agencies or arrangements, *or other peaceful means of their own choice*" (Article 33(1) - author's italics). The Charter does not indicate that any one of the methods for the pacific settlement of inter-state disputes mentioned in Article 33 should take precedence over any other.

In 1970, when — thanks to decolonisation — the membership of the UN had risen from about 50 in 1945 to more than 120, the Declaration on Principles of International Law concerning Friendly Relations and Co-operation among States in accordance with the Charter of the United Nations confirmed that situation.

That international agreement is the pivot on which everything hinges in the field of pacific settlement implies that the organisation of the community of states can be described as anti-authoritarian. In other words : the international community is based upon the sovereign equality of states — one of the seven Principles considered by the Special Committee — which means that the settlement of international relations rests on the negotiation and inter-action of states.

The phenomenon of law within itself is a form of communication between men like language, art and playing together. Legal security is a token of intelligibility and confidence, which are the basis of all forms of communication between men.

The legislator — both national and international — can be considered in a way as the personification of the practice of negotiation of legal subjects. A smooth interplay between the legislature, the judiciary and the executive is essential to the satisfactory functioning of society. In national legal systems the judge can normally operate within the legal framework which the state is building up in such a way that all kinds of motives can play their part. The international judge does not always have a truly international legislative body as his counterpart taking care of the balancing of interests in the abstract. The fact that states which conclude general treaties usually draw a distinction between legal and political disputes and limit the jurisdiction of the International Court to the former kind emphasises that the international community does not always feel that public international law is an adequate framework for the Court in resolving a dispute. The significance of the distinction is more political than juridical. States which limit judicial settlement to legal disputes imply that they are not ready and willing to submit all disputes to judicial settlement. This situation requires that the role of the judge be represented as clearly as possible.

Judicial settlement can be considered as a form of institutionalisation of negotiation between the parties to a dispute regarding the juridical consequences of a certain pattern of facts. However the judge has his own responsibility for the interpretation and application of legal rules in a concrete dispute between legal subjects. The difference between the functions of the legislative body and the judiciary is that the legislator binds all legal subjects while the judge only binds the parties to the dispute and their assigns in a specific relation. In no way are the parties at the mercy of the judge as a mere "bouche de la loi". By their questioning and argumentation they can also determine the words which that "bouche" will be able to pronounce.

The criterion for the stage of development — or humanity — which a social order has reached is the extent to which people and their institutions are ready and willing to communicate, even when disputes are arising, and to outlaw the use of uncontrolled force, which reduces the other party to a mere object, as a means for the settlement of a dispute. However this communication does not only depend on the application of judicial settlement, which indeed can be seen as *one* of the methods by which the community members can settle their disputes peacefully.

The 7 methods for the pacific settlement of inter-state disputes have no precise content. They do not perform different specific functions but are directed to the same purpose : to enable the pacific settlement of disputes by encouraging and maintaining communication between parties. They are to be considered as alternatives to direct negotiations between the parties themselves — good offices, mediation, conciliation or inquiry — or attempts to institutionalise the willingness of states to negotiate a settlement when a dispute arises : arbitration and judicial settlement.

In practice states conclude treaties whose sole or main subject is the pacific settlement of disputes — referred to in the analysis as general treaties — or they insert provisions for pacific settlement into treaties covering specific sectors of international cooperation like commerce, transport, navigation, mutual security or social and humanitarian interest, with regard to the settlement of disputes arising out of the application or interpretation of those treaties, referred to in the analysis as special provisions.

Most general treaties and special provisions aim at filling the gap in the pacific settlement of inter-state disputes which the failure of direct diplomatic negotiations would cause. The aim is to ensure that the dispute is removed as far as possible from the area of high political feelings, which prevents a more rational consideration of the problem.

Altogether 301 general treaties were classified according to whether they include conciliation, arbitration or judicial settlement for all disputes, legal disputes or political disputes, and whether the application of those methods depends (—), or not (+) on the cooperation of all parties to the dispute or the parties took special measures to obtain this cooperation (:⁚:). The same was done with 258 special provisions, without, however, the subdivision into the different categories of disputes, because the special provisions only have regard to the settlement of disputes concerning the application or interpretation of those treaties (i.e. legal disputes).

The classification of the general treaties shows that conciliation is mainly provided for in combination with other methods for the pacific settlement of inter-state disputes, either as a prelude to one of these methods, or in a more independent role for the category of all disputes or political disputes in treaties which limit arbitration or judicial settlement to legal disputes. The latter type of general treaty more than the former one underlines the significance of conciliation in the present-day international community as a possible way out of a situation in which the legislative function does not operate at all, or if so only inadequately.

The purpose of conciliation is to reach a settlement of a concrete dispute. Unlike diplomatic negotiations, conciliation in the international community is akin to the function of the judicature, though its very existence can be considered to be due to the inadequate operation of the legislative function. The comparatively low number of general treaties including conciliation only confirms that conclusion, for most of those treaties — 15 out of 22 — arrange the conciliation procedure in a similar way to that of arbitration and judicial settlement. The remaining 7 treaties, to all of which the USSR is party, arrange the conciliation procedure in a similar way to that of direct negotiations on a non-diplomatic level. This kind of conciliation may be called administrative conciliation.

Unlike the general treaties the special provisions arrange the conciliation procedure in a similar way to that of direct negotiation at the technical administrative level. This situation therefore does not correspond to the Convention on the Law of Treaties, intended as a framework for treaties. A comparatively small number of general treaties stipulate that, when special provisions only include a conciliation procedure and according to the general treaty the dispute could be settled by arbitration or judicial settlement, the latter methods apply, when the former is unsuccessful.

The attitude of Soviet states regarding the application of arbitration or judicial settlement at the request of one of the parties proceeds from their general point of view that in each particular case the agreement of all parties to the dispute is essential for the submission of that dispute to the International Court of Justice.

If not explicitly excluded, states may insert reservations when they ratify or accede to multilateral treaties, even with regard to the pacific settlement of disputes. These reservations only apply to other states which have accepted them. Multilateral or regional general treaties and special provisions thus embody a system of bilateral international relations.

The application of methods for the pacific settlement of international disputes confirms the conclusion drawn from the analysis of general treaties and special provisions : when states are prepared to settle a dispute peacefully, they prefer arbitration or judicial settlement to conciliation. The subject of the disputes in which conciliation, arbitration or judicial settlement were applied, usually belongs indeed to the category of legal disputes. The most important exception is formed by conciliation within the framework of multilateral or regional arrangements.

When one takes into consideration the treaty pattern of the disputing states with regard to the pacific settlement of disputes, the conclusion to be drawn from the practice of the application of the methods for the pacific settlement of international disputes, especially conciliation under bilateral arrangements, is that, apart from its application under multilateral arrangements, conciliation has usually been no more than a mere alternative to arbitration or judicial settlement, also provided for between the states in question. This conclusion establishes that the emphasis on the application of conciliation under bilateral arrangements, as laid by the report on "La conciliation internationale", included in the "Annuaire de l'Institut de Droit International", of 1959 and 1961 overlooks the treaty pattern of states regarding the pacific settlement of disputes. For in view of the aim of the report—to indicate ways for the promotion of the peaceful settlement of inter-state disputes in the very situations in which no provision has been made for arbitration or judicial settlement — it would have been more natural to concentrate the attention as well, if not exclusively, on conciliation under multilateral or regional arrangements.

There is a clear connection between the cooperation of states in the application of the methods for peaceful settlement and the results of that application for the claimant. This is self-evident with regard to conciliation. In case of arbitration it is clear that most applications were made under provisions of the — class and that in a number of disputes judgment was made in favour of the claimant. With regard to judicial settlement one has to conclude that in a number of cases the Court has found against the claimant, either as a consequence of its decision on the preliminary objections to its jurisdiction, or not.

In cases submitted under a provision of the — class the Court gave judgment for the claimant in a greater number of cases than in those submitted under provisions of the + class.

Apart from the merits of each case one might consider this situation as an indication that the International Court is rather more inclined to give judgment for the claimant when the acceptance of *both* parties of its competence in a concrete dispute is clearly established. In any case this situation is not surprising within the context of the pacific settlement of international disputes, in which negotiation still plays a predominant part.

The importance of the element of negotiation in the pacific settlement of disputes, even in the case of arbitration, appears from the fact that most applications were made under ad hoc provisions (39) and that also the remaining number (29), except for 6, were made under bilateral general treaties or bilateral and multilateral special provisions of the — class. The application of judicial settlement underlines even further the significance of agreement between states as the basis of their willingness to submit a dispute to the International Court, by virtue of the fact that in international relations where a case was submitted to the Court under a provision of the + class, the defendant state usually — in 21 out of 35 cases — challenged the competence of the Court, and in a comparatively large number of cases — — 10 out of 21 — did so successfully. Only in 7 cases was the Court's jurisdiction not challenged. In 8 cases submitted under a + class provision the claim was waived for political reasons or because the dispute was settled by mutual agreement before the judgment (illustrative in itself of the freedom of states with regard to peaceful settlement).

The basic criterion of the International Court in deciding upon its jurisdiction is that its competence depends on voluntary acceptance by states. The Court has carefully avoided adjudication upon legal disputes between *states* without their consent under cover of the advisory procedure provided for in Article 92 of its Statute. This is in conformity with the present-day pattern of international relations, in which the sovereignty of states is still the foundation of the international community.

As soon as an arbitration tribunal or the International Court has given its judgment, it has finished with the case, apart from a request for interpretation. It is up to the parties to ensure compliance with the Court's decision. In doing so, the parties, apart from their own sanctions, may appeal for the cooperation of international organisations or national judicial bodies. Regarding the sovereignty of states as the foundation of the present structure of the community of states, the cooperation of the states parties to the dispute is essential for the execution of a judgment. The judgment in other words is, depending on the relationship between the states in question, a more or less decisive factor in the negotiating process which aims at the pacific settlement of the dispute.

BIBLIOGRAPHY

BOOKS AND ARTICLES

ASBECK, F.M. VAN, "Une Commission d'Experts", in *Symbolae Verzijl*, pp. 9-21.

— "Nieuwe proeven in de beslechting van statengeschillen", *N.T.I.R.*, 1964, pp. 109-128.

— "La procédure suivie par la Commission permanente de la conciliation franco-suisse", *N.T.I.R.*, 1956, pp. 209-219.

— "Quelques aspects du contrôle international non-judiciaire de l'application par les gouvernements de conventions internationales", in *Varia Juris Gentium*, pp. 27-41.

— "La tâche et l'action d'une commission de conciliation", *N.T.I.R.*, 1956, pp. 1-9.

BASTID, S., "La Commission de conciliation franco-siamoise", in *La Technique et les Principes du Droit Public, Études en l'honneur de George Scelle*, Paris 1950, pp. 1-20.

— *Droit des Gens, le droit des crises internationales*, Paris 1958.

— "Une nouvelle commission de conciliation?" In *Mélanges Rolin*, pp. 1-12.

BLIX, H., "The Principle of Peaceful Settlement of Disputes", in *The Legal Principles governing Friendly Relations and Co-operation among States*, Leyden 1966, pp. 45-68.

BOLLA, P., "Quelques considéiations sur les Commissions de Conciliation prévues par l'article 83 du Traité de Paix avec l'Italie", in *Symbolae Verzijl*, p. 67-88.

BOS, M., "The Franco-Italian Conciliation Commission", *Acta scandinavica juris gentium 1952*, vol. 22, pp. 133-159.

BOUTROS-GHALI, B., "The Addis Ababa Charter", *International Conciliation 1964*, No. 546.

BOWETT, D.W., "The United Nations and Peaceful Settlement", in *Report of a Study Group on the Peaceful Settlement of International Disputes*, London 1966, Annexe III, p. 161-190.

BOYD, A., *United Nations, Piety, Myth and Truth*, Harmondsworth 1964.

BRINKHORST, L.J. and H.G. SCHERMERS, *Judicial Remedies in the European Communities, a Case Book*, Deventer 1969.

BÜRGERTHAL, Th., "Proceedings against Greece under the European Convention of Human Rights", *A.J.I.L.*, 1968, pp. 441-480.

BYSTRICKÝ, R., "On the Principle of Obligatory Co-operation of States", in *The*

Legal Principles governing Friendly Relations and Co-operation among States, Leyden 1966, pp. 99-114.

CAVARÉ, L., "L'arrêt de la C.I.J. du 18 novembre 1960 et les moyens d'assurer l'exécution des sentences arbitrales", in *Mélanges Rolin*, pp. 39-54.

CLARK, G. and L.B. SOHN, *World peace through World Law*, Cambridge (Mass.) 1962.

COLIJN, H.A., *La Décision de la Société des Nations concernant les Iles d'Aland*, 1923.

"La Conciliation internationale", in *Annuaire de l'Institut de Droit International* 1959, pp. 5-130 and 1961, pp. 193-271.

COT, J.-P., *La Conciliation Internationale*, Paris 1968.

CUKWURAH, A.O., *The Settlement of Boundary Disputes in International Law*, Manchester 1968.

DALTON, R.E., see KEARNEY, R.D.

DEGAN, V.D., *L'Équité et le Droit International*, The Hague 1970.

DELBEZ, L., "L'Evolution des idées en matière de règlement pacifique des conflits", *R.G.D.I.P.*, 1951, pp. 5-22.

EFREMOFF, J., "Organe Centrale de Conciliation", *Conciliation Internationale*, 1933, No. 1-2, pp. 71-204.

— "Organisation de la conciliation comme moyen de prévenir les guerres", *R.d.C.*, 1937, Part I, pp. 99-223.

ELIAS, T.O., "The Charter of the Organization of African Unity", *A.J.I.L.*, 1965, pp. 243-267.

— "The Commission of Mediation, Conciliation and Arbitration of the Organization of African Unity", *B.Y.I.L.*, 1964, pp. 336-354.

FARNSWORTH, E.A., *An Introduction to the Legal System of the United States*, New York 1963.

FENWICK, Ch. G., "The Dominican Republic : Intervention or Collective Self-Defense", *A.J.I.L.*, 1966, pp. 64-67.

— "International Law : The Old and the New", *A.J.I.L.*, 1966, pp. 475-483.

— "The Organization of American States : the transition from an unwritten to a written constitution", *A.J.I.L.*, 1965, pp. 315-320.

FRANÇOIS, J.P.A., "L'Avenir de la Cour Internationale de Justice ", in *Volkenrechtelijke Opstellen Gesina van der Molen*, pp. 73-76.

— "Le développement futur de la Cour permanente d'Arbitrage", *N.T.I.R.*, 1962, pp. 264-272.

— *Grondlijnen van het volkenrecht*, 3rd. ed., Zwolle 1967.

— "Le Palais de la Paix en 1956", *N.T.I.R.*, 1957, pp. 69-74.

FRIEDRICH, C.J., *Die Philosophie des Rechts in historischer Perspektive*, Berlin 1955.

GLASTRA VAN LOON, J.F., *Norm en handeling, bijdrage tot een kentheoretische fundering der sociale wetenschappen*, Haarlem 1957.

— *Recht en menselijke natuur*, intreerede Leyden, Haarlem 1959.

— See also *Norms and Actions*.

GOODRICH, L.M., *The United Nations*, London 1960.

GOODRICH, L.M. and A.P. SIMONS, *The United Nations and the Maintenance of International Peace and Security*, Washington 1955.
GROS, A., "Peaceful Settlement of International Disputes - Mediation and Conciliation", in *International Law in a Changing World*, New York 1963, pp. 44-53.
— "Remarques sur la conciliation internationale", in *L'Evolution du Droit Public, études offertes à Achille Mestre*, Paris 1956, pp. 279-283.
GROSS, L., "The International Court of Justice : Consideration of Requirements for Enhancing its Rôle in the International Legal Order", *A.J.I.L.*, 1971, pp. 253-326.
Guide to ICC Arbitration, a Study by International Headquarters of the International Chamber of Commerce, Paris 1963.

HABICHT, M., *Post-War Treaties for the Pacific Settlement of International Disputes, a Compilation and Analysis of Treaties of Investigation, Conciliation, Arbitration, and Compulsory Adjudication, concluded during the first Decade following the World War*, Cambridge 1931.
— *The Power of the International Judge to give a Decision « Ex Aequo et Bono »*, London 1935.
HAERSOLTE, R.A.V. VAN, *Een nieuw rechtstheoretisch klimaat, inleiding Ver. Wijsb. des Rechts*, Zwolle 1970.
HAMBRO, E., *The Case Law of the International Court*, Leyden, 1952.
HAMZEH, F.S., *International Conciliation with special reference to the work of the United Nations Conciliation Commission for Palestine*, diss. Amsterdam, The Hague 1963.
HART, H.L.A., *The concept of Law*, Oxford 1961.
HEIDE J. TER, *Rechtsvinding, inleiding Ver. Wijsb. des Rechts*, Zwolle 1965.
— *Vrijheid, over de zin van de straf.* The Hague, 1965, (with Summary in English).
HERMAN, G., *De adviesprocedure van artikel 96 van het Handvest der Verenigde Naties in het bijzonder bezien als geschillenprocedure*, diss. Amsterdam., The Hague 1956, (with Summary in English).
HETTE, J.-G.P., *L'évolution de la conciliation internationale*, Paris 1934.
HOEVEN, J. VAN DER, *De plaats van de grondwet in het constitutionele recht*, Zwolle 1958, (with Summary in English).
HOUBEN, P.-H., "Principles of International Law concerning Friendly Relations and Co-operation among States", *A.J.I.L.*, 1967, pp. 703-736.
HOIJER, O., *La solution pacifique des litiges internationaux avant et depuis la Société des Nations*, Paris 1925.
HUDSON, M.O., *The Permanent Court of International Justice, 1920-1942*, New York 1943.

IKLÉ, F.CH., *How Nations negotiate*, New York 1967.
The Inter-American System, its Development and Strengthening, New York 1966.
International Law, a textbook for use in Law Schools, publ. Academy of Sciences of the U.S.S.R. Institute of State and Law, Moscow ± 1960.

JACKSON, J.H., *GATT as an Instrument for the Settlement of Trade Disputes*, Proc. ASIL 1967, pp. 144-155.
JENKS, C.W., *The Prospects of International Adjudication*, London 1964.

JULLY, L., "Arbitration and judicial settlement recent trends", *A.J.I.L.*, 1954, pp. 380-407.

KAHNG, T.J., *Law, Politics and the Security Council, an Inquiry into the Handling of Legal Questions involved in International Disputes and Situations*, The Hague 1964.

KEARNEY, R.D. and R.E. DALTON, "The Treaty on Treaties", *A.J.I.L.*, 1970, pp. 495-561.

KELSEN, H., *The Law of the United Nations, a Critical Analysis of Its Fundamental Problems*, London 1951.

LADOR-LEDERER, J.J., *International Non-Governmental Organizations and Economic Entities, a Study in Autonomous Organization and Ius Gentium*, Leyden 1963.

LALL, A., *Modern International Negotiation, principles and practice*, New York 1966.

LANGEMEIJER, G.E., *Inleiding tot de studie van de wijsbegeerte des rechts*, 2nd. ed. (revised), Zwolle 1970.

LANGENHOVE, F. VAN, *Le rôle proéminent du Secrétaire Général dans l'opération des Nations Unies au Congo*, Brussels 1964.

LAUTERPACHT, H., "Some Observations on the Prohibition of 'Non Liquet' and the Completeness of the Law", in *Symbolae Verzijl*, pp. 196-221.

LEE, L.T., *China and International Agreements, a study of compliance*, Leyden 1969.

— "The International Law Commission re-examined", *A.J.I.L.*, 1965, pp. 545-569.

The Legal Principles governing Friendly Relations and Co-operation among States in the spirit of the United Nations Charter, lectures, publ. WFUNA, Leyden 1966.

LERCHE Jr., CH.O., *Development of Rules Relating to Peacekeeping by the Organization of American States*, Proc. ASIL 1965, pp. 60-66.

LILLICH, R.B., "The Gut Dam Claims Agreement with Canada", *A.J.I.L.*,1965, pp. 892-898.

— "International Claims : Their Settlement by Lump Sum Agreements", in *Liber Amicorum Martin Domke*, pp. 143-156.

MAIER, G., "The Boundary Dispute between Ecuador and Peru", *A.J.I.L.*, 1969, pp. 28-46.

MCMAHON, J.F., "Settlement of Disputes in Special Fields", in *Report of a Study Group on the Peaceful Settlement of International Disputes*, publ. David Davies Memorial Institute of International Studies, London 1966, Annexe IV, pp. 193-267.

MCNAIR, A., "The General Principles of Law recognized by Civilized Nations", *B.Y.I.L.*, 1957, pp. 1-20.

MCNEMAR, D.W., *The Post-Independence War in the Congo*, Proc. ASIL 1967, pp. 13-18.

MCWHINNEY, E., "The « New » Countries and the « New » International Law : The United Nations' Special Conference on Friendly Relations and Co-operation Among States", *A.J.I.L.*, 1966, pp. 1-33.

METZGER, S.D., "The Settlement of International Disputes by Non-Judicial Methods", *A.J.I.L.*, 1954, pp. 408-421 .

MEUWISSEN, D.H.M., *De Europese Conventie en het Nederlandse Recht*, diss. Amsterdam, Leyden 1968, (with Summary in French).

MOLEN, G.H.J., VAN DER, "The Present Crises in the Law of Nations", in *Symbolae Verzijl*, pp. 238-255.

MOSLER, H., "Die Erweiterung des Kreises der Völkerrechtssubjekte, *Z.f.a.ö.R.V.*, 1962, pp. 1-48.

NANTWI, E.K., *The Enforcement of International Judicial Decisions and Arbitral Awards in Public International Law*, diss. Utrecht, Leyden 1966.

Norms and actions, National Reports on Sociology of Law, ed. by R. Trewes and J.F. Glastra van Loon, The Hague 1968.

OPPENHEIM, L., *International Law*, vol. II, 7th ed., ed. by H. LAUTERPACHT, London 1952.

PANHUYS, H.F. VAN, "Regional or General International Law? A misleading dilemma", *N.T.I.R.*, 1961, pp. 146-165.

PEASLEE, A.J., *International Governmental Organizations, constitutional Documents*, rev. 2nd. ed., 2 parts, The Hague 1961.

PINK, G.P., *The Conference of Ambassadors (Paris 1920-1931)*. The Hague 1942.

POPPER, D.H., *Lessons of United Nations Peacekeeping in Cyprus*, Proc. ASIL 1970, pp. 1-9.

POTTER, P.B., *Article XIX of the Covenant of the League of Nations, a Study in the problem of International Government*, The Hague 1941.

RE, E.D., "The Presettlement Adjudication of International Claims", in *Liber Amicorum Martin Domke*, pp. 214-225.

REISMAN, W.M., *The Enforcement of International Judgments*, Proc. ASIL 1968, pp. 13-25.

Report of a Study Group on the Peaceful Settlement of International Disputes, publ. David Davies Memorial Institute of International Studies, London, 1966.

ROETHOF, H.J., *De norm in het volkenrecht*, The Hague 1962.

— *De universaliteit van het volkenrecht, inleiding Ver. Wijsb. des Rechts*, Zwolle 1963.

ROLIN, H., "L'arbitrage obligatoire : une panacée illusoire", in *Varia Juris Gentium*, pp. 254-262.

— "Une conciliation belgo-danoise", *R.G.D.I.P.*, 1953, pp. 353-371.

RÖLING, B.V.A., *Berust het huidige volkenrecht nog op universele grondslagen? Inleiding Ver. Wijsb. des Rechts*, Zwolle 1963.

— *International Law in an Expanded World*, Amsterdam 1960.

ROSENNE, SH., *The Law and Practice of the International Court*, 2 parts, Leyden 1965.

RUSSELL, R.B., *Development by the United Nations of Rules Relating to Peace-keeping*, Proc. ASIL, 1965 pp. 53-60.

SCHACHTER, O., "Conciliation Procedures in the United Nations Conference on Trade and Development", in *Liber Amicorum Martin Domke*, pp. 268-274.

— "The Enforcement of International Judicial and Arbitral Decisions", *A.J.I.L.*, 1960, pp. 1-24.

SCHERMERS, H.G., *Het Europese Verdrag tot bescherming van de rechten van de mens en de fundamentele vrijheden*, Zwolle 1964.

— See also BRINKHORST, L.J.,

SCHÜCKING, W., *Das völkerrechtliche Institut der Vermittlung*, The Hague 1923.

SCHURMANN, C.W.A., *A Center For International Fact-Finding : A Review and a Proposal*, New York 1963.

SCHWARZENBERGER, G., "The Arbitration Pattern and the Protection of Property Abroad", in *Liber Amicorum Martin Domke*, pp. 313-321.

SCHWEBEL, S.M. and J. GILLIS WETTER, "Arbitration and the Exhaustion of Local Remedies", *A.J.I.L.*, 1966, pp. 484-501.

SCOTT, J. BROWN, "La Conférence panaméricaine et le conflit de la Bolivie et du Paraguay, 1929" in MAURTUA, V.M., J. BROWN SCOTT and J. EFREMOFF, *Nouvelles tendances de la Conciliation Internationale*, Paris 1933.

SEIDL-HOHENVELDERN, I., "Arbitration by Organs of International Organizations", in *Liber Amicorum Martin Domke*, pp. 322-337.

— "General Principles of Law as applied by the Conciliation Commissions established under the Peace Treaty with Italy", *A.J.I.L.*, 1959, pp. 853-872.

SEYERSTED, F., "Settlement of Internal Disputes of Intergovernmental Organizations by Internal or External Courts", *Z.f.a.ö.R.V.*, 1964, pp. 1-121.

SIMONS, A.P., see GOODRICH, L.M.

SIOTIS, J., *Essai sur le Secrétariat International*, Genève 1963.

SOHN, L.B., see CLARK, G.

STUYT, A.M., *Survey of International Arbitrations 1794-1970*, The Hague 1972.

SUCHARITKUL, S., "Good Offices as a Peaceful Means of Settling Regional Differences", in *Liber Amicorum Martin Domke*, pp. 338-347.

SYATAUW, J.J.G., *Decisions of the International Court of Justice, a digest*, Leyden 1962.

TAMMES, A.J.P., *Hoofdstukken van Internationale Organisatie*, The Hague 1951.

— *Internationaal Publiekrecht*, Haarlem 1966.

— *Het universele rechtstelsel beschreven aan de hand van een classificatie*, Meded. Kon. Ned. Akademie van Wetensch., Amsterdam 1969.

Technics of Mediation and Conciliation, International Social Science Bulletin 1958, vol X, No. 4, pp. 507-628.

TRUYOL, A., "Doctrines contemporaines du Droit des Gens", *R.G.D.I.P.*, 1950, pp. 369-341 and 1951, pp. 22-40 and 199-236.

VALLAT, F., "The Peaceful Settlement of Disputes", in *Cambridge Essays in International Law, Essays in honour of Lord McNair*, London 1965, pp. 155-177.

VERZIJL, J.H.W., "International Court of Justice, Case concerning the Temple of Preah Vihear (Cambodia v. Thailand)", *N.T.I.R.*, 1962, pp. 229-263.

— The Jurisprudence of the World Court, a case by case commentary. 2 parts, Leyden 1965-66.

VISSCHER, CH. DE, *Théories et réalités en droit international public*, 3me éd. rev. et augm., Paris 1960.

VULCAN, C., *La conciliation dans le droit international actuel*, Paris 1932.

WEHBERG, H., "La convention européenne pour le règlement pacifique des différends", in *Varia Juris Gentium*, pp. 391-399.
— "Die Vergleichskommissionen im modernen Völkerrecht", *Z.f.a.ö.R.V.*, 1958, pp. 551-593.
WETTER, J. GILLIS, "The Rann of Kutch Arbitration", *A.J.I.L.*, 1971, pp. 346-357.
— See also SCHWEBEL, S.M.
WIONCZEK, M.G., *Economic Cooperation in Latin America, Africa and Asia, A Handbook of Documents*, Cambridge 1969.
WRIGHT, Q., *The Middle Eastern Crisis*, Proc. ASIL 1970, pp. 71-77.

De Zaak Zuid-West Afrika, het vonnis van het Internationaal Gerechtshof critisch bezien, Leyden 1967, with Summary in English.

PRINCIPAL DOCUMENTS (INCL. REPORTS AND YEARBOOKS)

Annuaire de l'Institut de Droit International, 1959 and 1961.
Atti relativi alla vertenza per l'applicazione ai cittadini svizzeri dell'imposta straordinaria italiana sul patrimonio; (report of the) Commissione Permanente di Conciliazione fra la Repubblica Italiana e la Confederazione Svizzere, Roma 1960.
International Organisation and Integration, a Collection of Texts of Documents relating to the United Nations, its Related Agencies and Regional International Organisations, with annotations; ed. by H.F. VAN PANHUYS, L.J. BRINKHORST and H.H. MAAS, Deventer 1968.
The Kutch-Sind Border Question, A collection of documents with comments, publ. under ausp. of the Indian Society of Int. Law, New Delhi 1965.
LEAGUE OF NATIONS, Doc. C. 400. M. 147. 1925. VII. — Question on the Frontier between Turkey and Iraq; Report of the Commission of Enquiry.
— Doc. C. 727. M. 270. 1925. VII. — Report of the Commission of Enquiry into the Incidents on the Frontier between Bulgaria and Greece (publ. in Official Journal LoN 1926, pp. 196-209).
— Doc. C. 663. M. 320. 1932. VII. — Appeal by the Chinese Government; Report of the Commission of Enquiry.
— PCIJ Series.
Recueil des Décisions de la Commission de Conciliation Franco-Italienne, instituée en exécutión de l'article 83 du Traité de Paix avec l'Italie, publié sous les auspices de la Représentation Française à la Commission de Conciliation Franco-Italienne, Rome 1950.
Report of the Commission of Enquiry established by the Government of the United Kingdom of Great Britain and Northern Ireland and the Government of the Kingdom of Denmark on November 15, 1961 — Investigation of certain incidents affecting the British trawler "Red Crusader" (the "Red Crusader" incident), publ. Bureau Int. de la Cour Permanente d'Arbitrage.
Synopses of United Nations Cases in the Field of Peace and Security 1946-1965, publ. Carnegie Endowment for Int. Peace, New York 1966.
UNITED NATIONS, Annuaire Cour Internationale de Justice 1967-1968, No. 22.
— Doc. A/C. 6/L. 537 — Consideration of Principles of International Law

concerning Friendly Relations and Co-operation among States in accordance with the Charter of the United Nations; Selected background documentation, 1963.
— Doc. A/AC. 119/L. 2 — Summary of the Practice of the United Nations and of views expressed in the United Nations by Member States in Respect of four of the Principles of International Law concerning Friendly Relations and Co-operation among States in accordance with the Charter of the United Nations, 1964.
— Doc. A/5694 — Report of the Secretary-General on methods of fact-finding, 1964.
— Doc. A/5746 — Report of the Special Committee on Principles of International Law concerning Friendly Relations and Co-operation among States, 1964.
— Doc. A/6230 — Idem 1966.
— Doc. A/6799 — Idem 1967.
— Doc. A/AC. 125/L. 86 and Doc. A/L. 600 — Declaration on Principles of International Law concerning Friendly Relations and Co-operation among States, 1970.
— Doc. A/Conf. 39/27 — Convention on the Law of Treaties, 1969.
— I.C.J. Reports.
— Organization and Procedure of United Nations Commissions, series X Nos. I-XII, 1949-50.
— Repertoire of the Practice of the Security Council.
— Repertory of Practice of United Nations Organs.
— Reports of International Arbitral Awards, parts I-XVI, 1948-69.
— A Survey of Treaty Provisions for the Pacific Settlement of International Disputes 1949-1962, 1966.
— Systematic Survey of Treaties for the Pacific Settlement of International Disputes 1928-1948, 1948.

Yearbook of the European Convention on Human Rights; *The European Commission, and European Court of Human Rights*, parts II, IV, VI and X.

ANNEX I

Treaties of which the pacific settlement of disputes between states is the main theme (general treaties), classified according to whether they provide for conciliation (C), arbitration (A) or judicial settlement (J) for all disputes (I), legal disputes (II) or political disputes (III), or only contain a general obligation on pacific settlement (P), and whether application of the method concerned is dependent (—) or not (+) on the cooperation of all parties, or special provisions have been made to obtain such cooperation (:⁚:).

It should be noted that, with some exceptions, in the combinations of arbitration with judicial settlement for the same group of disputes – I (all disputes), II (legal disputes) and III (political disputes) – the arbitration method is given as optional in the treaty and is not elaborated. This combination has been classified in columns —, :⁚: and + on the basis of the cooperation of parties that is needed to submit the dispute to the International Court.

We have confined ourselves to indicating the number of the treaties as they are listed in Post-War Treaties, Survey I and Survey II. The numbers not given relate to treaties that prolong existing treaties or have been replaced or supplemented by subsequent treaties.

Class			Treaty numbers as listed in :			Total
—	:⁚:	+	*Post-War Treaties*	*Survey I*	*Survey II*	
						22
IA			1,4,6,8,13,14,31, 32,83	23,88,104,111, 142,197,199,215	Chap. I, Nos. 6 and 29	
	IA		×	×	Chap. I, No. 7	
		IA	9	×	Chap. I, No.11	

Class			Treaty numbers as listed in :			Total
—	⁘	+	*Post-War Treaties*	*Survey I*	*Survey II*	
						9
IJ			×	231	Chap. I, Nos. 3,9, 10,19,27, 30	
		IJ	20	200	×	
						2
IAJ			12	×	×	
		IAJ	×	156	×	
						18
ICA			3,34,35,39,62, 64,72	24,47,107,208, 209,218,229,230	Chap. I, Nos. 5, 13,45	
						16
ICJ			×	232	×	
		ICJ	29,44,78,88,92	9,31,33,170,171, 179,193	Chap. I, Nos. 8, 18,32	
						20
	ICAJ		×	41	×	
		ICAJ	58,63,70,71,73, 74,90	1,14,84,100,121, 146,147,155,166, 167,186,234	×	
						62
ICA IIJ			49	201	×	
ICA	IIJ		×	38	×	
ICA		IIJ	38,65,67,77,79, 80,84,85,86	5,7,11,15,19,21, 22,35,44,67,87, 90,91,103,110, 118,126,127,140, 152,157,159,162, 168,169,180,204, 205,223,224	×	
	ICA	IIJ	89	34,50,72,75,79, 97,102,109,116, 124,133,143,144, 154,165,217	×	
		ICA IIJ	×	82,85,184	×	

Class			Treaty numbers as listed in :			Total
—	⁘	+	*Post-War Treaties*	*Survey I*	*Survey II*	
						5
		IC IIJ IIIA	×	×	Chap. I, No. 37	
IC IIIA		IIJ	56,57	134,178	×	
						7
IIICA		IIJ	51,54,55,59	135,136,137	×	
						48
IC		IIAJ	7(with SI 32),19, 28(with SI 76), 36(with SI 46), 45,46,47,48,53, 61,69,76,81,91	2,6,8,18,49,53,78, 83,86,89,98,99, 101,105,108,117, 120,122,125,128, 139,141,148,150, 151,172,182,183, 185,191,194,195, 202,216	×	
						34
IC IIA			×	3,10,12,16,20,25, 27,29,36,40,42, 51,54,56,59,61, 65,66,68,70,73, 92,94,113,114, 130,131,138,149, 221	×	
IC	IIA		42,66,68	45	×	
						6
ICIIJ			×	UN Charter	×	
IC		IIJ	43,52,82	39,119	×	
						1
IIIC		IIJ	×	×	Chap. II, No. 6	
						13
IICA			×	63,64,77,81,112, 129,161,163,196, 212	×	
		IICA	×	80,123,198	×	
						2
		IICAJ	×	48,192	×	

Class			Treaty numbers as listed in:			Total
—	⁘	+	*Post-War Treaties*	*Survey I*	*Survey II*	
IIA			16,21	153,188	Chap. I, Nos. 1 and 14	6
IIAJ			33	×	×	1
IIJ			×	203	ODECA	7
		IIJ	50	×	Chap. I, Nos. 4, 12,35,36	
IC			2,5,11,17,18,30, 37,40,41,75,87	58,106,164,173, 174,175,176,177, 181,189,206	×	22
P			×	96,145,214	Chap. I, Nos. 2, 15,16,17, 20-26,28, 31,33,34, 38,39,41-44; Chap. II, Nos. 2,3, 7,9,10,12, 13,15,18, 19 and 21	35
Total			83	196	57	336

ANNEX II

Survey of provisions on the pacific settlement of disputes between states arising out of the interpretation or application of the treaties in which the provisions are contained — special provisions — classified according to whether they provide for conciliation (C), arbitration (A) or judicial settlement (J) or only contain a general obligation on pacific settlement (P) and to whether application depends (—) or not (+) on the cooperation of all parties.

In grouping the special provisions the same categorisation was used as in Survey II. The treaties marked ') are not included in the tables in Chapter II but are in those in Chapter III. They are special provisions that have not been included in Survey II, Peaslee or International Organisation and Integration (I.O.) but have been applied. If a treaty is shown in brackets in the arbitration class (e.g. [IMF]), this means that arbitration was applied by the organs set up under the treaty, and it was therefore a case of administrative arbitration along the lines of administrative adjudication. The administrative procedure for dispute settlement has been counted as arbitration because the parties themselves are represented in the organ and thus codetermine the case, although, unlike in conciliation, they have to abide by the majority view.

Class		Provisions in treaties in category :	Total	
—	+		—	+
		I. Alliance, mutual security and military assistance	16	4
A		Neuilly Peace Treaty ') Art. 181; Trianon Peace Treaty ') Art. 304 with St. Germain-en-Laye Peace Treaty Art. 320; agreement on ending financial disputes between Germany and Romania ') Art. 7; Washington Agreement ') Art. 1;	4	
	A	*Survey II*, Chap. II No. *11* Art. 7 p. 133;		1
J		Versailles Peace Treaty ') Art. 386; Washington Statement '); *Survey II*, Chap. II Nos. *1* Art. 13 p. 88; *4* Art. 14 p. 100; *5* Art. 6 p. 102; *14* Art. 7 p. 140;	6	
	J	Memel-Convention ') Art. 17; Eastern Reparation Agreements ');		2
	AJ	Japanese Peace Treaty Art. 22 with Agreement for the Settlement of Disputes arising under Art. 15(a) of the Treaty of Peace with Japan ');		1
CA		Italian Peace Treaty '); Property Agreement Germany (Federal Republic) - Israel ') Art. 7;	2	

Class −	Class +	Provisions in treaties in category :	Total −	Total +
C		Lausanne Peace Treaty ') Art. 3 para. 2; *Survey II*, Chap. II Nos. *8* Art. XVI p. 127; *20* Art. 17 p. 155; *22* Art. 14 Protocol p. 163.	4	
		II. Regional cooperation	8	8
	A	[African Development Bank] Art. 62 Wionczek p. 439; [Asian Development Bank] Art. 61 Wionczek p. 475; [Inter-American Development Bank] Art. 13 Peaslee p. 849; *Survey II*, Chap. III No. *6* Art. 8 p. 217;		4
J		*Survey II*, Chap. III No. *7* Art. 14 p. 223;	1	
	J	*Survey II*, Chap. III No. *3* Art. 33 p. 198;		1
A		*Survey II*, Chap. III No. *13* Art. 41 with 51 pp. 319 and 321;	1	
CA		Benelux Protocol ') Art. 5;	1	
	CA	EEC Association Treaty Art. 51, I.O. p. 885		1
CJ		*Survey II*, Chap. III Nos. *2* Art. 45, 46, 48 p. 193; *5* Art. XI p. 215;	2	
	CJ	*Survey II*, Chap. III Nos. *8* Art. 164 with 170 and 219 pp. 235, 236 and 241 and *10* Art. 136 with 142 and 193 pp. 291. 292, 293 and 298;		2
C		*Survey II*, Chap. III No. *14* Art. IV p. 324; *15* Art. 35 p. 332; OECD art. 6, I.O. p. 1020.	3	
		III. Communications and transport	38	25
A		UPU Art. 32, I.O. p. 418; *Survey II*, Chap. IV Nos. *1* Art. 25 with Annex 3 pp. 342-344; *2* Art. 45 p. 353; *3* Art. 11 p. 354; *4* Art. 9 p. 354; *5* Art. 5 p. 355; *9* Art. IX p. 362; *10* Art. 9 p. 362; *11* Art. XVI p. 363; *12* Art. 10 p. 364; *13* Art. X p. 365; *21* Art. 9 p. 376; *23* Art. 12 p. 379; *26* Art. IX p. 384; *32* Art. 9 p. 391; *34* Art. VIII p. 394; *36* Art. 11 p. 396; *38* Art. X p. 398; *41* Art. XVIII p. 402; *44* Art. 14 p. 407; *48* Art. 8 p. 411; *51* Art. 25 p. 415.	22	
	A	Postal Union of the Americas and Spain Art. 26, Peaslee p. 1731; Universal Postal Convention Art. 33, Peaslee p. 1830; *Survey II*, Chap. IV Nos. *8* Art. 10 p. 360; *14* Art. XVI p. 366; *15* Art. XVI p. 368; *17* Art. XI p. 372; *24* Art. XV p. 380; *25* Art. XI p. 383; *27* Art. VII p. 384; *28* Art. 10 p. 386; *29* Art. 11 p. 387; *31* Art. X p. 390; *33* Art. VIII p. 393; *35* Art. 14 p. 395; *40* Art. XII p. 401;		

Class −	Class +	Provisions in treaties in category :	Total −	Total +
		42 Art. XII p. 404; *50* Art. IX p. 413; *52* Art. X p. 416; *54* Art. 10 p. 418; *55* Art. 8 p. 420;		20
	J	*Survey II*, Chap. IV No. *7* Art. 47 p. 360;		1
AJ		*Survey II*, Chap. IV No. *39* Art. 11 p. 399;	1	
	AJ	ICAO, Art. 84 and 85, I.O. pp. 456 and 457; *Survey II*, Chap. IV Nos. *19* Art. XVI p. 374; *30* Art. XI p. 389; *43* Art. X p. 406;		4
CA		*Survey II*, Chap. IV Nos. *6a* and *6b* Art. 57 and 60 with Annex X pp. 355-358 and Peaslee pp. 219 and 247; *18* Art. 17 p. 372; *49* Art. 11 p. 412;	4	
C		*Survey II*, Chap. IV Nos. *16* Art. 13 p. 369; *20* Art. 13 p. 375; *22* Art. 12 p. 378; *37* Art. 12 p. 397; *45* Art. XV p. 408; *46* Art. XVI p. 409; *47* Art. XII p. 410; *53* Art. XVI p. 417; IMCO Art. XV Peaslee p. 912; air transport agreements France-USA ') Art. X and Italy-USA ') Art. 12.	11	
		IV. Economic matters (multilateral)	9	6
	A	[Bank for International Settlements] Art. 2 with Agreement regarding the complete and final Settlement of the Question of Reparations of 20 January 1930, Art. XV Peaslee p. 69 and League of Nations Treaty Series 1930 vol. CIV pp. 252-254; [IMF] Art. 18, Peaslee p. 1280; [IBRD] Art. 9, Peaslee p. 963; [IFC] Art. 8, Peaslee p. 1186; *Survey II*, Chap. V No. *9*, [IDA] Art. 10 p. 458; *Survey II*, Chap. V No. *6* Art. 38 p. 451;		6
J		IAEA Art. 17 Peaslee p. 923;	1	
CA		*Survey II*, Chap. V Nos. *7* Art. XXV p. 454; *10* Art. XXIX p. 461;	2	
C		*Survey II*, Chap. V Nos. *1* Art. XXIII p. 438; *3* Art. III p. 446; *4* Art. IX p. 449; *5* Art. XI p. 450; *8* Art. 32 p. 456; UNCTAD, Art. 25 I.O. pp. 345-348;	6	
		V. Commodities	2	5
	A	*Survey II*, Chap. VI No. [*1*] art. 40 p. 464; [*4*] Art. XVII p. 486; [*5*] Art. 22 p. 492;		3
	CA	*Survey II*, Chap. VI No. [*8*] Art. 61 p. 506;		1
CJ		*Survey II*, Chap. VI Nos. *6* Art. XI p. 497; *7* Art. XIII p. 498;	2	
	CAJ	*Survey II*, Chap. VI No. [*9*] art. 12 para. 2 with 35 p. 509 and 515;		1

Class −	Class +	Provisions in treaties in category :	Total −	Total +
		VI. Social and humanitarian interest	12	10
J		ILO Art. 37 Peaslee p. 1245; WHO Art. 75 Peaslee p. 1891; FAO Art. 17 Peaslee p. 672; *Survey II*, Chap. VII No. *9* Art. 48 p. 578	4	
	J	Minority Treaty ') Art. 12 para . 3 and 72 para. 3; Mandate agreement South-West Africa ') Art. 7; Mandate agreement Palestine ') Art. 26; Trusteeship agreement Cameroun ') Art. 19; *Survey II*, Chap. VII Nos. *1* Art. IX p. 522; *3* Art. 22 p. 544; *4* Art. IX p. 545; *6* Art. 9 with 10 p. 556; *7* Art. 54 p. 565; *8* Art. 16 p. 566;		10
AJ		UNESCO Art. 14 Peaslee p. 1809; *Survey II*, Chap. VII No. *5* Art. 8 p. 552;	2	
CA		Germany-Poland ') on Upper-Silesia Art. 563; *Survey II*, Chap. VII No *2* (*a*) Art. 52 p. 532; (*b*) Art. 53 p. 534; (*c*) Art. 132 p. 536; (*d*) Art. 149 p. 538;	5	
C		Protocol instituting a Conciliation and Good Offices Commission to be responsible for seeking the settlement of any disputes which may arise between States Parties to the Convention against Discrimination in Education of 18 December 1962 — Tractatenblad 1964 No. 102.	1	
		VII. Economic matters (bilateral)	22	2
A		*Survey II*, Chap. VIII Nos. *2* annex B Art. 8 p. 583; *15* Art. XXI p. 609; *19* Art.VI p. 612; *20* Art. XX p. 615;	4	
	A	*Survey II*, Chap. VIII No. *21* Art. 12 p. 616;		1
CA		*Survey II*, Chap. VIII Nos. *4* Art. 7 p. 586; *5* Art. IV with annex 15 pp. 588-591;	2	
	CA	*Survey II*, Chap. VIII No. *6* Art. 11 p. 595;		1
C		*Survey II*, Chap. VIII Nos. *1* Art. 6 with 8 pp. 581 and 582; *3* Art. IV p. 585; *7* Art. 7 with 8 p. 601; *8* p. 602; *9* Art. 7 p. 604; *10* Art. 10 p. 604; *11* Art. 6 p. 605; *12* Art. 4 with 27 p. 606; *13* Art. 7 p. 607; *14* Art. 6 p. 607; *16* Art. 8 p. 609; *17* Art. 8 p. 610; *18* Art. 4 p. 611; *22* Art. 6 p. 618; *23* Art. 20 p. 618; *24* p. 619.	16	

Class −	Class +	Provisions in treaties in category :	Total −	Total +
		VIII. Treaties on behalf of nationals		
		a. commerce and navigation	19	4
A		Navigation treaty UK-USA ¹) Art. 4; *Survey II*, Chap. IX Nos. *1* Art. 14 p. 623; *2* Art. 16 p. 623; *3* Art. VIII p. 625; *5* Art. 29 p. 626; *6* Art. 7 p. 628; *10* Art. VI p. 631; *11* Art. VI p. 633; *14* Art. 6 p. 636; *16* Art. 6 p. 638;	10	
	A	Commerce and navigation treaty Greece-UK ¹) Art. 29;		1
	J	*Survey II*, Chap. IX Nos. *8* Art. VII p. 629; *9* Art. 8 p. 630; *13* Art. XVII p. 634;		3
J		*Survey II*, Chap. IX Nos. *7* Art. XXIII p. 629; *12* Art. XXVI p. 633; *17* art. XXVII p. 639;	3	
AJ		*Survey II*, Chap. IX Nos. *18* Art. XXVII p. 639; *20* Art. VII p. 642	2	
CAJ		*Survey II*, Chap. IX No. *4* Art. 33 p. 625;	1	
P		*Survey II*, Chap. IX Nos. *15* Art. VI p. 637; *19* Art. 14 p. 640; *21* Art. VII p. 643.	3	
		b. consular agreements		7
	J	*Survey II*, Chap. X Nos. *1* Art. 34 p. 651; *2* Art. 49 p. 652; *3* Art. 34 p. 653; *4* Art. 35 p. 654; *5* Art. 36 p. 655;		5
	AJ	*Survey II*, Chap. X No. *7* Art. 41 p. 656;		1
	CAJ	*Survey II*, Chap. X No. *6* Art. 44 p. 655.		1
		c. establishment and emigration	4	2
	J	*Survey II*, Chap. X No. *11* Art. 31 p. 664;		1
AJ		[ICEM] Art. 30 Peaslee p. 898;	1	
CA		*Survey II*, Chap. X Nos. *8* Art. 54 with 58 pp. 659 and 660; *9* Art. 12 p. 661;	2	
	CAJ	*Survey II*, Chap. X No. *10* Art. 13 p. 662		1
P		*Survey II*, Chap. X No. *12* Art. 11 p. 665	1	
		d. social security	4	19
	A	*Survey II*, Chap. X Nos. *18* Art. 10 p. 671; *19* Art. 12 p. 672; *24* Art. 36 p. 677; *30* Art. 36 p. 704;		4
CA		*Survey II*, Chap. X Nos. *17* Art. 32 p. 670; *31* Art. 21 p. 706; *32* Art. 38 p. 707;	3	

Class −	Class +	Provisions in treaties in category :	Total −	Total +
	CA	*Survey II*, Chap. X Nos. *13* Art. 18 p. 666; *14* Art. 34 p. 667; *15* Art. 39 p. 668; *16* Art. 29 p. 669; *20* Art. 32 p. 673; *21* Art. 32 p. 674; *23* Art. 26 p. 676; *25* Art. 33 p. 679; *26* Art. 11 p. 683; *27* Art. 11 p. 692; *28* Art. 20 p. 701; *29* Art. 45 p. 703; *33* Art. 38 p. 708; *34* Art. 37 p. 709; *35* Art. 21 p. 710;		15
C		*Survey II*, Chap. X No. *36* Art. 25 p. 711.	1	
		e. property and investment	1	31
A		Agreement on private property France-Poland ¹) Art. 16;	1	
	A	*Survey II*, Chap. X Nos. *54* p. 738; *56* p. 742; *57* Art. III p. 744; *58* Art. 5 p. 746; *59* p. 748; *61* Art. 5 p. 760; *62* p. 762; *63* p. 765; *64* p. 769; *65* p. 771: *66* p. 774;		11
	AJ	*Survey II*, Chap. X Nos. *37* Art. X p. 713; *38* Art. X p. 715; *39* Art. X p. 718; *40* Art. X p. 720; *41* Art. X p. 721; *42* Art. X p. 722; *43* Art. IX p. 724; *44* Art. X p. 727; *45* Art. XI p. 729; *46* Art. X p. 730; *47* Art. X p. 731; *48* Art. X p. 732; *49* Art. IX p. 733; *50* Art. IX p. 734; *51* Art. X p. 735; *52* Art. IX p. 736; *53* Art. 8 p. 738; *55* Art. VIII p. 740; *60* Art. 11 p. 752;		19
	J	Agreement on settlement of financial problems arising from the liquidation of financial and monetary relations between France and the Lebanon ¹) Art. 23.		1
		IX. Regime in frontier areas	15	2
CA		*Survey II*, Chap. XI Nos. *12* Art. 7 with annex 9 pp. 847 and 848; *Survey II*, Chap. XI No. *13* Art. 8 p. 852	2	
	CA	*Survey II*, Chap. XI No. *6* Art. 7 p. 813; *15* Art. IX p. 869 with annex G;		2
C		*Survey II*, Chap. XI Nos. *1* Art. 5 with protocol Art. 6 pp. 781 and 784; *2* Art. VII p. 791; *3* Art. 8 p. 797; *4* Art. 25 p. 800; *5* Art. 3 p. 807; *7* Art. 16 p. 816; *8* Art. 11 with 16 pp. 820 and 821; *9* Art. 29 p. 825; *10* Art. 20 with 27 pp. 830 and 833; *11* Art. 33 p. 839; *14* Art. 32 p. 861; *16* Art. 43 p. 882; *17* Art. II p. 886.	13	
		X. Miscellaneous	8	4
A		WMO Art. 29 Peaslee p. 1912	1	

J		*Survey II*, Chap. X Nos. *1* Art. 27 bis p. 891; *2* Art. XV p. 892; *6* Art. XI p. 900;	3	
	J	Montreux Convention of 8 May 1937 regarding the Abrogation of Capitulations in Egypt ') Art. 13; *Survey II*, Chap. XI Nos. *4* Art. XIII, p. 894; *5* Art. I p. 895; *7* Art. I p. 900;		4
AJ		International Institute of Refrigeration Art. 33, p. 1222; International Relief Union Art. 14 Peaslee p. 1348;	2	
CJ		Convention on the Law of Treaties UN Doc. A/ Conf. 39/27 p. 699;	1	
C		*Survey II*, Chap. XII No. *3* Art. XVII p. 892.	1	
		Grand Total	158	129

ANNEX III

Survey of cases of conciliation and the use of arbitration and judicial settlement independent of the cooperation of all parties (+).

We have confined ourselves to indicating the party relationship within which conciliation, arbitration or judicial settlement was used. The countries involved are given in alphabetical order in each case. In the party relationships marked ') the treaty concerned was applied more than once. In grouping the cases the chronological order was used of the years in which the dispute was submitted to the organ concerned. The figures after the party relationships refer to the pages in which the dispute is discussed. If the dispute is connected with or arose out of the threat or use of force between neighbouring states, usually in boundary questions, or between colonising powers and dependent territories striving for independence, usually in tense political situations, the states concerned are printed in *italics*. In the other cases the dispute can be counted among the category of legal disputes as defined in Art. 36, para. 2 of the ICJ Statute.

CONCILIATION

1. Bilateral agreements

General treaties

1928

Germany - Lithuania, 133

1929-1932

Germany - USSR '), 133

1934

Belgium - Luxembourg, 134

1935

France - Portugal, 134

1938

Denmark - Lithuania, 135

1946

France - Thailand (Siam), 138 et seq.

1949

Romania - Switzerland, 135

1952

Belgium - Denmark, 135

1954

France - Switzerland, 136

France - Switzerland, 136

* ECR = European Convention for the protection of human rights and fundamental freedoms, of 4 November 1950.

Inter-American Conciliation Convention = Convention of Inter-American Conciliation of 5 January 1929 (*Survey I*, No. 52).

LoN = League of Nations Covenant of 28 April 1919.

** German Reparations Scheme = Agreement regarding the complete and final settlement of the Question of Reparations, of 20 January 1930 Art. XV.

UPC = Universal Postal Convention of 12 July 1952, Art. 31.

Peace Treaty = Japanese Peace Treaty of 8 September 1951, Art. 22 with Agreement for the Settlement of Disputes arising under Art. 15(a) of the Treaty of Peace with Japan.

*** British Mandate = British Mandate on Palestine of 24 July 1926, Art. 26.

British Trusteeship = Trusteeship Agreement for the Territory of the Cameroons under British Administration, of 13 December 1946, Art. 19.

ERA = Agreement II, Art. X of the Eastern Reparation Agreements of 28 April 1930.

Mandate South-West Africa = Mandate on German South-West Africa of 17 December 1920, Art. 7.

Memel Convention = Memel Convention of 18 May 1924, Art. 17.

Minority Treaty = Minority Treaty of 28 June 1919, Arts. 12, para. 3 and 72, para. 3.

Montreux Convention = Convention regarding the Abrogation of Capitulations in Egypt, Art. 13, of 8 May 1937.

INDEX

<u>GPSR Compliance</u>

The European Union's (EU) General Product Safety Regulation (GPSR) is a set of rules that requires consumer products to be safe and our obligations to ensure this.

If you have any concerns about our products, you can contact us on ProductSafety@springernature.com

In case Publisher is established outside the EU, the EU authorized representative is:

Springer Nature Customer Service Center GmbH
Europaplatz 3
69115 Heidelberg, Germany

Batch number: 10824476

Printed by Printforce, the Netherlands